# No Student Left Indoors:

## *Creating a Field Guide to Your Schoolyard*

**By Jane Kirkland**

**Edited by:**
Dorothy Burke
Guy Kirkland
Melanie Palaisa

Stillwater Publishing
Lionville, PA

## Dedication

***To Rob and Patti with love and gratitude.***

Whether we know it or not, most of us travel through life with blinders on—with a narrow view of a narrow world experienced by a narrow mind. We don't know what we don't know. Nor do we know *who* we don't know. Therefore, we exist happily in our narrow little universes. But over time our experiences broaden our world, making us smarter, stronger, more tolerant, more forgiving—more mature. And at some point (usually by middle age) we recognize that we got to where we are in spite of living an insulated life. We feel part of a bigger purpose and a larger world. We might even feel a bit insignificant, from our new global perspective. But we feel, in a much more compelling way than we've ever felt, that we want the world to be a better place. Some actually answer the call—they drop the blinders to see more clearly.

The journey to such clarity doesn't always take half a lifetime—for some it happens in an instant, with a single and sudden realization, illumination, or intuition. A thought or experience that many call a "revelation" or an "epiphany".

I dedicate this book to two extraordinary people: my husband Guy Robinson Kirkland ("Rob") and my friend Dr. Patti Vathis. These two generous, compassionate, tolerant, and wise friends possess a special gift—the gift of giving. They are pied pipers dropping epiphanian crumbs of possibility and opportunity for those ready to see themselves in the world from a new perspective. They showed me a bigger world and helped me discover my role as both one of six billion and one of a kind.

## able of Contents


CREATING A FIELD GUIDE TO YOUR SCHOOLYARD

**Foreword** ..... xi

**Preface** ..... xiii

**Acknowledgements** ..... xvii

**Introduction** ..... xix

CHAPTER ONE

**What is a Field Guide to Your Schoolyard?**

What is a Field Guide Project (FGP)? ..... 1
How Long Will It Take? ..... 2
What Skills Do You Need? ..... 2
Who Will Participate? ..... 3
What Materials Do You Need? ..... 4
Which Disciplines Are Involved? ..... 4
What About Multiple Intelligences? ..... 7
What Defines Nature? ..... 9
What if You Have No Nature? ..... 10
How Much Work is This—Really? ..... 11
In Conclusion ..... 12

CHAPTER TWO

**Planning and Launching a Field Guide Project**

Step One: Choosing Your Subjects ..... 16
Begin with Birds ..... 16
Guarantee Success with Bird Feeders ..... 18
Other Subjects ..... 20
Step Two: Choosing Your Content ..... 23
Suggestions For Bonus Content ..... 24
Step Three: Defining Your Property ..... 26
Step Four: Scheduling Observations ..... 26
Step Five: Assessing Material and Equipment Needs ..... 28
Budgeting for Binoculars ..... 29
Budgeting for Field Guides ..... 29
Other Equipment and Materials ..... 32
Step Six: Creating a Budget ..... 32
Funding & Launching Your Project ..... 34
Introducing the FGP to Your Students ..... 35
In Conclusion ..... 36

CHAPTER THREE

**Observing Nature and Collecting Data**

Observing Nature ..... 37
Step One: Master the 20-Second Nature Break™ ..... 37
Step Two: Master the Tools of the Trade ..... 39
Choosing and Using Binoculars ..... 39

Choosing and Using Field Guides ... 43
Step Three: Master Nature Observation Skills ... 44
Observing Birds ... 45
Observing Trees ... 46
Observing Butterflies ... 46
Observation Tips for Urban Schools ... 47
Prepare for Damage Control ... 48
Do You Know the Laws? ... 48
Finding Injured Animals ... 49
Controlling the Urge to Touch ... 50
Addressing Field Etiquette ... 51
Data Collection: Notes and Journals ... 52
In Conclusion ... 54

CHAPTER FOUR
**Creating Your Book**
Creating Hand-drawn Page Templates ... 56
Creating a Custom Paper Size ... 60
Choosing a Slide Design ... 61
Choosing a Slide Layout ... 63
Sourcing Images ... 67
Copies and Distribution ... 67
Choosing Binding ... 68
Creating Files for the Web ... 69
In Conclusion ... 70

CHAPTER FIVE
**Exercises, Lessons, and Forms**
Field Guide Planning Workbook ... 72
Bird Observation *from* Take A Backyard Bird Walk ... 76
Caterpillar Observation *from* Take A Walk With Butterflies and Dragonflies ... 77
Butterfly Observation *from* Take A Walk With Butterflies And Dragonflies ... 78
Nature Observation *from* Take A City Nature Walk ... 79
Field Notes *from* Take A City Nature Walk ... 80
Tree Observation *from* Take A Tree Walk ... 81
Habitat House Hunt *from* Green Teacher Magazine ... 82
Glorious Weeds! *from* Green Teacher Magazine ... 85
Bird Sleuth *from* Cornell Laboratory of Ornithology ... 89
Creating a Dichotomous Key *from* Bridges to the Natural World ... 95
Making Maps—A Different Point of View *from* Discovering Barnegat Bay ... 98
Quick Quadrat Exercise *from* Discovering the Naturalist Intelligence ... 102
A Reflection Page *from* Keeping a Nature Journal ... 107
Making Connections *from* Walk on the Wild Side—Explore Your Public Lands ... 108

CHAPTER SIX
**Resources and Recommendations**
Contests ... 110
Films ... 110
Grants and Donor Programs ... 111
Websites ... 112
Books: Field Guides ... 114
Books: Journals ... 120

Books: Recommended Reading (Grades 9 to adult) ... 121
Books: Recommended Reading (Educators) ... 123
Books: Reference ... 124

APPENDIX A
**Jane Kirkland's Books, Assembly Programs, and Workshops ... 129**

APPENDIX B:
**Hands-on Science, New Friends Are Magnet School's Draw ... 139**

APPENDIX C:
**If You Find an Injured Animal ... 145**

APPENDIX D:
**Gardening to Attract Birds and Butterflies ... 149**

APPENDIX F:
**Native Plants in Elementary School Learning ... 153**

APPENDIX F
**Park Forest Inquiry ... 161**

**Index ... 175**

www.istockphoto.com/fredven

# Foreword

***By Sue Slotterback***

I met Jane about five years ago when she walked into the Nature Center of Cape May. I showed her around the Center and when Jane saw the Monarch caterpillars and chrysalises we had on display, she became very excited and ran for her camera. She was like a kid in a candy shop, just sucking in all the information she could get about Monarchs and rattling off questions as fast as a hummer's wings. Her enthusiasm was infectious. We became immediate friends, Jane and I, both enthralled by the tiniest wonders and sharing the same view of turning kids on to the world around them.

Shortly after my day with Jane, I led a group of third and fourth graders from Cape May Elementary School on a two hour bus tour of Cape Island. We visited fourteen different habitats. It was striking to find how many students and teachers had never known about, let alone had never been to, many of the sites on their own small island. On the way through the dense vegetation, down the bumpy, single-lane dirt road at the Higbee Wildlife Management Area, one of the students asked, "Is this the rainforest?" He knew about the Amazon rainforest, but had never been to the maritime forest less than a ten minute ride from his house. I told Jane about the experience next time we met.

"I am totally frustrated over the focus we put on the rainforest in our elementary school education," she replied. "It's not that rainforests aren't important, but I do wish we'd spend more time focusing on our local environment. Few kids will ever travel to the rainforest and, until they experience it, how can they possibly and truly relate? They can, however, head out their back doors to find local nature. If we focused more on the local wildlife, children will have a better understanding of the importance of native plants as a source of food, shelter, and nesting sights. Then we can really say we are teaching our children to think globally, act locally."

I told Jane that I'd employed her *20-Second Nature Break* at several sites along the island tour. This term was first coined by Jane who visited the school about two years ago for another program in conjunction with the Nature Center. During a *20-Second Nature Break* students are instructed to remain in one place, standing or sitting, eyes opened or closed, no talking, no writing, just observing with their senses, just absorbing what is around them. When the 20 seconds are up, the students are invited to share their observations. Many saw things they never would have noticed (a small, metallic green insect on the side of a tree or the geese far out on the other side of a pond). Some felt things they never would have experienced ( Quiet. Calming. The breeze tickling my face.) Others heard things and were able to make connections they would never have realized (So many birds here so close to the road. It's so still I can hear the ocean. I didn't know we were that close. I could feel my heart beating.) Who would have thought 20 seconds could be so powerful?

That's Jane's legacy (and mine, too). You don't have to have any special training (or 'blessing'); you are already special just being who you are. You don't have to spend any money on high (or low) tech gadgets; the only tools you need are the senses you were born with. You don't even have to go to some famous "out there" area; just open your door. As Jane puts it, "Nature is not a destination. It is not a season. It's not just the rainforest. It is here, with us, all day, all night, every day of the year. It only takes a few seconds to see it, understand it, appreciate it, benefit from it, and care for it. We [only] need to open our eyes."

*No Student Left Indoors: Creating a Field Guide to Your Schoolyard* will help educators help their students to see and value the nature that is their legacy.

Sue Ann Slotterback
Program Director
New Jersey Audubon Society
Nature Center of Cape May

www.istockphoto.com/Gloria-Leigh

# Preface

One February day—amid suburban sprawl, retail shopping strips, and construction sites—as I was loading my groceries into the back of my van, I reached up to close the hatch door. The shadow of a large bird caught my attention. I looked up and could see a bird soaring overhead. It had a brown body, white head, and white tail. I recognized it immediately as a Bald Eagle. What a remarkable sight!

I wondered what the heck it was doing in my neighborhood. I stood frozen in place as it circled above. I began attracting attention with my upraised face and gaping mouth. A few shoppers joined me in looking up and became excited. As we chatted enthusiastically, the small group grew into a crowd of about 20 people! We all admitted that we were watching our first Bald Eagle ever!

I thought it might be important to report this incredible sighting. As soon as the eagle flew away, I drove to the ranger station at my nearby state park. I was breathless with excitement, and certain they'd be shocked and pleased to learn about the eagle. Instead, it was I who was shocked when one of the rangers explained, "This isn't unusual. We've been seeing eagles here for a good many years, mostly in the winter."

I was disappointed that my sighting wasn't special. I pondered for days about why I—nor any of the others who gathered with me in the grocery parking lot that day—had never seen a Bald Eagle in my neighborhood before that day. I wondered what would happen if I took the time to look up more often. Would I see the eagle again? What else might I see?

That day changed my life—and ultimately my career. It marked the beginning of my "season of looking up," a season which has no end in sight. Determined to see what I'd been missing, I promised myself that I'd take a short "nature break" every day. Like most people, my life is full, I'm very busy, and time is a scarce commodity. I felt I couldn't devote much time to nature breaks so I committed to taking a 20-Second Nature Break, one second for each of us who saw that eagle in our grocery store parking lot. To my amazement, 20 seconds a day was all it took for me to see the most incredible wildlife and plants that I'd never noticed before. Twenty seconds a day was all it took for me to become hooked on nature.

You can't imagine the nature I've discovered in my own backyard, neighborhood and, well, everywhere I go! I once saw a Praying Mantis on the side of a high-rise building in the middle of downtown Philadelphia. I saw a dragonfly trapped in the cell phone store at my local mall. I watched a dove build her nest on the top of my neighbor's garage door opener and she fledged two young from that quaking nest. The following year she did it again nesting on the garage door opener of a different neighbor and fledged two more. I once saw thousands of migrating Common Green Darners in the middle of Central Park, New York! I saw three species of woodpeckers in a city neighborhood park that was home to several basketball courts and only about 15 trees! I found toads mating and laying eggs in a puddle in the parking lot of my local train station. I find nature whenever and wherever I look.

Over the next year nature took more and more of my time away from my work until ultimately it consumed me. All I wanted was to be outdoors—no matter what the weather. The more I looked, the more I discovered. The more I shared my discoveries with others, the more I realized that most people (adults and children) knew little of the nature that surrounded them. In fact, most people are oblivious to the nature around them.

A strong desire to share my experiences with others came over me. I took every opportunity to show anyone and everyone what was just above their heads, under their feet, and within earshot. I wanted to impart the joys that nature observation brought to me: a sense of place, a sense of peace, a heightened awareness of my surroundings, an excitement about nature, and an awareness of the fragility of our natural world. To that end, I left behind a lucrative career as a successful author of more than 30 books on computer software to develop a series of books for young readers called Take A Walk® books. That award-winning series led me to this book, a manual to help educators help their students discover the nature in their own schoolyards.

Nature is something every child relates to. When a butterfly lands in a child's hand it etches an indelible memory in the heart and mind. When a simple walk turns into a chance meeting with a deer and her young, it registers a magic moment forever. When we see our first Bald Eagle in the wild, that breathless moment generates a new sense of awe and awareness of our natural environment. Encounters like these are possible for all of us and they can happen in our backyards, neighborhoods, and even our schoolyards. These exciting encounters also define some of the most quiet and intimate moments of our lives, creating memories of a simpler time. Moments like these have always been and will always be a right of passage for all children and you can create opportunities for such moments by stepping outside the classroom with your students.

If you think that you won't find nature in your schoolyard, think again. Nature is not a destination. It is in your schoolyard, neighborhood, park, back yard, and everywhere you go. I know. I've seen it and I see it every day. Now you know. Now you'll see it every day. Take your students outdoors. Look up. Take a 20-Second Nature Break. Seeing is believing.

www.istockphoto.com/Studio1One

# Acknowledgements

Every book is a collaborative effort. This book is collaboration on steroids—beginning with the educators. Some shared their expertise by providing exercises, lessons, articles, or sidebars. Others "tested" our manuscript, giving us feedback and suggestions. All gave their time, expertise, and encouragement. Among them are old friends, new friends, and even newer acquaintances to whom I will always feel a kinship and gratitude. Their contributions are a key component to this book. Thank you Lauren Boerlin, Dana Byer, Kathleen Geist, Kathy Gingerich, Mary Judge, Denise Hansen, Cait Harris, Michele Huey, Gail Heintzelman, Lois Leggett, Sherry McVeigh, Joyce Mitchell, Barbara Norris, Tom Pearson, Christine Raabe, Catherine Renzi, Cary Rosillo, Linda Rowan, Sue Slotterback, Donann Stoicovy, Robin Squier, and Tim Vargo.

Thanks also to author Maggie Meyer, and to the following organizations for generously allowing us to share their materials with you: Education World, Johnson Books, the New Jersey Audubon Society, Nikon U.S.A., Green Teacher Magazine, Cornell Lab of Ornithology, and Storey Publishing.

And a special thanks to you for your plans to explore your schoolyard with your students. On behalf of all the wild plants and animals that have no voice or language understood by human, I thank you for taking your students outdoors to meet them.

See you in the outdoors!

www.istockphoto.com/og-vision

# Introduction

Welcome to *Creating a Field Guide to Your Schoolyard*—your personal guide to helping students discover, observe, and record nature in your urban, suburban, or rural schoolyard. Our goal is to provide you with the definitive resource for place-based and project-based environmental education and to show you how this project streamlines directly into your current teaching methods, curriculum, objectives, and standards.

This compilation of Jane Kirkland's instructions, tips, experiences, and recommendations has been several years in the making. She's reached out to other educators, publishers, and commercial and nonprofit companies too, so you can benefit from their experiences, suggestions, and resources. Here you'll glean the information and confidence you need to raise your students' environmental and ecological IQ (EIQ) through this multidisciplinary project.

## How to Use This Book

*Creating a Field Guide to Your Schoolyard* is comprised of six chapters and several appendices as well as a comprehensive *Index* to help you navigate quickly to the information you need—when you need it. Here are the chapters at a glance:

- **Chapter One, *What is a Field Guide to Your Schoolyard,*** provides answers to the most-asked questions about a field guide project. Even if you were committed to creating a field guide to your schoolyard before you purchased this book, you'll find purposes and benefits to your project you might not have considered.

- **Chapter Two, *Planning Your Field Guide Project,*** prepares you to make informed decisions about the length and breadth of your field guide project. Here you'll learn that there's more than one way to conduct a Field Guide Project. You'll plan your project, assess your material needs, and create a budget. As you read the chapter you can (optionally) fill in the provided *Planning Workbook.*

- **Chapter Three, *Observation and Data Collection,*** discusses schoolyard nature observations: what to look for, when and how to observe nature, and suggestions for taking field notes, writing nature journals, and collecting data.

- **Chapter Four, *Creating Your Book,*** presents options for designing your field guide. You'll find ideas for creating your pages by hand as well as instructions for using Microsoft PowerPoint for book layout. You'll also learn about scanning and sourcing images for your book.

- **Chapter Five, *Exercises, Lessons, and Forms,*** contains the companion Planning Workbook for planning your field guide as well as forms for your students to use when writing field notes or observation notes. You'll also find nature-related exercises and lessons from other teachers, organizations, and publications. Some forms may be reproduced—they are noted as such—and you can copy them directly from this book or download PDF files at our Website, **www.takeawalk.com.**

- **Chapter Six, *Resources and Recommendations,*** contains lists of recommended books, Websites, and other resources. Here you'll also find coupons and special offers for supplies and equipment.

**Appendices** offer supplemental information for your Field Guide Project, including information on Jane Kirkland's Take A Walk® books and programs, a report from Park Forest Elementary (one of our example schools), and information on schoolyard habitats and native plants.

**Sidebars present** different perspectives about chapter topics and are categorized by the following icons:

 **Caution** (eye) a caution or warning.

 **Meet** (handshake) profile of school or person.

 **Note** (pencil icon) a comment or sidebar from the author

 **Recommended** (diamond) a product recommendation.

 **Student Reference** (book) a cross-reference to Take A Walk® book pages.

 **Worth Repeating** (musical note) advice from an educator, quote from a celebrated person, or essay from winners of a Take A Walk® books elementary school writing contest called *Why I Love the Nature in My Schoolyard* .

It is our intention that this book serve as a "living document". Please check our Website regularly as we add new exercises and updates. We encourage you to write to us with your schoolyard nature exploration questions, experiences, and anecdotes. Write to: *editor@takeawalk.com.*

We hope you find *Creating a Field Guide to Your Schoolyard* a definitive resource for your environmental education efforts. We welcome your comments. We wish you luck with your project.

Guy Kirkland
Vice President and Executive Editor
Stillwater Publishing, Take A Walk® Books
P O Box 500, Lionville, PA 19353
610-458-4000

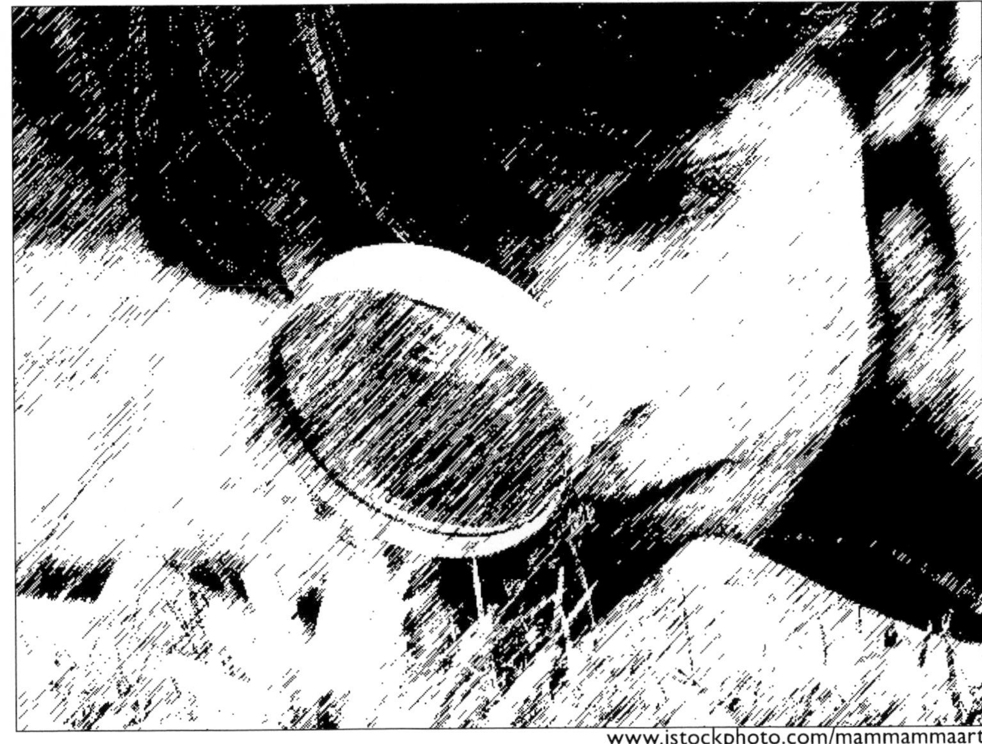

www.istockphoto.com/mammammaart

In This Chapter


What is a Field Guide Project?

How Long Will it Take?

What Skills Do You Need?

Who Will Participate?

What Materials Do You Need?

Which Disciplines are Involved?

What about Multiple Intelligences?

What Defines Nature?

What If You Have No Nature?

How Much Work Is This—Really?


CHAPTER ONE

# What is a Field Guide to Your Schoolyard?

A field guide to your schoolyard is a species account, a catalog of the animals and/or plants found in your schoolyard. *Which* plants and animals, *how much* information your guide contains about each, and *who* contributes to the guide are up to you.

Your field guide can be a small book about the birds in your schoolyard, created by a single class. Alternatively, it can be a comprehensive study and complete inventory to which the entire student body contributes over the course of the school year—or a living document that expands every year. Big or small, your field guide is what you need and want it to be to help you engage your students in an exciting and challenging environmental education experience.

## What is a Field Guide Project (FGP)?

In order to create a field guide to your schoolyard, you must first explore, observe, collect data, conduct research, and write about the plants and animals in your schoolyard. The entire process—from your first schoolyard observation to the creation of the last page of your field guide book—is what I call the *Field Guide Project*, or FGP.

A Field Guide Project is divided into three parts: planning; observation and data collection; and book creation. Here is a summary of those parts, or steps:

**Worth Repeating**

*They took all the trees and put them in a tree museum.*

*And they charged all the people a dollar and a half just to see 'em.*

*Don't it always seem to go that you don't know what you've got till it's gone?*

*They paved paradise and put up a parking lot.*

**From *Big Yellow Taxi* by Joni Mitchell**

1. **Planning.** Here you decide *who* will participate in the field guide project and *what* information you'll gather for your book content. You'll also plan *where, when,* and *how* the observations, study, and research will take place and for what period of time. You'll determine some of the content of your field guide book and prepare a budget for your project.

2. **Observation and data collection.** This is when the project comes to life for your students. They'll explore your schoolyard and, with your guidance, they'll find, observe, and identify species of plants and animals. They'll take field notes and compile their findings. Every plant and animal found in the boundaries of your schoolyard and every bird flying overhead is a potential subject for your field guide. Your subject list can grow with every type of habitat or landscaping you find in your schoolyard, and with every season you observe and investigate.

3. **Book creation.** When your observation and data collection period is complete, you're ready to create the final book. Field guides can be hand written and created on construction paper stitched together, or created on a PC. You can include nonfiction book elements such as captions, a table of contents, an index, a list of contributors, and so forth.

**Meet Don Jenny**

I recently read an article in the Allentown, PA, *Morning Call* newspaper about Don Jenny, a school Maintenance Director at the Bethlehem Area Vocational Technical School in Bethlehem, Pennsylvania. Jenny, as a result of his nature observations, has made a difference in the lives of hundreds of students. He noticed that hawks found the rabbits on the school property as easy prey because there was no place for the rabbits to find cover. He stopped cutting a 2 acre area of the property so the rabbits could hide in the grass. As a result, he essentially created a new habitat, which bloomed with wildflowers and teemed with insects. The insects attracted birds, the grass provided cover for wildlife, and Jenny approached the staff suggesting the area become an outdoor classroom. With staff help and grant money, the school is now turning the plot into an outdoor classroom. Perhaps you have a Don Jenny among your staff or faculty.

Each step of the FGP is covered in detail in the following chapters of this book: Chapter Two, *Planning your FGP,* Chapter Three, *Observation and Data Collection* and Chapter Four, *Creating Your Book.*

## How Long Will It Take?

Your field guide can be a one-day project, a semester-long project, a year-long project, or a multi-year project. You can schedule schoolyard observations weekly, biweekly, or monthly. The more time you invest, the more opportunities you present for students to learn and participate.

The time you need is a direct correlation to the time you can invest. But even a one-day project should be revisited once a season. As birds and other animals move and migrate, as plants blossom and trees drop their leaves, your students will have the opportunity to experience seasonal changes.

## What Skills Do You Need?

You won't need special skills for this project—but you might need to know how to choose and use binoculars and field guides (see Chapter Three, *Observation and Data Collection)* before you begin your project. If you're concerned because you don't have a science background, view the FGP as an opportunity to learn alongside your students. Your role in a field guide project is to motivate, plan, coordinate, and support your students—skills you've already mastered.

If you just can't get comfortable with the thought of teaching about nature, consider taking a naturalist-led nature or bird walk or two. Most local watershed organizations, Audubon chapters, birding, wildflower, and butterfly clubs hold regularly scheduled public walks. Many are free, and those that charge usually ask only a nominal fee. You can learn a lot during these walks. Most of the people who lead nature walks for nonprofit organizations are volunteers or get paid little for their services. They are people who do what they do out of love for nature— enthusiastic people who love their work and who will put you at ease with nature exploration.

## Who Will Participate?

The FGP can be a class project, a project for an entire grade, or a project for the entire student body. During your planning stage you'll determine who will contribute what to your project. Those participants might include any or all of the following:

- **Students.** Assignments can be made by grade or by task. You might have a group of illustrators, writers, researchers, and so forth. Lower grades can focus more in illustrations than extensive writing. Upper elementary, middle, and high school grades can create a more comprehensive guide with room for teams of writers, editors, researchers, fact checkers, photographers, illustrators, graphic artists, designers, cover designer, and indexers. In many ways creating a field guide to your schoolyard is similar to creating a yearbook. Consider consulting with your yearbook committee or school newspaper staff to solicit their input to your project. Why reinvent the process if someone in your school is already producing books?

- **Faculty and staff.** Don't keep the field guide project to a single class—invite other teachers and their classes—at the very least, those at your grade level. Heck, invite the entire staff to participate: perhaps the school nurse can help students make posters about nature observation *safety*—with drawings and descriptions of poison ivy, how to avoid bee stings, and how to stay safe while exploring the outdoors. The librarian could help with research and book design. The rest of the staff could post their schoolyard bird sightings in a central location for everyone to see.

- **Parents, families and community members.** Invite parents to observe the schoolyard and take notes for a few minutes after they drop off their children, or in the afternoon after school closes. Ask if families can observe during holidays and school breaks, or over the summer. If you plan to include a history page in your field guide, consult with parents, grandparents, and older community residents to help. Another good source for historical information is your local historical society, librarians and newspaper reporters. They might even contribute a story about a personal experience with nature or about a memory of your school property—perhaps from a time before the school was built. A bonus of community involvement is that it can nurture a stronger *sense of place* and a *sense of pride* for your students.

In the end, *you* will determine who will participate in and contribute to your FGP: a group, club, single class, single grade, the entire student body, and/or community members and businesses. Keep in mind that as you invite faculty

**Note**

Consider creating a **multi-lingual** field guide to your schoolyard. Multi-lingual guides can benefit your ESL students and their families and help bridge language gaps in the classroom. Did someone say, "las plumas del pájaro de bebé están borrosas"? I sure hope this translates to "the feathers of the baby bird are fuzzy" or I might be in trouble here!

**Worth Repeating**

*Include administrators (principals, supervisors, board of education members, etc.) in your field guide project because their inclusion can lend immediate perceived value to the project. Administrative support can help carry the project from year-to-year. Don't keep an important project like this within the walls of one classroom.*

**Christine Raabe**
**Education Outreach Specialist**
**Ocean County Soil Conservation District**
**Forked River, NJ**

Snail

and administrators to participate, you're helping to secure the future (and hopefully the funding) of your project.

## What Materials Do You Need?

You already have many of the tools you'll need for a field guide project. The obvious ones are: drawing and painting implements, paper, and art supplies. But at a minimum you'll also need binoculars and field guides.

- **Binoculars.** You'll need at least one pair. Two pair are better. One pair for every two-to-four students is best. You'll need to know how to use binoculars properly. Learn about buying and using binoculars in Chapter Three, *Observation and Data Collection.*

- **Field Guides.** You need field guides to identify the plants and animals you find in your schoolyard. I recommend at least one field guide for each group of plants or animals you plan to include in your guide: trees, butterflies, birds, insects, and so forth. Field guides are for the field, not just the bookshelf. Your library might have field guides but you'll need a set dedicated to your project—available and accessible when and where the students need them. It's important to select the appropriate field guide for your students. You'll learn how to choose and use field guides in Chapter Three, *Observation and Data Collection.*

If you have the money, there's a plethora of tools to help with your project. You might want binders for data collection, weather instruments, journals, a digital camera, a scanner, photo correction software, and clipboards. But the operative word here is *want;* you don't *need* those things for your FGP.

As you consider tools and materials for your project, avoid items that encourage children to pick or collect living plants and animals. Read more about materials in Chapter Two, *Planning Your Field Guide Project.*

## Which Disciplines Are Involved?

Like nature itself, the FGP is multidisciplinary. Figure 1.1 illustrates the disciplines interconnected in a Field Guide Project. A large part of your FGP is data collection through nature journaling and field notes which is also multidisciplinary as shown in Figure 1.2 on page 6. Here are some ways in which the FGP incorporates multiple disciplines:

- **Science, environment and ecology.** Science is the basis of the FGP. Your students learn to think like scientists, act like scientists, and write like scientists. This is a great project to teach students species categorization and classification, adaptations, life cycles, habitats, ecosystems, watersheds, and the impact of humans on our environment.

Mallard

- **Language arts, reading and writing.** The FGP is a reading and writing workshop: students research and write about the species they discover. They learn new scientific terms, scientific names, how to write for their intended audience, and how to use nonfiction elements, or signposts.

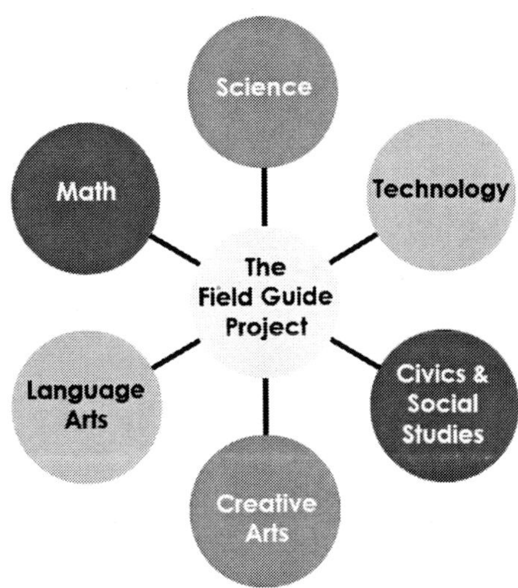


**Figure 1.1 A Field Guide Project combines multiple disciplines.**

- **Creative arts.** Art plays a critical role in your FGP, whether your field guide contains illustrations, photographs, or both. Students will also design the layout and cover for your book.

- **Math.** Counting and totaling species, mapping, measurements, statistics, charts, and graphs are just a few examples of the role math plays in the FGP.

- **Technology**. Technology plays an optional role in your field guide. This is the perfect project for teaching students how to use their computers for research. Older students can learn how to use software such as desktop publishing, word processing, graphics, or digital photography programs as they design, lay out and construct the field guide. You might even want to create a database or spreadsheet to record your statistics.

- **Civics and social studies.** There's a place for history in the FGP. Consider a chapter in your field guide about the natural history of the school property, how the schoolyard works (or doesn't) as a wildlife habitat, or even how the schoolyard can be improved. Community involvement and current events have optional roles in your field guide, too. If your school is newly constructed, consider a research project and chapter about how the construction impacted the environment and the community.

The Field Guide Project also lends itself to the integration of numerous educational strategies, theories, and techniques including, but not limited to:

- **Character building, values, and ethics.** Students learn about environmental ethics, respect, kindness, and caring for the environment. They will witness the effects of human impact on our natural world.

- **Collaborative and cooperative learning.** The FGP is a team project requiring students to collaborate and cooperate.

**The FGP by Task**

Assign FGP task groups for middle and high school students. Example groups are research, content writer, copy and technical editor, illustrator, photography, design and layout teams.

Cecropia Moth

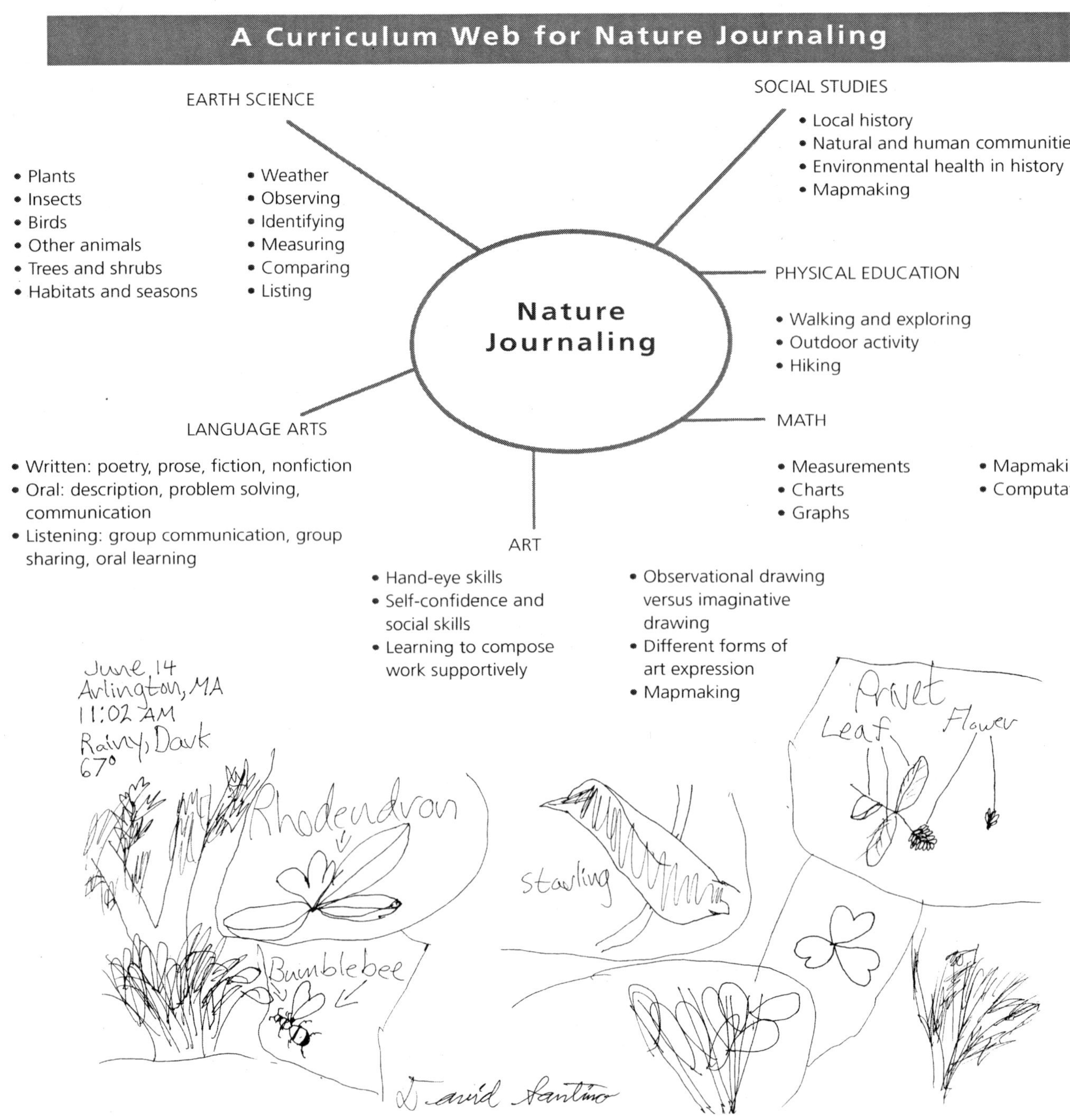


**Figure 1.2 Nature journaling, as part of a FGP, involves many disciplines, as illustrated in this Curriculum Web excerpted from *Keeping a Nature Journal* by Claire Walker Leslie. Copyright ©2005 By Claire Walker Leslie. Used with permission from Storey Publishing, LLC, North Adams, Massachusetts.**

- **Community and place-based learning.** The FGP has real-world context, linking the classroom to the community and environment.

- **Constructivism.** Students gain knowledge through exploration and active learning in the schoolyard.

- **Curriculum integration, multidisciplinary and interdisciplinary teaching.** Environmental topics are interdisciplinary by nature. Content for the field guide is drawn from many subject areas; science, math, social studies, language arts, creative arts, and technology.

- **Direct instructions.** The FGP provides opportunities for structured overview, lecture, and explicit teaching. Topics include science, the environment, ecology, social studies, current events, reading, writing, and research workshops.

- **Experiential learning.** The Field Guide Project provides numerous hands-on learning opportunities through exploration and discovery.

- **Independent study.** Autonomous writing in journals, computer-based research, and assigned questions can all be a part of the field guide project.

- **Indirect instructions.** Research involved in the field guide project is a perfect example of *reading for meaning,* and the field guide itself is an exercise in writing to inform.

- **Interactive Instruction.** The field guide project offers almost endless opportunities for stimulating debate and brainstorming, discussions, and cooperative learning across the curriculum. Students can be involved in discussions about the field guide content, research, development, and creation, while learning about the implications of those decisions.

- **Problem-based learning and critical thinking**. A FGP is hands-on learning through inquiry and investigation. It offers opportunities for critical thinking, problem solving, and effective decision-making.

 **Worth Repeating**

*The fact that we have the same intelligences means that we can communicate with one another. But the fact that we represent things mentally in numerous symbolic systems to one another means that we are not necessarily going to construe things in the same way or see the same options.*

**Howard Gardner**
**In an interview about his book, *Intelligence Reframed.***

## What About Multiple Intelligences?

At first blush, it might seems as if this is a project for those students with a strong naturalist intelligence—and, of course, it is. But the project is really bigger than that and has something for many different intelligences such as:

- **Linguistic**. Every student has an opportunity in this project to read, write, research, and edit—even if they are only editing their own work. Optional tasks include creating word definitions and pronunciation keys, glossaries, and indices for the field guide.

- **Logical-mathematical**. Students will use analysis and investigation during the project through measuring and statistics. Optional tasks include charting, graphing, projections, and analysis.

Chickadee

- **Musical.** Students with musical abilities should be encouraged to learn to identify birds by their calls. Encourage them to teach other students, too.
- **Bodily-kinesthetic.** Students learn and practice sitting still and being quiet during nature observation.
- **Spatial**. Students with spatial abilities can create maps and diagrams for the field guide.
- **Interpersonal**. Students learn and practice collaboration and working in a team environment.
- **Intrapersonal**. Students have opportunities to learn about themselves through independent study, observation, and research.
- **Naturalist**. Encourage your students with naturalist abilities to lead and help others to discover, observe, and identify nature.

To help you develop the naturalist intelligence in your students, I share this excerpt from an article by Maggie Meyer, author and elementary teacher from Washington State. The article appears at *New Horizons for Learning* Website, **www.newhorizons.org**. Permission to reprint was given by Maggie.

> *Developing the naturalist intelligence is no different than teaching math or reading skills. Teachers must provide the opportunity for this intelligence to grow.*
>
> *We need to stop and consider the implications this identified intelligence has on our educational settings. Getting on a bus and moving to an appropriate expedition site extends learning beyond walking down the hall to the gym or the art room. Doing field studies extends experiential learning beyond working with pattern blocks in math class. By observing outside we can see those same patterns in nature and understand connections. Employable success in the future requires that our children be computer literate. We have stocked our classrooms and constructed computer labs to provide this opportunity. The quality of life on this planet requires that our children have experience with nature. We must provide the best educational learning opportunities for the Naturalist Intelligence.*
>
> *All teachers are facing reforms that include state essential learnings and national standards. Naturalist topics and themes make some of the best curriculum integrations that will help us reach these goals. An example would be the themes of change, cycles, and connections. Topics that help enrich curriculum could revolve around the ecosystem where the school is located. Teachers in the Pacific Northwest could establish integrated studies around marine ecology, watersheds, forests, aquatic life. The instructors in the Southwest could focus on the desert environment. After all, intelligence has been defined as solving problems and fashioning products valued in one culture or community. Knowing and understanding your community environment and using it as an extended classroom just makes sense.*
>
> *One simple way to encourage the Naturalist Intelligence is to take students outside to explore their school community. Careful observation will find weeds*

Raccoon

*in the cracks of almost any playground surface. The eaves of a roof provide nesting places for birds. Water from storm runoff pours down storm drains in the parking lot. Data collected can be returned to the classroom and distributed in tables, charts and graphs . One trip outside can generate enough questions for inquiry that a school's library and research lab could be utilized all year. These consistent short experiences outside on your school grounds provide a learning environment that will empower kids. Let them research solutions to problems they may identify. Allow them to make a plan of action, design a project based on certain criteria and then implement it . Invite community resource professionals to support you. Celebrate with your entire school community when the problem is solved and the project is completed. Howard Gardner defines understanding as the capacity to apply knowledge in new situations. Providing for the Naturalist Intelligence is one way to encourage true understanding.*

*A teacher's primary responsibility is to be sure all children experience success and learn. We must consider each child and provide the skills they need to grow. We must consider all ways to deliver curriculum. We must consider all intelligences when planning and organizing lessons. Tom Hoerr, Principal of New City School in St. Louis, states, "The Naturalist Intelligence offers one more way to help students understand and learn.*

You can learn more in Maggie Meyer's book, *Discovering the Naturalist Intelligence: Science in the Schoolyard.* You'll find her book listed in Chapter Six, *Resources and Recommendations.* An excerpted lesson called *Quick Quadrat Exercise,* appears in Chapter Five, *Exercises, Lessons, and Forms.*

## What Defines Nature?

Sooner or later your students are going to ask you, "What is nature?" I've been asked this question at every school I've visited by at least one student. Whenever possible, I don't answer the question but I open it up to the students to answer. I do that for a selfish reason: I want to understand kids' perception of nature. As kids offer their definitions of nature, others inevitably challenge them and more questions arise. "If plants must be *wild* to be part of nature, does that mean that if I plant a seed from a wild plant, it's no longer wild?" "Is weather part of nature—are meteors—is the solar system?" "Is acid rain part of nature or did man make it?" "If nature is the physical world that has been untouched or unaltered by human interaction—where on earth have we not touched—does that mean there is no nature left?" "If nature includes all living things, then isn't man part of nature?" "Are rocks part of nature—even though they aren't living things?" "Is Mother Nature related to Mother Goose?" "Are *you* Mother Nature?"

If I'm on the spot and must answer the question I usually say something like "Nature, for me, is the things (living and otherwise) that are not man made. To me, nature is the sun and the moon and the birds and the bees. It's our gardens, our lawns, our rivers, our seas. And I believe that man is part of nature—because if we weren't related to nature we couldn't possibly feel so connected to it. I also believe that we are all the caretakers of nature. And sometimes being the caretaker means not interfering."

House Wren

## What if You Have No Nature?

I compiled a list of plants and animals I've seen in schoolyards in the mid-Atlantic area over the past year or so. I didn't go to these schools for the purpose of looking for nature; I went to conduct a school assembly. My time outdoors was limited to the walk between my car and the school and perhaps out and in again during lunch. Table 1.1 on page 11 lists some of the plants and animals I've seen while visiting these "typical" suburban schools, meaning that they haven't improved their property for wildlife and aren't located near the coast or any large body of water. If, in reading this table, you discover a number of species you don't recognize or even ones you've never heard of—good! That could mean that you have more nature than you realize because you wouldn't know these plants and animals if you ran into them! A typical urban schoolyard would have fewer species than a rural or suburban school, but they are no less exciting. I think it would be fair to say that you could find several species of birds, insects, and trees for starters.

The more you *look*, the more you *see*. How do I know? Well, to start with, we're living closer to nature than ever before. We're encroaching on wildlife with urban sprawl and development. As a result wildlife has no place left to escape us. Some stay in and around the suburbs, others migrate to what's left of more rural areas and still others head in the opposite direction—toward our cities.

Wildlife is adapting to the changing landscape, finding new or different shelter, places to nest, sources of food, and paths for movement and migration. We witness these adaptations every time we see bears, raccoons, or crows raid our trash and gulls feed from our landfills. Pigeons have adapted to our cities, using buildings and underpasses in the same way they previously lived and nested on cliffs and rocks. Skunks raise their young under unsuspecting suburban homeowners' front doorsteps—often the last shelter in a newly altered landscape. Robins nest on the crossbeams of our wooden decks—in place of nesting in the large trees that once stood where our soccer fields stand. Deer eat the expensive shrubs we plant in our new neighborhoods. Deer, squirrel, and possum carcasses litter our roads and insect carcasses are splattered on our windshields as animals try to cross our roads.

Wildlife *is* closer. It's practically knocking at our doors. We face many problems living this close to wildlife, but there's also at least one benefit. Living closer means having more opportunity to observe wildlife.

If, after you explore your schoolyard, you still think it has no nature, choose a nearby park to study or have your students create field guides to their backyards. Remember, the FGP is about getting kids outdoors.

**Nature Deficit Disorder**

There was a time when kids and nature were synonymous—kids were always outdoors. But today kids spend more time indoors than out and much less time in the outdoors than previous generations. Are they nature deprived? In *Last Child in the Woods* author Richard Louv says our kids are so disconnected from the outdoors some suffer from what he calls "nature deficit disorder". Louv says nature deficit disorder is "the human costs of alienation from nature. An alienation that damages children and shapes adults, families, and communities."

Scientific studies suggest that spending significant time in the outdoors helps build healthier immune systems in children. But few children are spending "significant" time in the outdoors these days. Perhaps that's why we have seen such an increase in allergies, colds, infections, and asthma in children. Nature deprivation leads to other kinds of deprivation, too. We live in an increasingly homogeneous world where one neighborhood looks like the other. Our culture, food, art, dress, local and familial languages, accents and colloquialisms seem to be blending into one look and sound. From what can we form our sense of place if all places are the same? From nature, that's what. And from our seasons, native plants, wildlife, ountains, rivers, and natural landscape that remain unique. In many places and for many people, nature is what defines their sense of place. Deprived of one, they are deprived of the other. Maybe it's time we all took a little nature break.

**Table 1.1 Common Plants and Animals of Mid-Atlantic Suburban Schoolyards.**

**Birds**
American Robin
White-breasted Nuthatch
Blue Jay
American Crow
Red-tailed Hawk
Sharp-shinned Hawk
Turkey Vulture
Northern Mockingbird
Carolina Wren
Carolina Chickadee
House Wren
House Sparrow
House Finch
European Starling
Tree Sparrow
White-throated Sparrow
Mourning Dove
Northern Cardinal
Downy Woodpecker

**Wildflowers**
Queen Anne's Lace
Dandelion
Chicory
Fleabane
Clover
Ragweed
Goldenrod
Crown Vetch

**Amphibians**
American Toad

**Insects**
Tiger Swallowtail
Black Swallowtail
Monarch
Tent Caterpillar
House Fly
Carpenter Bee
Japanese Beetle
Lady Bird Beetle (Ladybug)
Locust
Katydid
Praying Mantis
Cabbage White
Crescent Butterfly
Silver-spotted Skipper
Common Green Darner

**Trees**
Red Maple
Silver Maple
Norwegian Maple
White Pine
Paper Birch
Blue Spruce
Flowering Dogwood
Red Oak
Sycamore

**Mammals**
White-tailed Deer
Eastern Squirrel
Groundhog
Red Fox
Eastern Cottontail Rabbit
Feral cat

**Worth Repeating**

*One of the biggest misconceptions of urban children (and adults) is that they have to get in a car and drive far away to find nature.*

**Tim Vargo, Urban Ecology Center of Milwaukee**

## How Much Work is This—Really?

Based on the size of this book you might think a Field Guide Project looks like a lot of work. But some teachers think FGP is actually an opportunity to work *smarter*, not *more*. The FGP can focus on nature as the topic of all disciplines—utilizing the skills and experiences of all faculty and staff toward a single goal of creating responsible stewards of our planet while meeting your existing educational missions and goals.

Queen Anne's Lace

A FGP is exciting, enlightening, creative, and educational for the participants and it can make great improvements in their lives. If you peel through the layers of the curriculum Web that entwine the Field Guide Project, you'll find a common thread throughout. That thread is *observation skills.* Although observation isn't an academic discipline, it isn't a course in elementary schools, and students aren't tested on their observation skills, it is a huge benefit and bonus of participating in a Field Guide Project.

We use observation skills not only to observe nature, but in every facet of our daily lives. As we observe our surroundings we become more conscious and conscientious citizens. At times our very health and safety are dependent upon good observation skills—skills that help us to avoid dangerous or unhealthy places, things, and even people. Observation skills involve many of our senses and hone our ability to focus and to learn. Your Field Guide Project, your field guide book, and your experiences exploring your schoolyard begin and end with observation. At some point in their lives your students (like most people) might "outgrow" nature exploration, allowing the business of earning a living and raising a family to overtake their desire or ability to get outdoors. They might never again be a part of a such a collaborative endeavor and might never illustrate or take another photo of a leaf. But they will carry and apply their observation skills with them for the rest of their lives—more cognizant of everyone and everything around them.

## In Conclusion

You've taken the 30,000 foot view of a field guide project and you can see how flexible it is. The FGP can easily adapt to suit your teaching methodologies and challenge and stimulate the multiple intelligences. It will correlate to your academic standards and fit securely into your core curriculum.

Remember when it comes to outdoors exploration—don't sweat the small stuff. You can't have too few species or even too many species of plants and animals in your schoolyard. If you think you do, simply learn more about the "too few" or restrict yourself to only a few of the "too many".

Now it's time to get to the details of the project. In Chapter Two, *Planning Your Field Guide Project,* you'll learn the six steps to planning your Field Guide Project along with some insider tips on guaranteeing a successful project for you and your students.

**Worth Repeating**

*Stress management opportunities are everywhere in nature. Children who are classroom bound during the school day are often the most in need of direct stress relief. A brisk walk or playtime outdoors during any season fills lungs with oxygen, increases heart rate and respiration, and invites reflection of the surroundings. Keeping field notes or a nature journal directs the observer (children) away from tensions or problems, offering a brief hiatus.*

**Barbara Norris**
**Teacher, Gifted Education**
**Downingtown Area School District**
**Downingtown, PA**

## Meet Green Woods Charter School

Throughout this book you'll read the experiences and advice written by or about other teachers. Kathleen Geist is one of those teachers who stepped up to offer her schoolyard experiences. Kathleen teaches eighth grade at Green Woods Charter School in Philadelphia, Pennsylvania. She holds two PA Teaching Certifications: K-12 Environmental Science and Middle School Science. She writes:

*Every day, the Green Woods teaching team provides students with learning experiences that focus on the relationship between humans and the natural world. Our location on the grounds of Schuykill Center for Environmental Education (SCEE) provides Green Woods with a "learning laboratory" complete with ponds, streams, forests, and fields, while our partnership SCEE enhances the curriculum created and delivered by our staff. Our school stresses integration between the core subjects, so our 7th grade teaching team planned a unit meshing Lewis & Clark (social studies), biographies and journals of expedition members, journal-writing (ELA), database management (technology) and creating a field guide to the school grounds (life science). In science we discussed why scientists give each living thing a unique scientific name. Different organisms with the same common name are confusing; there are at least five "snakeroot" plants but they are unrelated; at least one is medicinal and another is poisonous. Also, one organism may have many common names, such as pill bug, sow bug, wood louse, potato bug, or roly-poly.*

*We explored classification by using dichotomous keys. We keyed out the classroom ("Student is a boy, straight black hair, brown eyes, no freckles: he's Jack"). That was easy; next we keyed out leaves. Students found that any mistakes (such as deciding the leaves were opposite instead of alternate) led to an incorrect ID and they had to start over. Most of the class now feels that field guides, with their pictures, are more "user friendly" than dichotomous keys.*

*Our data gathering will be during the winter, so I chose birds for our first field guide. The students brainstormed the features they thought would be most helpful in a bird guide. Groups each reviewed a bird field guide, ranked it (up to "five stars") and reported back to the class. We'll use one of our "five star" choices to do our ID work.*

*The next step is for students to learn bird parts and field marks. In the field students will fill worksheets with simple bird diagrams, habitat and behavior notes. After making an ID the data will be input onto computers. Finally we'll decide how to set up our field guide pages.*

(Note: find an exercise for creating your own dichotomous keys in Chapter 5, *Exercises, Lessons, and Forms, on page 95*).

### Worth Repeating

*No teacher should be intimidated by the size and complexity of the outdoors. Everything out there does have a name, but triple doctorates in botany, zoology, and ecology are not necessary to teach some of the basic concepts. "I don't know" is a perfectly acceptable answer to "What is that?" Better still, "I don't know, but I wonder why it is here?" puts the question to both teacher and student, leading into a dialogue of "how come," "why," "what if," and "suppose." Of course there is always a guide book for identification but knowing the names of things is not as interesting or as important as knowing about them: what they need, what makes them flourish, why they live in this particular place. It's like getting to know new friends: we are not attracted by a name as much as we are by unique characteristics, behavior, or similar interests. Any field trip to the schoolyard can be successful and the secret to that success is preparation.*

**From Bridges to the Natural World, Patricia F. Kane, et al. ©New Jersey Audubon Society**

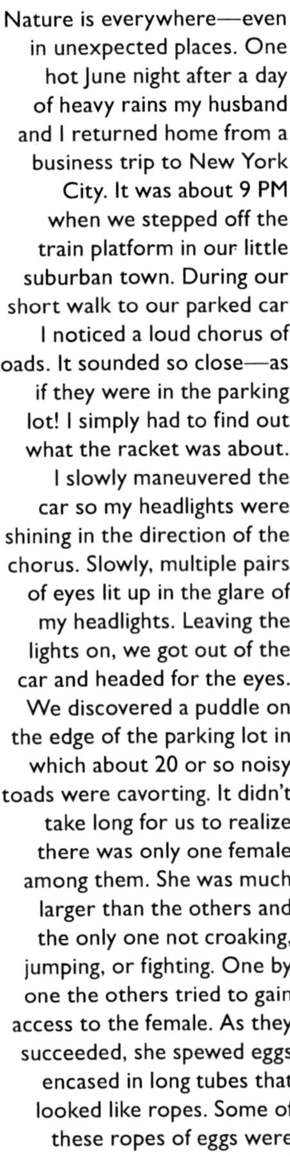

**Toads at the Train Station**

Nature is everywhere—even in unexpected places. One hot June night after a day of heavy rains my husband and I returned home from a business trip to New York City. It was about 9 PM when we stepped off the train platform in our little suburban town. During our short walk to our parked car I noticed a loud chorus of toads. It sounded so close—as if they were in the parking lot! I simply had to find out what the racket was about. I slowly maneuvered the car so my headlights were shining in the direction of the chorus. Slowly, multiple pairs of eyes lit up in the glare of my headlights. Leaving the lights on, we got out of the car and headed for the eyes. We discovered a puddle on the edge of the parking lot in which about 20 or so noisy toads were cavorting. It didn't take long for us to realize there was only one female among them. She was much larger than the others and the only one not croaking, jumping, or fighting. One by one the others tried to gain access to the female. As they succeeded, she spewed eggs encased in long tubes that looked like ropes. Some of these ropes of eggs were several feet long!

We drove home to retrieve our cameras and back to the parking lot to take photos. The toads kept us entertained for a few hours, and we managed to get some great photos. As I looked at the photos I realized that I'd seen toad eggs several times in my life. But I never gave any thought to what they were—they were just "ropes" in the mud. What a discovery—toads at the train station—who would have thought?

## Meet Park Forest Elementary School

Park Forest Elementary (PFE) is located in State College, Pennsylvania, on a 22-acre, mostly-wooded, rural property. Since 1990, it has been under the leadership of Principal Donnan Stoicovy, a very talented, energetic, and innovative environmental educator. That year, Donnan set a goal to provide the ultimate placed-based environmental education for her students using her school site for learning. She began by blazing trails—literally. She worked with her district high school, recruiting student volunteers to create a trail in the wooded school property. When the trail was completed, it was labeled the "Trail of Life". The entire PFE staff is committed to environmental education. Thanks to Donnan and her staff's efforts there have been numerous environmental projects, programs, grants, and successes, and PFE is also the recipient of a special recognition from the Pennsylvania Department of Education for their commitment to environmental education.

Donnan's work continues today with garbage-less lunch activities, garden sites, tree planting, grants, and a butterfly garden. She conserved and preserved their established outdoor learning sites while their school building was razed and a new one constructed on the very same property! Throughout this book, Donnan shares her newest schoolyard project with us—the one in which she led 450 students, 90 faculty and staff, and 20 classrooms, in a study of their schoolyard plants and wildlife during 8 visits a day at 4 sites in one schoolyard over the course of one school year. Her goal was to record a natural field history of the four sites. Data collected from the students will help her determine how to use each of the sites in the future—such as to plant a butterfly or vegetable garden, or use an area for birdwatching.

Donnan and her staff are an inspiration and model for every educator, and I thank them for sharing invaluable experiences and immeasurable knowledge for your enrichment and enjoyment.

www.istockphoto.com/bonniej

In This Chapter

Choosing Your Subjects
Choosing Your Content
Defining Your Property
Scheduling Observations
Assessing Material and Equipment Needs
Creating a Budget

CHAPTER TWO

# Planning and Launching a Field Guide Project

To help you make informed planning decisions I have provided a significant amount of background information on each of the planning steps. This chapter also contains stories from other educators, product recommendations, and an example budget from an elementary school studying their schoolyard.

You'll plan your FGP in six easy steps by:

1. Choosing which plants and animals to include in your FGP.
2. Determining what data you want to collect on each.
3. Defining your school property for observation purposes.
4. Scheduling observation times and locations.
5. Determining equipment needs.
6. Creating a budget.

If you haven't been outside you might want to take time to do so before you begin your planning. You only need a few minutes to take a quick assessment of the nature in your schoolyard. Invite another teacher (or two) to walk the

 **Worth Repeating**

*Thank God they cannot cut down the clouds.*

**Henry David Thoreau**

**Recommended: A Field Guide to Your Region**

A ***field guide to a region*** covers a variety of species of plants and animals within a given geographic area. This type of field guide can help you during the planning phase of your FGP because it will help you to understand the wealth and variety of plants and animals you might find in your schoolyard. It can help you determine which subjects to include in the field guide to your schoolyard. If you need a quick, basic, understanding of your local flora and fauna, this is the way to go.

The National Audubon Society has a series of field guides to regions of the U.S. (such as the Rocky Mountains). Each guide contains more than 1,000 of a region's birds, wildflowers, trees, mammals, mosses, fishes, amphibians, reptiles, and butterflies. You'll also find a region's natural history, best parks and preserves, geology, wildlife habitats, ecology, fossils, rocks and minerals, clouds and weather patterns, and even a guide to the night sky. The books are organized so that the information is directly below the photograph.

Eastern Cottontail

schoolyard with you. Count every different plant each of you sees and every animal you see or hear. It isn't necessary to identify each one, simply count the different things you see or hear, such as 10 birds, 8 flowers, 3 trees, and so forth.

If you can't do an assessment, don't like surprises, and have *no clue* which plants and animals are likely in your neighborhood, get your hands on a field guide to your region. Otherwise, allow me to guide you in selecting the plants and animals to include in your project.

I've created a form to assist you in the planning process called the *FGP Planning Workbook.* There are two versions of this: a hard copy located in *Chapter Five, Exercises, Lessons, and Forms* on page 72 and an electronic version which you can download from our Website. These workbooks can double as a meeting agenda when you are recruiting others and campaigning for support for your project. To download the electronic workbook, visit the FGP section of our Website at **www.takeawalk.com** and double click the file. Microsoft Excel will launch on your computer with the workbook file opened. Save the file before you use it so you have a new, blank copy should you need it later. Use the "Save as" menu command in Excel to save different versions by giving different file names to your workbook. Not only will the electronic workbook calculate your project costs, it can easily be distributed electronically as an attachment to email.

## Step One: Choosing Your Subjects

In Table 1.1, *Common Plants and Animals of Mid-Atlantic Schoolyards* (see page 11), I listed some of the plants and animals I've seen in Mid-Atlantic schoolyards over the past year. I created the list from memory. If I had actually kept a list it would no doubt contain many more species than I can recall. The point is, there are probably more plants and animals in your schoolyard than you realize, and it's best to choose which ones you want to include in your book before you begin your project. How do you decide which plants and animals you should include in your FGP? You begin with birds.

### Begin with Birds

Birds are an exciting subject for children. Birdwatching is a wildly popular hobby and one of the fastest-growing outdoor hobbies in the United States. It's easy to understand why. One can watch birds anywhere and during any season. It's inexpensive, easy to do, and requires little equipment (a pair of binoculars and a field guide). From the birds in our backyards, in the parking lots of our shopping centers, in our parks, at our beaches, in bodies of water, in the skies overhead, birds are simply everywhere we go. There are more than 600 species of birds in North America. For these reasons and more, I suggest you begin your FGP with birds.

Kids and birds are a natural. This has been observed and written about time and time again by those who spend time with and write about kids and nature. Even middle and high school students (believe it or not) are easily captivated by birds, given the opportunity to do a little birdwatching.

Whether you decide to begin your project with birds alone or birds and trees, insects, or other plants and animals, you should still start with birds. Of all your prospective subjects, birds have the greatest power to captivate. The success of your project can just about be guaranteed if you start with birds, and here are a few more reasons birds make a great starting point:

- **Birds are plentiful.** With more than 600 species of birds in North America there's a good chance that a minimum of six species and as many as 20 can be seen or heard from urban schoolyards and 13 or more species from suburban and rural schoolyards.

- **Birds are ubiquitous.** You will find birds wherever you find their food source. Different species have different food sources, so which species you find depends on which food sources are present. Food sources for birds include: small mammals, fish, reptiles and amphibians, insects, berries, seeds, nuts, human food scraps, road kill and other carcasses, and even other birds. If you hang a bird feeder, not only will you attract the birds that eat the kind of food contained in that feeder, you will attract the birds that eat the birds that eat the food in the container.

- **Birds come in a wide range of colors and sizes.** From the largest of our birds of prey to the smallest of our hummingbirds, from red to blue to yellow and orange, birds come in enough variety of sizes and colors to interest those of us with even the shortest of attention spans.

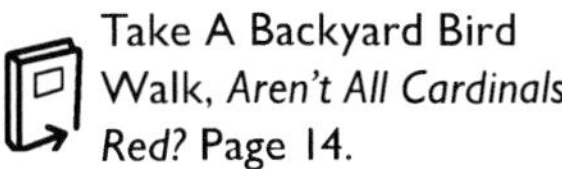
Take A Backyard Bird Walk, *Aren't All Cardinals Red?* Page 14.

- **Birds are present year-round.** Which species you see may change with the seasons. Some will nest in your region—maybe even in your schoolyard. Others will winter in your region. Still others will be present only during migration periods.

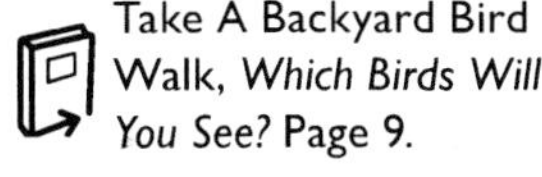
Take A Backyard Bird Walk, *Which Birds Will You See?* Page 9.

- **Birds offer something for all ages**. Younger students can study birds at the feeder, where they stay long enough for the inexperienced to identify them. Older students can observe and identify birds in flight, learning to identify not only by field marks but by flight patterns. Older students can also learn to identify or differentiate between juvenile and adult birds, and to identify seasonal markings in birds—a sometimes challenging task.

- **Birdwatching is possible for the physically impaired.** Visually impaired students can learn to bird-by-ear. Bird call recognition can often be the determining factor in identifying a bird. Physically impaired students can watch birds from the comfort of the classroom by observing activities at a bird feeder or from a single, easily-accessed location in the field. Hearing impaired students can be bird watchers as opposed to bird listeners and can also help identify birds by their behavior.

- **Birds exhibit different behaviors.** Bird behavior is fascinating to children and adults as well. Different species have definite and recognizable behaviors. Even without the other clues: shape, size, color, beak description, song or call, and location some bird behaviors are so species-specific that one can identify a bird on location and behavior description alone.

Bull Thistle

- **Birdwatching is a life-long hobby.** Birds are so charismatic that birdwatching often becomes a life-long activity. It's an inexpensive hobby that requires little equipment (a pair of binoculars and a field guide). Your study of the birds in your schoolyard will give students a skill and an activity they can use and participate in for the rest of their lives.

- **Information on birds is plentiful and accessible.** Birds are one of our most studied animals by both professionals as well as hobbyists. There are hundreds of Websites dedicated to wild birds and birdwatching such as Cornell Laboratory of Ornithology's **www.birds.cornell.edu.** There are thousands of books on the topic of wild birds and birdwatching, both fiction and nonfiction, such as *That Quail Robert* by Margaret Stanger, and even books on how to draw birds such as *How to Draw Birds,* one of a series on how-to-draw books for kids from Dover Publications. There are several CDs for learning bird calls, such as *Birding by Ear* (a Peterson Field Guide CD). There are award-winning movies and documentaries to show in your classroom, such as *Fly Away Home*, *Winged Migration*, and David Attenborough's *Life of Birds* (PBS). Among these resources are several age-appropriate materials for your students. You'll find an expanded list of resources in Chapter Five, *Exercises, Lessons and Forms.*

Birds certainly don't have to be the only subject for your FGP; but definitely begin with them. For more information on observing birds, see *Observing Birds* on page 45 Chapter 3, *Observation and Data Collection.*

## Guarantee Success with Bird Feeders

Before you take your students outdoors for nature observation, help Mother Nature along by stacking the deck to help ensure success. When it comes to nature, stacking the deck means supplying food and water; and this is especially true when you want to observe birds. Although bird baths are not a good option for most schools because keeping them filled can be a challenge, a small depression in the ground with a few flat stones where water can collect after a rain is a good alternative to a bird bath. Hang a filled bird feeder a few weeks before your students start their outdoor observations to guarantee that they'll see birds. Urban schools should be cautious and remove the feeder if you are attracting too many pigeons. Know that feeding birds often means feeding squirrels, so buy a feeder that is sturdy (metal) and not likely to be destroyed by squirrels. You could also recycle old soda bottles as feeders—which the squirrels will destroy but which cost nothing to replace.

Monarch

Be assured that by feeding the birds you are not interfering with their ability to find food. Also, the feeders should be taken down during the summer. Birds won't even bother with the feeders in the summer (except for hummingbirds, which will take sugar water from hummingbird feeders). In summer months when birds are breeding, they search for insects to feed their young. Bacteria breeds in the heat of summer—another good reason to remove your feeder. Lastly, clean the feeder occasionally with bleach and water. Please—*please* don't let your school deter you from hanging a feeder because of Avian flu. There have been no reports yet in the U.S. of Avian flu. To learn more about bird feeders and feeding birds visit **www.cornell.edu/birds**.

The beauty of a bird feeder is that you can observe even in inclement weather if the bird feeder is visible from within the school. You might want to start young students' observations of nature indoors regardless of weather. They'll be less likely to scare off the birds with their chatter and movements if there is a window between them and the birds.

Birds are attracted to feeders for two reasons. The feeder contains the preferred food for that species of bird and the feeder is designed to dispense food in a manner accessible to a particular species. For example, there are platform feeders (flat beds) and platform eaters (Mourning Doves). There are thistle feeders (long tubes with or without perches that the tiny thistle seed will fit through but not spill out of) and thistle eaters (American Goldfinch). There are feeders with perches (little bars protruding from the feeder) and birds that prefer perches over platforms. So how do you decide on the best feeder for your schoolyard?

If you can only have one feeder, choose a feeder that has both a platform at the bottom and perches or a mesh that the perch feeders and woodpeckers can grasp. One of my favorite feeders is my original *Mobi Mesh* feeder that I purchased from my local Wild Bird Center of America store. If you have a problem with your feeders attracting larger mammals such as bears or raccoons, change the food in your feeder (don't use suet), remove the feeder for several weeks, move the feeder to a different location, or bring the feeder in at night.

The best seed for attracting a variety of species is sunflower seed. Seed mixes that include millet attract a lot of "unwanted" species that hang out on or near a feeder. These Mourning Doves, European Starlings, Grackles, Starlings, and House Sparrows might make it difficult for smaller birds to access the feeder. Large birds also have large bird droppings.

Suet is a good choice for attracting woodpeckers. You'll need a suet feeder. Don't feed seed or suet in hot months. Birds depend on insects and fruits during those months and they won't visit your feeder frequently. Also, your seed or suet will go bad in the hot weather.

Bird feeders can be breeding grounds for birds to pass diseases on to other birds. It's important to clean your feeder regularly with hot soapy water. The Cornell Laboratory of Ornithology recommends every two weeks. Rinse the feeder well and then disinfect it with a mixture of one part bleach to 9 parts water. Rinse and dry it before filling it again.

Hang the bird feeder in a place that can be viewed from a public area from within the school such as a hallway, courtyard, or cafeteria. Or hang it outside your classroom window.

For more information on types of feeders, feeding birds, and maintaining bird feeders and birds at school, visit the Cornell Website at: **www.birds.cornell.edu/AllAboutBirds.**

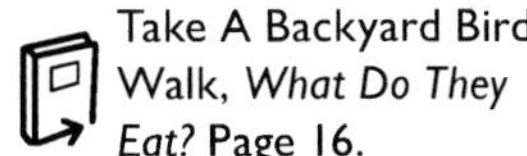

Take A Backyard Bird Walk, *What Do They Eat?* Page 16.

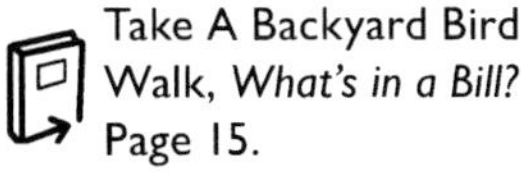

Take A Backyard Bird Walk, *What's in a Bill?* Page 15.

**Worth Repeating Out the Window**

*Sometimes life's best lessons are learned when staring outside the window. I used to hang a feeder about 10 feet from my classroom window. The teacher and the students can immediately spot new species. The proximity also allows the students good viewing for drawing and studying behavior up close. A good teacher would not be worried about being upstaged by the birds. Some of my former third graders (now young adults) still talk about the birds "they discovered". I also suggest that the children help clean up and fill the feeders. My third graders loved doing this after which they'd form a quiet line and stand about 10 feet away and watch five or six different species land while they watched. Yes, 15 kids can be quiet when they are motivated!*

**Joyce Mitchell**
**Retired teacher**
**Glasford, IL**

****Caution** Peanut Allergies**

If you buy mixed bird seed be aware that it may contain peanuts, peanut pieces, or dust from peanuts. Suet often contains peanuts and peanut products, too. Play it safe and protect students with peanut allergies from exposure to any bird seed or suet products.

## Other Subjects

Depending on the number of students, the amount of time you want to dedicate to this project, and the physical characteristics of your schoolyard, you should begin your FGP with at least two subjects, with one of them being birds.

If you are a truly urban school with little or no plant life in your schoolyard, no parks nearby, and only a sampling of wildlife, you might want to include all of these subjects in your FGP. Consider expanding your species information too, so your FGP keeps students motivated. For example, if you include butterflies in your project and then find only two species, include detailed information on the butterfly life cycle. If you find mostly pigeons, include a detailed pigeon study. My seven-point criteria for selecting FGP book subjects is:

**Note on Migration** 

Ask an elementary student "what animals migrate?" Most will answer "birds". Unless, of course, they get excited and confused and answer "bears". Ask "*why* do birds migrate?" And most will say, "because it's cold". Someone is teaching our children that birds migrate because of the weather—is it you? Students should be taught that all animals that migrate do so to *follow their food source*. There's an important distinction here—the cold weather is affecting the food source, not the birds' desire to keep warm. Please teach this to your students. It will help them understand why whales and other mammals migrate, as well as birds.

1. Plants and animals widely distributed throughout North America north of Mexico.

2. Plants and animals that are easy to spot and which can be observed safely from a distance or up close.

3. Plants and animals familiar and attractive to kids.

4. Plants and animals for which there are a variety of field guides well suited for different skills, reading levels, and age groups.

5. Plants and animals for which there are a lot of data available and accessible in books, movies, and Websites.

6. Plants and animals for which there are organizations and clubs that educate the general public about those plants and animals (such as the National Audubon Society, National Wildlife Federation, National Gardening Association).

7. Plants and animals that are generally not threatening or harmful. In other words, I have avoided *bees, flies, alligators, rats, mice, and snakes* as a separate and focused subject in your project.

Take A Tree Walk. 

Using my criteria, I've developed a list of suggestions for subjects (other than birds) for your Field Guide Project:

- **Trees.** Like birds, trees are a terrific subject for kids. There are a huge number of species of trees in North America; in the U.S., more than 300 west of the Rocky Mountains, 364 east, and more than 300 in all of Canada. North Carolina is reported to have more species of trees than all of Europe so if your school is located in North Carolina, birds and trees would be a fabulous start for your FGP. In general, trees are plentiful and accessible. They're also easy to study because they don't move! Humans, animals and other plants benefit greatly from trees; trees have adapted to many climates and habitats; trees have played important parts in our history thus they make excellent subjects for botany, history, civics, and math—beyond the

Black Oak

scope of the field guide. For tips on tree observation, see Chapter Three, *Observation and Data Collection, Observing Trees,* on page 46

- **Insects and Spiders** There are more than 100,000 species of insects and spiders in North America—more than the sum of all other groups of plants and animals mentioned in this book! Most field guides cover about 600 to 700 of the widespread and most visible insects and spiders. You might want to start with a small group of insects—choosing those that are not considered threatening to students and those that don't bite or sting—such as butterflies, beetles, grasshoppers, and so forth. Don't overlook ants—kids love ants and they could look for ant colonies, observe behaviors and even set up an ant farm in the classroom.

- **Butterflies**. There are about 725 species of butterflies in North America and about 275 species in Canada. According to the North American Butterfly Association (NABA, **www.naba.org**) "in most places in the United States you can find about 100 butterfly species near your home". Wow! Different species have different *flight seasons*, some as short as two weeks. Different species also have different numbers of broods per season. Some butterflies can be seen only in the spring and only for a period of a few weeks. Others can be seen from spring to fall with several generations passing during that time. Still others produce only one brood and it might be present from spring to fall. The height of butterfly season is the summer but there are plenty of species in spring and fall. There are many reasons to include butterflies in your FGP: kids and adults are drawn to butterflies; they're harmless to humans; they're colorful and attractive; they're easy to spot and observe; and if you haven't done so already, this is as good a time as any for a butterfly life cycle study. For tips on observing butterflies, see Chapter Three, *Observation and Data Collection, Observing Butterflies,* on page 46.

- **Wildflowers.** There are more than 20,000 species of flowering plants in North America. I guess any of them might qualify as a "wildflower". Most wildflower field guides are divided by regions of North American and regional guides can contain as many as 600 species of wildflowers. Your students will likely be surprised to learn that wildflowers, such as dandelions, grow in their schoolyard and that many plants we call "weeds" are actually wildflowers. Wildflowers are the perfect topic for discussions about native, non-native, invasive, edible, endangered, poisonous, and medicinal plants. For a suggested wildflower lesson, read *Glorious Weeds* from *Green Teacher Magazine* in Chapter Five, *Exercises, Lessons, and Forms,* on page 85.

- **Gardens.** If your school has a garden and, in particular, if that garden hosts the only real plants in the schoolyard, include the garden in your Field Guide Project. The one problem you might face is that it can be difficult to identify cultivated plants and flowers. You won't find a simple field guide to garden plants. You could keep identification limited to families such as "chrysanthemums" or "tulips". A good source for helping identify garden plants is the National Gardening Association (**www.NGA.org**),

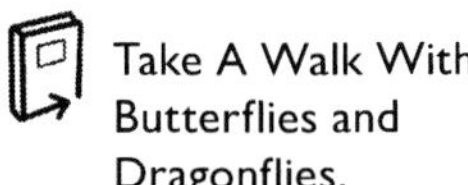

Take A Walk With Butterflies and Dragonflies.

**Multiple Species of Migrating Monarchs**

In September of 2003 my husband Rob and I drove from our home in Pennsylvania to southwestern Illinois for a school visit. While traveling the Ohio Turnpike, we couldn't help but notice the numbers of butterflies splattering over our windshield and the front of our car. I eventually ran out of washer fluid. We stopped at a rest stop to clean the windshield. There we saw that Painted Lady, Common Buckeye, and Red Admiral butterflies were all over the building and grounds. It was then that it occurred to us that we were in the path of a migration—a real eye opener for me because I thought only Monarchs migrated! During a 20 minute break at a rest stop in Ohio, I observed only one person who noticed the entire rest stop area was covered by butterflies. She called out to her husband, "Honey, look at all the Monarchs!"
At least she noticed.

where you'll also find a kids' section. Another helpful tool for plant identification is a seed or flower catalog such as Burpee Seed (**www.burpee.com**).

- **Rocks.** I wouldn't choose inanimate objects over animals. But as a third or fourth subject, or a subject for subsequent years, rocks are perfect for your field guide. Kids love rocks and the things that hide under them. And fossils, well, they're just the greatest, aren't they?

- **Mammals.** Generally speaking, mammals will be the smallest number of species of all your subjects. Keep in mind that mammals aren't as accessible for observation purposes as other animals such as butterflies and birds (except for squirrels, which are likely to visit your bird feeders). And it's important to stress to your students that they keep their distance from all mammals. If you have an area of the schoolyard that is frequently visited by mammals and visible from within your building, conduct your mammal observation from indoors. If you're concerned about safe distances between your students and mammals, or you don't actually see mammals but do see signs of them, create a mammal *tracks* section to your field guide.

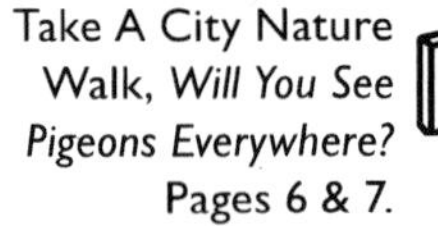
Take A City Nature Walk, *Will You See Pigeons Everywhere?* Pages 6 & 7.

- **Pigeons.** If you are in an urban school you might find only a small variety of birds, such as pigeons, starlings, and House Sparrows. To help make your project exciting for your students, consider focusing on pigeons for your FGP. There are seven color morphs of pigeons and there's a good chance you'll find them all in your schoolyard if you know what you're looking for. Cornell Laboratory of Ornithology has an ongoing study called *PigeonWatch* (go to **www.birds.cornell.edu** and search for "pigeon watch") where you can learn about pigeons and report your findings to their study, giving your students an opportunity to become "citizen scientists". Learn more about finding and observing pigeons in Chapter 3, *Observation and Data Collection, Observing Pigeons,* on page 47.

There are many more topics for your field guide and, of course, what you find depends on the habitats in and around your schoolyard. I've highlighted the most common plants and animals here. If you are still undecided about the right subjects for your project, answer the following questions:

1. **Which plants and animals fit within, expand, or compliment your current curriculum?** There is no sense creating more work for yourself or other teachers, so pick the subjects that fit your curriculum needs and wants.

2. **Which plants and animals help you address your science, environment, or ecology standards?** This is another key to working *smart* instead of working *more*. Use the FGP to achieve your standards requirements and goals.

3. **Which plants and animals do you believe will most excite and interest your students?** There are enough subjects in a field guide project that you can choose those you believe the students will embrace quickly.

Rock Pigeon

4. **Which plants and animals do you believe you will actually be able to find and observe in your schoolyard?**

Weigh the answers to those questions along with the information I provided on various subjects and you'll have your list of subjects. Scale down that list to two or three subjects to include in your new project. You can always add more later. If you're an urban school, include a wide range of subjects. When you decide on which subjects you want to include in your book, indicate so on your *Planning Workbook*.

Your next step is to determine how much species content you want to include in your book, whether or not you want to include other content such as a school history, and how you want to organize your book.

## Step Two: Choosing Your Content

How much information do you want to include about each species of plant and animal in your book? The more information you include, the more pages you'll need for each species. To keep things simple, think of your book in a single page per species format or a two-page spread per species. Using a single page, each species has its own page in your book and everything about that species (name, illustration, other information) must be designed to fit on one page. The more information you have, the smaller the print and photos will be. In a spread format, all species will have two facing pages on which to place the content. Because books start on the right page, your first page is a natural for your title page and your last page can be an index page. Either way, it's helpful to determine how many pages you want per species so that you can keep a handle on the size of your book during your project.

Some species content can be presented in list format—such as date, time, and location observed. Other information—such as physical descriptions and behavior—will need to be presented in paragraph form. The *content table* located on your *Planning Workbook* indicates which content is best suited for list (L) or paragraph (P) format. This will help you to determine whether or not you have chosen content that can realistically fit on one page per species.

Following are some suggestions for additional content.

- Scientific names (with pronunciation key).
- Common name.
- Size, physical description and field marks.
- Range.

Take A Backyard Bird Walk
*Recording Observations*, page 17,
*Bird Notes*, page 19.

Take A Tree Walk
*Recording Your Observations*, page 24,
*Tree Notes*, page 25.

Take A Walk With Butterflies and Dragonflies
*Caterpillar Observation Notes*, page 21
*Butterfly Observation Notes*, page 22
*Dragonfly Observation Notes*, page 23.

Take A City Nature Walk
*Go! Create a Nature ID Page*, pages 22 and 23.

Stellar's Jay

- An illustration or photograph, more than one if seasonal changes result in significant physical changes.
- How it is affected by seasons—such as the growing season, seasonal movements and migration.
- The habitat and food needs.
- Whether or not the species is native, non-native, endemic, invasive, threatened, or endangered.
- How the plant or animal reproduces.
- The value of the plant to wildlife, or the value of wildlife to the plant (pollinators) and any synergistic relationships with like kind or others.
- The time, date, and a map or written description of the plant's location.
- A theory or speculation about why the plant or wildlife is in your schoolyard. Was it planted there by someone? Is the animal a year-round resident? How does the schoolyard meet the survival needs of the species?
- A natural history of the species.
- Known conservation issues.
- Whether or not improvements to the schoolyard can help plants and animals survive and, if so, what improvements are needed.
- Whether or not the presence of a species is harmful, dangerous, or in any way a problem or nuisance.
- Observed behavior.
- Its value to humans, other wildlife and plants and/or its habitat.

Your *Planning Workbook* contains a *content table* that lists these content suggestions and that has room for you to add your own items.

## Suggestions For Bonus Content

When you inject the personality and culture of your school and community into your field guide it becomes much more than an inventory or species account. It becomes a *journal*, a *historical record,* a veritable *time capsule.* Here are some suggestions for additional content. Each of these content suggestions can represent one or more pages in your book. The number of pages is completely at your discretion. In Chapter Four, *Assembling Your Book,* we'll discuss the placement of these pages within your book. But for now it's good to know if you want to include them in your project so you can plan to assign them to a group of students.

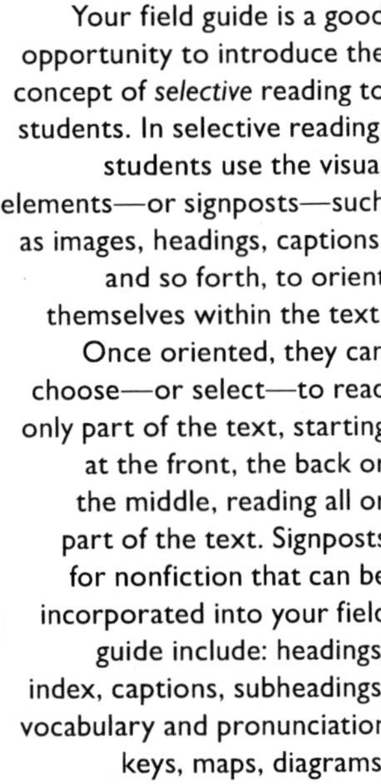
**Nonfiction Signposts**

Your field guide is a good opportunity to introduce the concept of *selective* reading to students. In selective reading, students use the visual elements—or signposts—such as images, headings, captions, and so forth, to orient themselves within the text. Once oriented, they can choose—or select—to read only part of the text, starting at the front, the back or the middle, reading all or part of the text. Signposts for nonfiction that can be incorporated into your field guide include: headings, index, captions, subheadings, vocabulary and pronunciation keys, maps, diagrams, photographs and sidebars.

- ***Foreword.*** A Foreword page usually contains a message from the author about the book. Your Foreword might contain your mission statement and even predictions of what you think you'll find when you explore your schoolyard. Whether you include a mission statement in your book, it would be useful in helping students to understand the scope and guidelines of the project.

- ***About Our Students.*** Make a permanent record of student involvement with a list of contributors. You might even want to create a multi-page "photo-documentary" of your project with photos of the students at work in the school and in the field.

- ***About Our School.*** Here students can write a brief description of the school, such as: when built, the architect, which school district, how many students, grades, and so forth. They might also include a history of significant events or a paragraph on celebrated alumni. This is a good place for a natural history of the school property—how was the land used before the school was built? How far back can students trace the history of the property? You could use this page to dedicate your field guide, to acknowledge a retiring staff or faculty member, or to list special school awards or recognitions.

- ***About Our Schoolyard.*** This page can contain a written description of the physical characteristics of the schoolyard. It can accompany your schoolyard map. Alternatively, this is a good place to express student views on the schoolyard as a habitat for plants and animals

- ***Our Watershed***. Reinforce your watershed lessons. Incorporate them into your FGP by giving students an opportunity to illustrate—with maps and writing—what they've learned about their watershed.

- ***Project History.*** This can't be written until the conclusion of your project—or the school year, whichever comes first. A history page can illuminate your findings by including funny or unusual experiences, significant or unexpected findings, and student conclusions. The information can be in essay or list format. For lists, have your students summarize their feelings about the project in one sentence. Add a "charm" effect to your book by scanning student conclusions and pasting the images on this page. Other options for a History page include: how and when you conducted observations, the number of students that participated in the project, unexpected findings, eventful encounters, information on special content contributors, thanks, and special recognitions. It should also address the things you wrote about in your Foreword.

- ***Map of Our Schoolyard***. A map can be a very simple diagram as shown in Figure 2.1. Or students can break the map into areas and create names or numbers for each. They can use the areas names to describe the location of a plant or animal. The location can be included in your species description. If you don't want to include a map in your field guide, it can still be useful to help students understand property lines when they are conducting field observations.

**What is a Watershed?**

Water doesn't stand still. It flows underground and from small streams into bigger creeks, rivers, or lakes. A watershed is the area that the water travels over and through on its way to a larger body of water. A watershed includes the land and the water that runs through it, as well as the plants, animals, and humans who live there. The health of the water you drink, bathe in, and do your laundry in depends on the health of your watershed. To find which watershed you live in, go to **www.epa.gov/surf.**

Take A Backyard Bird Walk, *My Map, page 5.*

Take A Tree Walk, *My Map*, page 5.

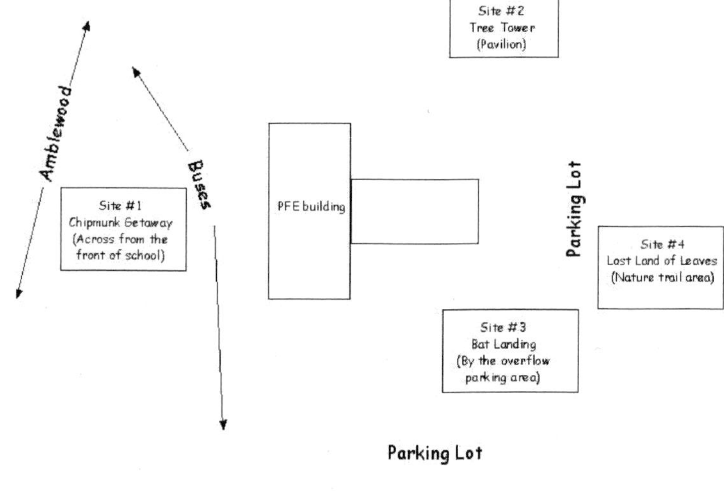


**Figure 2.1 A map to your schoolyard can be a simple diagram of your schoolyard like this one created by Park Forest Elementary Principal Donnan Stoicovy.**

In addition to this bonus book content, any number of components, such as an index, table of contents, and so forth, can be incorporated into your book. For more information on the parts of a book, consult your library for the *Chicago Manual of Style* by the University of Chicago Press.

## Step Three: Defining Your Property

What constitutes your schoolyard? When students see a plant or animal, how will they determine whether or not that plant or animal is "in" the schoolyard and whether or not it can be included in your field guide? Your schoolyard property line might seem like an obvious boundary but what should you do about birds flying overhead?

To avoid confusion, I suggest you set the boundaries and parameters for counting before you take your students outdoors. By counting all the birds you see, rather than just those "in" the schoolyard, you'll get a broader selection of species. You might want to apply the same to mammal observation. You don't want to encourage students to attract mammals to the schoolyard and you don't want to encourage them to get close to mammals. So a fox seen running through a neighboring field and a squirrel in the tree across the street should be counted.

You'd probably be inclined only to count the plants growing within your property boundaries but if the tree across the street is the only tree around, you might change your mind.

## Step Four: Scheduling Observations

If your FGP is comprised of a single class during a single marking period, you might not need a time line or schedule for observation. But if multiple classes are participating in the project and if your project will span more than one marking period, a schedule will ensure that all students have the opportunity to observe. You'll find a section on your *Planning Workbook* to write your

Luna Moth

observation schedule. To create different scheduling scenarios, save different versions of your workbook file.

As you plan *when* your students will conduct their observations and for *how long,* you need to consider such things as frequency, inclement weather, school closings, seasonal changes, and so forth. You'll also need to provide ample time for students to take notes outdoors or, if there is no place for note-taking in the schoolyard, schedule class time for them when they return from the outdoors. Here are some considerations for creating observation schedules:

- **Decide how you will handle inclement weather.** Park Forest, one of our example schools, sent their kids outside even in the rain. Animals have to deal with rain—why not us? How will you handle inclement weather?
- **Choose multiple locations.** Don't keep the children in one spot all the time. Different habitats have different food sources, shelter, and plants and animals.
- **Provide ample time for observations and writing.** If your school day is divided into periods you'll no doubt schedule observation/writing time to correlate with periods. Ideally, each student would have one period a week for project work (observation and book creation). Otherwise, set your schedule so students have no less than 20 minutes per scheduled observation plus sufficient time to travel from and to the classroom and field as well as sufficient time to take notes indoors if they can't take notes while outdoors.
- **Stagger schedules.** To ensure that students have an opportunity to observe nature in the morning as well as the afternoon, stagger their schedules. Animals may exhibit different behavior at different times of the day—birds are active in the early morning as they look for food, butterflies are most active between 11 AM and 3 PM when the sun is shining and the temperature is at its daily high.
- **Span seasons.** As seasons change, so do plants and animals. Maximize your students' nature experiences by spanning seasons when you schedule observation times.
- **Observe frequently.** Nature is constantly moving and changing. Animals migrate. Some insects have a life span of only a few weeks—or even days. Nature will engage your students when you send them outdoors to explore; and the more they observe, the more they'll see. In a perfect world, you'll have the flexibility to provide each student with a monthly opportunity to observe; and your schoolyard will be observed at different times of the day. Table 2.1 illustrates how Park Forest Elementary School scheduled their entire school body so that each student had an opportunity to observe the schoolyard once a month.

**Worth Repeating**

*One of the most tragic things I know about human nature is that 99% of all of us tend to put off living. We are all dreaming of some magical rose garden over the horizon instead of enjoying the roses that are blooming outside our windows today.*

**Dale Carnegie**

| Park Forest Observation Schedule by Teacher | | | | | | | | | |
|---|---|---|---|---|---|---|---|---|---|
| Meyers | Aug 31 | Oct 3 | Nov 6 | Dec 14 | Jan 24 | Feb 26 | Apr 5 | May 10 |
| Wilson | Sep 1 | Oct 4 | Nov 7 | Dec 15 | Jan 25 | Feb 27 | Apr 9 | May 11 |
| Bowman | Sep 5 | Oct 5 | Nov 8 | Dec 18 | Jan 26 | Feb 28 | Apr 10 | May 14 |
| Romig | Sep 6 | Oct 6 | Nov 9 | Dec 19 | Jan 30 | Mar 1 | Apr 11 | May 15 |
| Hartman | Sep 7 | Oct 9 | Nov 10 | Dec 20 | Jan 31 | Mar 2 | Apr 12 | May 16 |
| Daughenbaugh | Sep 8 | Oct 10 | Nov 13 | Dec 21 | Feb 1 | Mar 5 | Apr 13 | May 17 |
| Karwoski | Sep 11 | Oct 11 | Nov 14 | Dec 22 | Feb 2 | Mar 6 | Apr 16 | May 18 |
| Roth | Sep 12 | Oct 12 | Nov 15 | Jan 2 | Feb 5 | Mar 7 | Apr 17 | May 21 |
| Humphrey | Sep 13 | Oct 13 | Nov 16 | Jan 3 | Feb 6 | Mar 8 | Apr 18 | May 22 |
| Patrick | Sep 14 | Oct 16 | Nov 17 | Jan 4 | Feb 7 | Mar 19 | Apr 19 | May 23 |
| Stroschein | Sep 15 | Oct 17 | Nov 28 | Jan 5 | Feb 8 | Mar 20 | Apr 20 | May 24 |
| Shockowitz | Sep 18 | Oct 18 | Nov 29 | Jan 8 | Feb 9 | Mar 21 | Apr 23 | May 25 |
| Watson | Sep 19 | Oct 19 | Nov 30 | Jan 9 | Feb 12 | Mar 22 | Apr 24 | May 29 |
| Khayat | Sep 20 | Oct 20 | Dec 1 | Jan 10 | Feb 13 | Mar 23 | Apr 25 | May 30 |
| Mauk | Sep 21 | Oct 25 | Dec 4 | Jan 11 | Feb 14 | Mar 26 | Apr 30 | May 31 |
| Mattivi | Sep 22 | Oct 26 | Dec 5 | Jan 12 | Feb 15 | Mar 27 | May 1 | Jun 1 |
| Milutinovic | Sep 25 | Oct 27 | Dec 6 | Jan 16 | Feb 16 | Mar 28 | May 2 | Jun 4 |
| Vogt | Sep 26 | Oct 30 | Dec 7 | Jan 17 | Feb 19 | Mar 29 | May 3 | Jun 5 |
| DelReal | Sep 27 | Oct 31 | Dec 8 | Jan 18 | Feb 20 | Mar 30 | May 4 | Jun 6 |
| Valent | Sep 28 | Nov 1 | Dec 11 | Jan 19 | Feb 21 | Apr 2 | May 7 | Jun 7 |
| Abruzzo | Sep 29 | Nov 2 | Dec 12 | Jan 22 | Feb 22 | Apr 3 | May 8 | Jun 8 |
| Shenk | Oct 2 | Nov 3 | Dec 13 | Jan 23 | Feb 23 | Apr 4 | May 9 | |

**Table 2.1. Park Forest Elementary School observation schedule.**

Instead of excluding the summer months, consider reaching out to other teachers and your community. Teachers at schools that have summer programs and families who live close to the school might be willing to volunteer for 15-minute observation periods over the summer. With enough volunteers, you could schedule weekly observations that require volunteers to observe only once during the summer break. Summer observations might add considerably to your list of flowering plants and insects and, especially to your list of schoolyard butterflies.

Each day in nature brings changes. There is much to see year-round, even in the winter. To help you understand what to look for in different seasons, see the *Seasonal Guideposts Table* (Figure 2.2 on page 30) from my very favorite book on journaling, *Keeping a Nature Journal* by Claire Walker Leslie.

## Step Five: Assessing Material and Equipment Needs

The list of what you could use in your project could fill a page. Be conservative in your initial "wish list" and field test equipment before you make any major investment. I can't stress enough that you should avoid items that encourage children to pick, destroy, or collect living plants and animals. Your *Planning Workbook* contains a section for you to list your equipment and material needs and to calculate their costs.

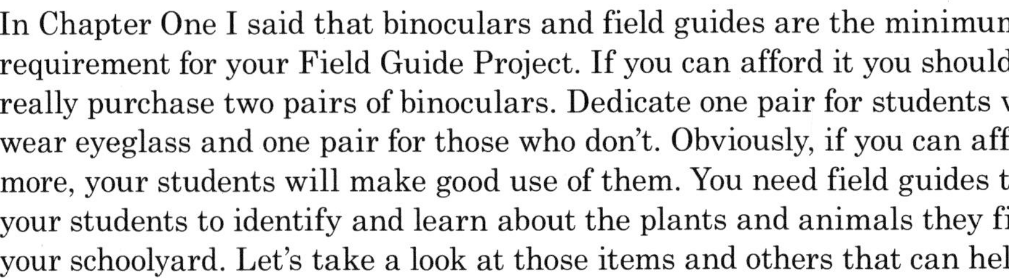

In Chapter One I said that binoculars and field guides are the minimum requirement for your Field Guide Project. If you can afford it you should really purchase two pairs of binoculars. Dedicate one pair for students who wear eyeglass and one pair for those who don't. Obviously, if you can afford more, your students will make good use of them. You need field guides to help your students to identify and learn about the plants and animals they find in your schoolyard. Let's take a look at those items and others that can help you in your Field Guide Project.

American Toad

## Budgeting for Binoculars

It's been my experience that many people who own binoculars, but rarely use them, don't know how to use them; and often they don't even know that they don't know how. To be certain that you understand how to use binoculars as well as how to adjust them for those who wear eyeglass and those who don't, please be sure to read more about binoculars in Chapter Three, *Observation and Data Collection, Choosing and Using Binoculars.*

An important consideration and key for buying binoculars for elementary students is size and weight. There's no sense paying for great optics if the binoculars won't fit small faces or they are too heavy or bulky for young students to carry with them. Pay special attention to the the distance between the pupils of the eyes as it is shorter on children than adults.

Binoculars can range from $20.00 to over $400.00. Park Forest Elementary school is quite happy with the binoculars they purchased for $29.00 from the *Acorn Naturalists* catalog (**www.acornnaturalists.com**). Learn more about them on page 40.

For budgeting purposes you have a choice among three binocular prices: 1) a $29.00 pair for the Acorn Naturalists binoculars, 2) a $75.00 per pair if you want to step up the quality a little, and 3) a $150.00 per pair for middle and high school students.

## Budgeting for Field Guides

You might find the field guides you need for your FGP in your own school library. But a field guide is most useful when it's available and accessible *in the field*, at the time you see something and need to identify it. Because it's easier to identify something when you are looking at it than trying to identify it from memory, you should purchase field guides that can travel with your students every time they are in the field. If multiple classrooms participate in your FGP, one set of guides could move from the class that was scheduled one day to the class that is scheduled the next. Or you could create "mobile labs" that move with the students. *Which* field guides you'll need depends on which subjects you plan to include in your FGP—if your content is birds and trees, you'll want a field guide to the birds of your region and another for trees.

Be advised that all field guides are not created equal. Before you purchase field guides for your students be sure to read *Master the Tools of the Trade* on page 39.

For your budgeting purposes consider that you'll need at least one field guide per subject of your book and that each field guide will cost an average of $10.00. If you have multiple classes observing simultaneously in separate locations, you'll need a copy for each of them, too. This figure is for budgeting purposes only.

House Sparrow (male)

### Seasonal Guideposts

A seasonal journal is essentially your personal record of riding the planet earth through one annual journey around the sun. That journey takes us past four key marker points — the two solstices and two equinoxes.

## Subjects to Observe, Draw, Record throughout the Seasons

| SEASON | BIRDS | ANIMALS |
|---|---|---|
| AUTUMN | Observe change in activity and preparations for winter or migrations south among starlings, hawks, geese, shorebirds.<br>What fruits are robins, mockingbirds, and sparrows eating? | Look for signs of winter preparations, including butterfly migration, and dragonfly migration, and changes in cricket, cicada, and grasshopper calls.<br>Salamanders, slugs, spiders, sowbugs, and fish head for dark places. |
| WINTER | What birds stay through winter and where can you find them?<br>Observe the habits of feeder birds: cardinals, house sparrows, mourning doves, blue jays.<br>Look for wilder birds: owls, hawks, turkeys, ducks, vultures, crows. | What creatures stay active?<br>What do they eat?<br>What creatures disappear to hibernate or die?<br>Observe animals that are active: houseflies, spiders, centipedes, rabbits, red and gray squirrels, foxes, raccoons, deer, elk, and moose.<br>Look for tracks in the mud or snow. |
| SPRING | Watch for the first birds returning from the south: bay and sea ducks, warblers, sparrows.<br>Observe activities of nearby nesting birds: starlings, house sparrows, crows, robins, cardinals. | Focus on the birth, awakening, or return of butterflies, earthworms, chipmunks, insects, frogs and toads, salmon, herring, caribou, dall sheep. |
| SUMMER | Learn to identify birds by their calls and habitats.<br>Read bird guidebooks and practice drawing bird shapes: blue jay, chickadee, magpie, red-tailed hawk, song sparrow, mallard duck, herring gull, common loon. | This is the height of productivity for frogs, toads, snakes, salamanders, turtles, spiders, and earthworms. Document who is doing what.<br>Focus on night sounds: crickets, owls, mice.<br>Learn your local animals and draw them, learning about their habits. |

**Figure 2.2 As you can see from this Seasonal Guideposts chart, every season offers subjects for your Field Guide Project.**
Excerpted from *Keeping a Nature Journal* by Claire Walker Leslie. ©2005 By Claire Walker Leslie. Used with permission from Storey Publishing, LLC, North Adams, Massachusetts.

Within each of these periods, there are many natural objects and events to observe and record. See the box below for some ideas of natural activities, objects, and changes to study at various points in the year. These are just a starting point; you may want to change the questions and focuses depending on where you live and what your interests are.

| PLANTS AND TREES | WEATHER, SKY, LANDSCAPES | SEASONAL CELEBRATIONS |
|---|---|---|
| Which plants bloom the latest: asters, goldenrod, chicory, marigolds, or butter-and-eggs?<br>What trees and shrubs lose their leaves, turn colors?<br>Observe and draw the varieties of tree seeds, nuts, and fruits. | Watch for weather changes.<br>Draw cloud shapes, sunsets, rain patterns.<br>What sounds in nature are changing?<br>Days are noticeably shorter after September 22.<br>Draw a little landscape scene showing tree shapes and color changes. | Autumnal equinox<br>Sukkot<br>Halloween<br>Thanksgiving Day<br>Fall festivals<br>Year's End in Celtic calendar |
| Draw silhouetttes of winter trees.<br>Observe the twig, leaf, and flower bud shapes on deciduous trees.<br>Observe the seeds and cones of evergreens.<br>Observe the leaves and buds of broad-leaved evergreen. | Focus on weather changes.<br>Draw snowflake shapes.<br>Observe rain patterns.<br>Record moon phases.<br>Draw constellation shapes.<br>Days get longer after December 22.<br>Draw a little landscape scene showing the tree and land shapes this time of year. | Winter solstice<br>Hanukkah<br>Advent and Christmas<br>Kwanza<br>Winter and New Year festivals<br>Groundhog Day |
| Look for the first flowers. In the North: spring bulbs of crocus, snowdrop, daffodil. In the South: cactus, amaryllis, poinsettia.<br>Record the first leaves and tree flowers you see.<br>Draw sequence of flowers blooming, in high to low elevations. | Record the rain, mud, snow, and slush. Record signs of warm- and cold-weather changes.<br>Look for animal tracks in mud.<br>Days get noticeably longer after March 21 or 22.<br>Draw a little landscape scene showing early signs of spring in trees and land. | Vernal equinox<br>International Earth Day<br>Easter<br>Passover<br>May Day<br>Spring planting festivals<br>First day of summer in Celtic calendar |
| Record the productivity of backyard gardens, parks, abandoned lots, fields, and meadows.<br>Plant your own garden and draw and record its growth.<br>Get out a field guide to plants and learn to identify what's growing where. | Use your local newspaper, radio station, TV, planetarium, and almanacs to learn about weather. Document the weather daily for a month.<br>Days are getting shorter after June 21 or 22.<br>Draw a little summer landscape. | Summer solstice<br>Native American sun-dance festivals<br>August 1 is Lammas, fall in the Celtic calender<br>International harvest festivals |

**Recommended: Bird Identiflyer** 

This handy portable device called an Identiflyer is as useful in the classroom as it is in the field. Slip one of the Song Cards into this talking dictionary of sounds and hear the bird call as you look at the illustrations. Use the Identiflyer in the field to help identify birds and in the classroom to learn bird calls. I know of a school where the principal plays a different bird call every day for his students over the morning announcements. Now ***that's*** my kind of school! I own a Bird Identiflyer and I used it frequently with kids and beginner bird watchers. Each Song Card contains an illustration, name, and song of 10 birds. You can buy different cards of bird calls—grouped by habitat or region and you can even buy frog call cards. The IdenfiFlyer retails for $34.95, cards about $10.00 each. The inventor and President of ***For the Birds***, Terry Allen, has offered to give a discount to our readers. Simply call his company, mention my name (Jane Kirkland) and provide your school tax ID number for a teacher discount. For The Birds, Inc., 1209 A Stamp Creek Rd. Salem, SC 29676 Phone 877-261-6556

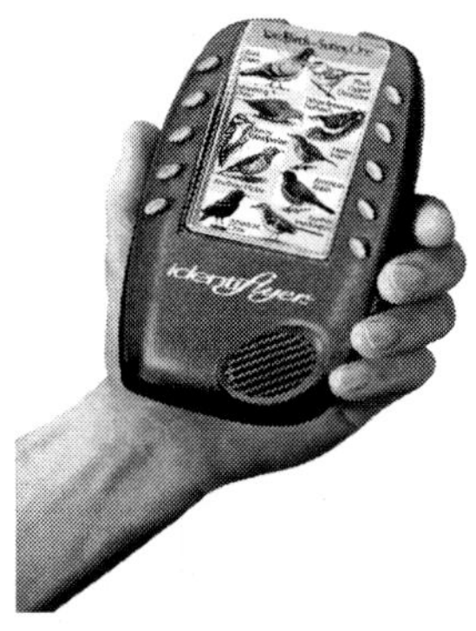

## Other Equipment and Materials

If you have sufficient funding, your students can benefit from additional equipment and supplies for your project. You might be tempted to include a birding scope on your list of equipment needs. This is a very expensive item ($500.00 and up). Before you invest in a scope be sure that you understand its application. A scope helps you focus on a distant object that is motionless—not birds in flight. Binoculars are better for tracking. On the other hand, if there is a bird nest in the schoolyard, a bird perched on a distant tree, or a large body of water in or near your property, a scope can be invaluable. Scopes are also useful in the city where birds on tall buildings (even your own school) might be difficult to view through binoculars. Kids love scoping even if distant plants and animals won't "count" for your field guide. Scopes give students a completely new perspective on their world. But it's an expensive item with limited application, and I would make this a low priority until you have purchased the other basics such as books, journals, magnifying glasses, and so forth. Magnifying glasses, insect boxes (with magnifying covers), and other kinds of magnifiers are helpful for your project.

Books for your wish list should include trade reference books and even fiction on the topic of nature, workbooks and journals for each student to keep his field notes and journals, and even coloring books for younger students. Clipboards and/or steno pads (the kind with cardboard covers) are helpful when taking notes in the field.

To incorporate technology into your project, consider a digital camera, a scanner, and even a GPS device. Older students can make good use of digital photography, database, and desktop publishing software, too.

## Step Six: Creating a Budget

As I suggested in Chapter 1, *What is a Field Guide to Your Schoolyard,* you can manage your Field Guide Project with existing supplies, two pairs of binoculars, and enough field guides to help you identify various groups of plants and animals. If your FGP focuses on birds and your school library has a field guide to birds of your region, you only need to purchase or borrow binoculars to be up and running.

In the publishing world, page count and distribution are one of the first considerations in estimating book costs. The largest expense in this project *could* be the cost of reproducing your book for distribution to your students. But we're going to suggest ways of distributing your book and controlling page count so you can keep costs down. Until you have a grasp on the number of species you want to include in your book, the content for each of those species, and the final look and feel of your book, you can't really budget for book costs. Save the book details of your budget workbook until you've read Chapters Three and Four. Then you can estimate your book costs on your budget sheet. Alternatively, pick a conservative and random number of pages, say 20, to work with your budget sheet.

You can plug in equipment costs on your budget sheet based on the information provided in this chapter. See an example of Park Forest's equipment list in Table 2.2. Park Forest Elementary School took a creative approach to their equipment needs. Using a grant for their natural history study, they purchased two wagons to hold their field equipment. The wagons accompany each of two groups comprising a class and heading for different observation sites. Keep in mind that their Principal, Donnan Stoicovy, has been involved with environment and ecology education for many years. When she purchased equipment for her school she did so with a strong knowledge of nature and with extensive field experience. In other words, she had a good idea of what she needed and what was going to work for her students. Thanks to grant money, she was able to afford a lot of equipment that would, for other schools, be more a part of a wish list than a budget item. Keep in mind that all you really need to begin your project is a couple of pairs of binoculars and some field guides to help you identify what you find.

**Wagon/Field Equipment and Materials**

| Item | Wagon A | Wagon B | Total items | Cost per item | Total Amount |
|---|---|---|---|---|---|
| Wagon | 1 | 1 | 2 | 177.95 | 355.90 |
| Digital Cameras | 1 | 1 | 2 | 294.84 | 589.68 |
| Small Binoculars | 5 | 5 | 10 | 8.00 | 80.00 |
| Lapboards | 10 | 10 | NC | NC | 0.00 |
| 2-way magnifiers | 15 | 15 | 30 | 6.95 | 208.50 |
| Compasses | 1 | 1 | 2 | 14.36 | 28.72 |
| GPS Unit | 1 | 1 | 2 | 97.54 | 195.08 |
| Wildflower guidebook | 3 | 3 | 6 | 5.00 | 30.00 |
| Bird guidebook | 3 | 3 | 6 | 5.00 | 30.00 |
| Tree guidebook | 3 | 3 | 6 | 5.00 | 30.00 |
| Insect guidebook | 3 | 3 | 6 | 5.00 | 30.00 |
| Caterpillar guidebook | 3 | 3 | 6 | 5.00 | 30.00 |
| Rocks & Minerals field guide | 3 | 3 | 6 | 5.00 | 30.00 |
| Tape measures, metric rulers, standard rulers, 6 of each | 9 | 9 | 18 | 1.00 | 18.00 |
| Flashlight | 1 | 1 | 2 | 2.00 | 4.00 |
| Site map | 1 | 1 | 2 | 0.00 | 0.00 |
| Flashguide to Animal Tracks | 1 | 1 | 2 | 5.00 | 10.00 |
| Rain Ponchos | 15 | 15 | 30 | 4.00 | 120.00 |
| Golden Field Guide to Wildflowers | 3 | 3 | 6 | 6.95 | 41.70 |
| Binoculars (Acorn Naturalists) | 15 | 15 | 30 | 21.83 | 654.90 |
| National Audubon Animal Tracks | 3 | 3 | 6 | 8.10 | 48.60 |
| National Audubon Amphibians | 3 | 3 | 6 | 8.10 | 48.60 |
| Stokes Dragonflies | 3 | 3 | 6 | 4.95 | 29.70 |
| Stokes Eastern Birds | 3 | 3 | 6 | 8.05 | 48.30 |
| Stokes Hummingbirds | 3 | 3 | 6 | 4.95 | 29.70 |
| Stokes Butterflies | 3 | 3 | 6 | 4.95 | 29.70 |
| Subtotal (Wagon items) | | | | | 2,721.08 |

**Table 2. 2 Park Forest Elementary Equipment Purchases**

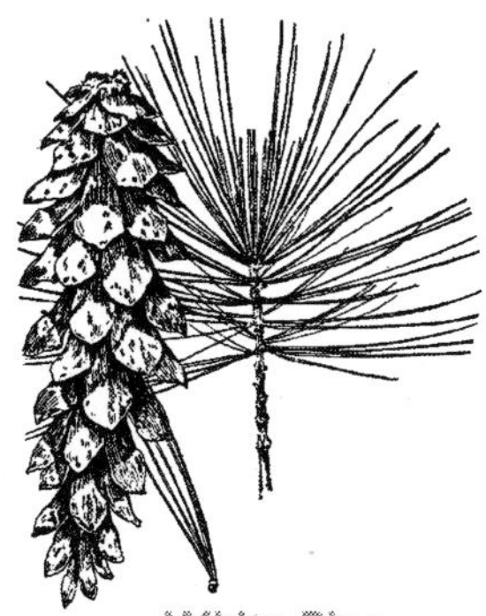

White Pine

To compare prices for equipment and supplies, even if you can't purchase online, try **www.pricegrabber.com, www.google.com/froogle,** or **www.bizrate.com.** A great source for equipment and supplies for your FGP is the Acorn Naturalists catalog (**www.acornnaturalists.com**). Acorn Naturalists is practically one-stop shopping for environmental education supplies and equipment—and they accept purchase orders. Once you create your project equipment and supplies list you can use the *Planning Workbook* to build your budget.

## Funding & Launching Your Project

You no doubt know better than I about funding school projects. But you'll find references to grant programs throughout this book. Beyond grants, the next obvious place to look for funding is your parents organization. Talk with them about sponsoring a nature-related fund-raiser with bird seed, feeders, or native plant sales and about providing parent volunteers for your project. Contact your local bird, garden, or butterfly club, nursery or seed store for help with a seed or plant sale. Consider featuring books about plants and wildlife, nature observation, and journaling at your next book fair.

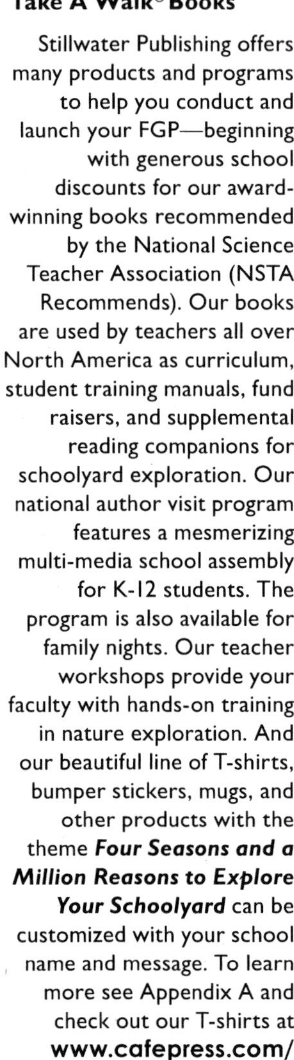

**Raising Funds with Take A Walk® Books**

Stillwater Publishing offers many products and programs to help you conduct and launch your FGP—beginning with generous school discounts for our award-winning books recommended by the National Science Teacher Association (NSTA Recommends). Our books are used by teachers all over North America as curriculum, student training manuals, fund raisers, and supplemental reading companions for schoolyard exploration. Our national author visit program features a mesmerizing multi-media school assembly for K-12 students. The program is also available for family nights. Our teacher workshops provide your faculty with hands-on training in nature exploration. And our beautiful line of T-shirts, bumper stickers, mugs, and other products with the theme ***Four Seasons and a Million Reasons to Explore Your Schoolyard*** can be customized with your school name and message. To learn more see Appendix A and check out our T-shirts at **www.cafepress.com/environmentaled**

A project launch is a good way to get students, faculty, and families excited about your Field Guide Project. Consider holding a luncheon in your cafeteria on a weekend. You might call it *Let's Do Launch* and make a nature theme for everything—even the food. You could make maple lollipops shaped like maple leaves, and decorate your hallways with construction paper trees, flowers, butterflies, and birds. You could sell items such as bird seed, books, native plants and even hold a silent auction or sale of students' original nature drawings and crafts by students as well as adults. Develop a short (5 to 10 slides) PowerPoint presentation describing your Field Guide Project goals. Include some nature photos. Let the presentation loop continuously during the lunch, projecting onto a screen or wall in your cafeteria. Add a little music and some bird calls to it and you can create a serene nature mood. Consider a one-line mantra or slogan for your project and post it around the school. Something like "We're Exploring Our Schoolyard—One Species at a Time!' If you can't come up with a tag line, feel free to use my Take A Walk® tag line "No Student Left Indoors™"—it's trademarked, but you may use it as long as you don't put it on products for sale.

How about an Earth Day theme for your project? One of the most original Earth Day celebrations I've ever seen is the one by The Lower Merion Conservancy in Gladwyne, Pennsylvania (**www.lmconservancy.org**). Each year the Conservancy sponsors a unique contest in celebration of Earth Day. About 1,000 students from many schools compete in teams to create and construct interpretations of creatures and trees that ultimately end up in a display of an Earth Day Forest. Some of the trees are as high as seven feet and they are erected to stand independently, giving the contest sponsors the ability to group them into little "woods" and tree-lined paths. The contest integrates science with art and writing. Prizes are given at several levels and the forest is displayed for several days over a weekend so kids and their parents can tour the exhibit. This would be a great project for your launch party—why wait until Earth Day? Imagine your cafeteria decorated with native trees, hand-made by your students.

If you do some kind of launch party or kick-off, invite a dynamic and animated naturalist-speaker, author, wildlife rehabilitator, celebrity, or even a visiting zoo to your school for an assembly program on nature, plants, or animals. To find authors and speakers search the Internet for "authors who visit schools", "wildlife rehabilitators" and "school speakers".

Whatever else you do or don't do to launch your project, remember to hang a bird feeder where students can observe the activity at the feeder. Watching birds at a bird feeder is a great way to spark interest in nature. You might even keep a bird list on the wall so students can add their sightings.

## Introducing the FGP to Your Students

I poll the class at the beginning of every workshop I teach. I need to know why people have come to the workshop, a little about their background and work, and what they expect to learn. I need this information so I can customize a workshop on-the-fly. By giving the attendees the information they actually need instead of what I assume they might need, I optimize our time together. I'm rewarded with interested and engaged attendees; they are rewarded with information they can use and everyone goes home happy.

Of course, you don't need to poll your classroom. You know your students and their capabilities—or do you? Do you know if you have birdwatchers in your classroom? Do you know who are the outdoor kids and who helps in the garden? Do you know if any students own their own pair of binoculars or field guides and how often they use them?

If you haven't yet, now is a good time to test your students' nature IQ. Share your project plans with them and engage them in a discussion that encourages their own ideas about a Field Guide Project. Ask them if they regularly see plants and animals in the schoolyard and, if so, which ones.

Use this time to learn who-knows-what about nature. Ask your students who among them are the current nature observers, who goes camping with their families, and who are the birdwatchers. Students with these experiences can assist you in teaching nature observation and species identification to the other kids. Ask if students have family members who lead bird walks, teach at environmental or nature centers, or work with wildlife rehabilitators. Those members can be a valuable asset to you and your project.

Ask if there are students who are willing to bring field guides or binoculars from home for use during your project—either for their own use or to share with other students. Equipment brought in from home might help you to cut an item or two from your budget.

Lastly, ask students how they feel about the Field Guide Project, if they feel the project is beneficial, and why.

These discussions are your window to understanding your students' view and current knowledge of nature. You'll quickly learn their interests, hot spots,

**Worth Repeating**

A schoolyard garden can be beneficial in many ways. It can beautify the school property and provide habitat for flora and fauna. Most importantly it will become an outdoor classroom. These are some of the things we considered when my school applied for a Wild Action Grant form the Pennsylvania Game Commission.

I learned about the grant opportunity while attending another workshop provided by the Game Commission. I requested the application and then a committee of students and teachers went to work to complete the application process. It was completed in about a month. We decided to create a butterfly garden, the size of the garden, what plants to purchase, and the jobs each grade level would perform as the garden was created. A time line was developed to keep the project on target.

When the school was notified that the grant was being awarded to us, we were thrilled. Then the hard work began. This was the physical labor of digging and removing sod, preparing the soil, planting, and spreading mulch. Every child in our PreK to eighth grade classes did some work in the garden. What a sense of accomplishment they all had on the day our Reflection Garden was dedicated and the first butterflies released.

**Linda Rowan**
**School Library**
**Media Specialist**
**Grey Nun Academy**
**Yardley, PA**

fears, and impressions about our natural world—allowing you to further customize the FGP to your own students' needs and interests.

**Worth Repeating**

*The best remedy for those who are afraid, lonely or unhappy is to go outside, somewhere where they can be quiet, alone with the heavens, nature and God. Because only then does one feel that all is as it should be and that God wishes to see people happy, amidst the simple beauty of nature.*

**Anne Frank**

## In Conclusion

Remember that you're in far more danger of finding *too many* species for your field guide project than of not finding enough. This will help you take on a FGP with confidence. If you do find only a small number of species in your schoolyard—no problem—simply research those species to a greater depth to inspire and motivate students.

Once you have your plans in place, you're ready to step outside and explore your schoolyard. Chapter 3, *Observations and Data Collection,* presents methods to help you teach your students how to observe nature. You'll learn about field notes and journaling. You'll also learn some best practices for field etiquette and damage control.

www.istockphoto.com/RBFried

**In This Chapter**

Master the 20-Second Nature Break

Master The Tools of the Trade

Master Nature Observation Skills

Prepare for Damage Control

Data Collection

CHAPTER THREE

# Observing Nature and Collecting Data

This chapter is divided into two main parts: the first on nature observation and the second on collecting data. It is during these phases of your project that it comes to life for your students. It is, perhaps, the most rewarding phase of the FGP because witnessing the power of nature to engage and excite your students will invigorate you.

## Observing Nature

Observation is the primary skill students need to explore their schoolyard. Like all skills, some people seem to be better at it than others; most people can be taught to a relatively successful degree; and the more one practices, the better one becomes.

To help you teach your students how to observe, I've broken the process into three easy steps. First, teach them my *20-Second Nature Break*. Second, teach them how to operate binoculars and use field guides. And third, tell them *when, where, and what* to look for when they are outdoors. Let's look at these steps in more detail.

### Step One: Master the 20-Second Nature Break™

One way to get kids to hone their observation skills is to challenge them to take a nature break. This is something they can do at home, on the way to school, while riding on the school bus, or while outside on recess. Encourage

Take A Backyard Bird Walk.

Take A Tree Walk.

Take A Walk With Butterflies And Dragonflies

Take A City Nature Walk.

**Worth Repeating**

*What we see depends mainly on what we look for.*

**Sir John Lubbock**

them to make their nature break a part of their daily life—like brushing their teeth—something they do every day. The objective of a nature break is to look around—up, down, all around, for 20 seconds to see what plants and animals they can find. Don't *tell* them why they should do this—*ask* them why they think they should do it. You'll love their answers and you'll realize quickly that this whole nature observation thing is going to be a very easy sell.

Begin preparing students for their nature break by practicing observation skills in your classroom. Instruct students to clear their desks of everything except one piece of paper and a pencil. Ask them to close their eyes or put their heads down on their desks while you give the instructions for the observation practice. Explain that, upon your signal, they'll raise their heads for 20 seconds while looking around the room in silence and making a mental note of everything they see. If you have vision-impaired students, include what students *hear* as well. After the 20 seconds elapse, they'll have another 60 seconds to write down what they saw (while looking only at their paper—no glancing around the room). Explain that this is neither a *test* nor a *contest*. There are no right or wrong answers and the objective isn't to find the most items, it is simply to notice. Also you may want to assure them that you haven't planted something for them to find so they don't waste time looking for something that's not there.

**Focus on the Obvious** 

Very young students might need help focusing during their first trip in the field. Help them by suggesting what they should look for. Give them something you know they can easily find such as ants on a tree trunk or robins on the front lawn of the school. It's OK if several students study the same object, so create teams if you're unable to come up with an extensive list of subjects for observation.

When time is up for listing, have students share their observations by reading their lists aloud. Lead a discussion about the observations. Did all students list the same items? Of course not—so why not? What was it about the items they listed that attracted their attention? Why are different students attracted to different things? What makes us observant? How can we benefit from observations? Why did some students list many items and others only a few? Can their lists be more descriptive? For example, is it enough to list "poster" or would it have been better to describe the poster? Talk about the importance of good observation skills and descriptive writing and the role each will play in your Field Guide Project. Repeat and expand the exercise until students are able to describe—without naming—the objects of their observations well enough that the rest of the class can identify the objects from those descriptions.

Make the *20-Second Nature Break* a frequent homework assignment so students practice and improve their observation skills. Suggest that they take a break after school—in the schoolyard, on the bus, or at home. Share observations as part of a regular follow-up to the homework assignment. You will be surprised by the number of things students admit to having never noticed prior to the nature breaks—I've lost track of the number of students who have told me that they discovered a huge tree in their yard. It's amazing what we fail to notice.

Dandelion

Adapt the *20-Second Nature Break* over the course of your project to improve students' listening skills with a *listening* break. Conduct a 20-second *feeling* break and create tree bark rubbings by placing a piece of paper on the bark and rubbing a pencil. After a spring rain, take a 20-second *smelling* break. Take 20-second *listening* breaks at different points in your schoolyard.

Make the *20-Second Nature Break* something *you* do every day, too. You'll enjoy the break; and practicing will keep you one step ahead of your students.

## Step Two: Master the Tools of the Trade

I'm a big believer in "the right tool for the job". But in order to buy the right tools for your FGP, you have to know what about them makes them *right.* All binoculars and all field guides are not created equal. The following information will help you to select the best tools for your students and your budget.

### *Choosing and Using Binoculars*

You'll need at least two pairs of binoculars for your field guide project; one for yourself and at least one for your students. If you have a tight budget, don't sacrifice your pair for a second student pair. Without a decent pair of binoculars for yourself, you won't be able to assist your students when they ask for your help identifying a bird passing overhead.

Binocular prices run from $15.00 to over $1,000.00. A beginner birdwatcher can easily spend $400.00 to $500.00 on their first pair of binoculars. But your students won't be relying on or even using their binoculars as often as birdwatchers and you won't need to invest that much money. You should be able to find binoculars for your students for between $25.00 and $80.00. Middle and high school students are more demanding of performance and a satisfactory pair should run you around $80.00 to $200.00. But understand that price is not the only consideration when buying binoculars. One size does not fit all, bigger is not always better and size *does* matter. Factors you need to consider are: magnification, lens diameter, focus length, distance between the pupils, construction of the eye cups, and weight.

- **Magnification and lens diameter** are those two numbers always found in binocular descriptions, such as 8x40. Magnification, or how many times the image is magnified, is represented by the first number (8X). The higher the first number, the larger the magnification. But higher magnification also means that the binoculars are more sensitive to movement (like shaky hands). Diameter, the distance (in millimeters) across each of the front lenses, is the second number (40). The higher the second number, the more light the lenses let in and the brighter your image will appear. An 8x25 binocular is not as bright as an 8x40 binocular. But bigger lenses also mean **heavier binoculars**—and kids will quickly tire of heavy binoculars. A good binocular for young students (K-3) would be one that magnifies less, like a 6x or a 4x giving you the brightness without the weight.

- **The minimum focus length** tells you how far away items must be to focus properly. Many nature enthusiasts own two pair of binoculars: one for close range (insects), one for far (birds). But kids can turn their binoculars backwards to view things up close—and it works!

- The **interpupillary distance (IP)** is the distance between the pupils of the eyes. Most binoculars can be adjusted to be opened wide or narrow for different size faces. Kids need binoculars with a smaller IP distance.

*Exploring my schoolyard is an adventure. Spider webs glinting in the half shadow half light fill the gap between tree trunks. Spinning beautiful silk, jumping so elegantly from thread to thread, they connect a highway of webs. A new kingdom of wildlife awaits discovery every day.*

**Dario Caminite**
**Grade 5**

**Recommended: Binoculars for Students** 

To help make your binocular selection easy, I recommend this little pair of binoculars that retail for $29.00. It's a good size and quality for elementary school students. The *ACORN NATURALISTS FIELD BINOCULAR*, 8x by 21mm features fully-coated lenses to reduce glare and produce crisp, bright images. Lenses provide unsurpassed infrared and ultraviolet protection, reducing eye strain and improving image contrast. Easy to adjust center focus knob with an independent right diopter adjusts for any differences in vision from one eye to the other. Although this photo doesn't illustrate the eye cups, the binoculars are equipped with roll-down eyecups for eyeglass wearers. It focuses from infinity down to 9 feet with a field of view of 379 feet at 1000 yards. Includes pouch case and wrist strap (many prefer to keep these smaller binoculars in pockets to protect them and also to keep them from flopping around when one bends over or jogs, as is the case when using neck straps). Perfect binocular for all but the youngest (K-1) or smallest of your students—from novice beginners to advanced users. Forest green.

www.acornnaturalists.com

- The **Eye Cups** are the rubber or plastic cups on which you rest your eyes or eyeglasses. If made of rubber, eyecups can fold up and down. If the eyecups are plastic they twist up and down. The reasons eyecups fold or twist up and down is to accommodate two kinds of viewers: those wearing eyeglass and those not. If you wear eyeglasses, don't remove them to look through binoculars. Instead, fold or twist the eye cups down. If you don't you'll see a narrow field of vision with vignetting around the edges. If you don't wear eyeglasses, make certain the eyecup is up, or unfolded—because if it's down or folded, you'll see black spots in the center of the lenses. If you can afford more than one pair of binoculars for your students, and the binoculars have rubber eyecups instead of ones that twist, keep one pair with the rubber eye cups folded back all the time for eyeglass users and the other pair unfolded. Frequent folding and unfolding of the rubber eyecups will ultimately lead to the rubber cracking or tearing.

- **The weight.** Young students need binoculars that are not too heavy around their neck. If the binoculars are heavy, students will be likely to carry the binoculars instead of wearing them—increasing the chances of dropping the binoculars—or worse, they might not want to use them at all. Consider the weight and consider purchasing a harness strap for your binoculars. The harness strap will take the weight off the neck and make it easier for students (and you) to wear and carry the binoculars without neck pain. Binocular harnesses go by several names such as bino-system and bino-strap. You can find them on the Web by searching for those terms, or at your local Audubon, camera, or nature center store. We are researching a customized *Take A Walk*® strap for our store so check our Website, too.

The four steps to using binoculars (on page 41) are provided by Nikon USA. If you follow these steps carefully, you'll quickly master using binoculars and have the necessary skills to teach your students how to use them. As you will see, using binoculars isn't difficult but it's not necessarily intuitive. I've met countless adults who own binoculars but don't use them—claiming that they can't see well enough through them. In as much as 90% of those cases the reason people don't see well is because they don't know how to use the eye cups and they don't understand how to focus the binoculars. If you have access to a pair of binoculars, practice with them before you purchase any for your project.

When you determine how many pairs of binoculars you want for your project, indicate the number on your *Planning Workbook*. Next we'll take a look at choosing field guides.

## Using Binoculars in correct ways.

Will ensure you much better viewing than ever before.

### Setting the eyecup

**<Setting the rubber eyecup>**

Eyeglass wearer

Fold back the rubber eyecup.

Non eyeglass wearer

Set the rubber eyecup up.

**<Setting turn-and-slide rubber eyecup>**

For those who wear eyeglass

Turn clockwise to fully ratracted position.

For those who do not wear eyeglass

Turn counterclockwise to the fully extended position.

(!) Once the rubber eyecup has been correctly set, you can use the binoculars to provide a sufficient field of view without any vignetting at the best suited eyepoint whether or not you wear eyeglasses.

### Adjustment of interpupillary distance

While you look at a distance object, carefully move the binocular tubes downward or upward.
(Photos are simulations for illustration purposes only)

Stop moving the binocular tubes when both fields are correctly aligned, forming a perfect circle.
(Photos are simulations for illustration purposes only)

(!) If interpupillary distance has not been properly adjusted, the image might give you an uncomfortable feeling.

**Figure 3.1 How to Focus Binoculars. ©Nikon USA. Reproduced with permission from the Nikon USA Website. For more information on choosing and using binoculars, please visit the Nikon Website at:** www.nikonusa.com.

****Caution****
**Kids and Binoculars**

Three things inevitability happen when kids and binoculars come together for the first time. First, kids swing the binoculars by their strap. To avoid this, instruct students to wear the straps around their necks or give the binoculars to someone who will. The second problem comes with sharing. When kids are sharing binoculars and one has the strap around his neck, with certainty, he will hand the binoculars to the other student before he removes the strap from his neck and, well, you get the picture. Lastly, kids (and adults) frequently follow something they've spotted in their lenses without removing the binoculars from their eyes. Walking while looking through the binoculars is, at best, dangerous. Spare yourself and your students from death by binoculars by reviewing safety tips before you head into the field.

**Recommended: Student Workshops and Tours**

Take your FGP to the next level with professionally-lead workshops to teach your students birding skills, plant identification skills, or digital photography skills. These workshops can be held at your school or a local park or nature center. Or give your students the memory of a lifetime by taking them on an eco-tour. To find out what's available in your area, contact your local Audubon Chapter where you might be able to find free workshops (but not free tours, of course).

If you have the budget, my personal recommendation for workshops and tours anywhere in the Western Hemisphere is *Wildside Tours*. Owner Kevin Loughlin is both my personal birding mentor and photographer instructor. I've taken trips with his company in several states as well as Belize. Every time I get a chance to take one of his tours or workshops, I'm there. Kevin was kind enough to put a special offer for teachers on page 126. Take advantage of his generous offer!
**www.WildsideToursInc.com**

**Dioptre adjustment**

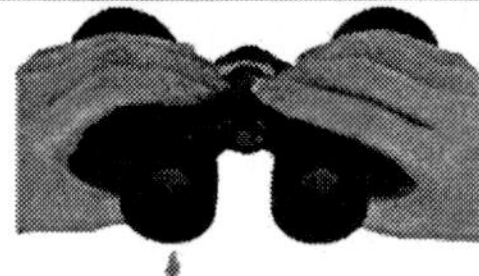

First look through the left eyepiece with your left eye and turn the central focusing ring to focus on a distant object.

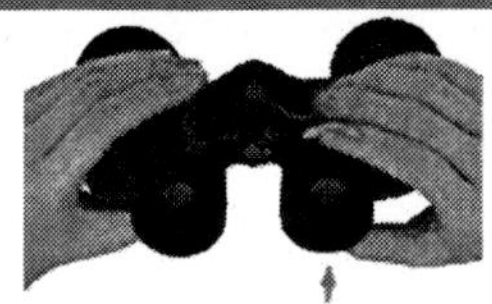

Then look through the right eyepiece with your right eye, rotating the dioptre adjustment ring to focus on the same object.

(!) First set the magnification to its maximum then adjust the diopter when using zoom binoculars.

(!) Making a diopter adjustment is also needed if there is a difference in visual acuity between your left and right eyes.

**Focusing on the object**

Now you can focus on any distant object by just turning the central focusing ring for both the right and left eyepieces simultaneously.

Never look at the sun directly.
Doing so may seriously damage the eyes.

**Figure 3.1 How to Focus Binoculars. ©Nikon USA. Reproduced with permission from the Nikon USA Website. For more information on choosing and using binoculars, please visit the Nikon Website at:** www.nikonusa.com.

### Choosing and Using Field Guides

Like binoculars, field guides come in all shapes and sizes; and one size does not fit all. You'll need to determine which field guides are best suited for your students before you purchase. I should point out that I don't count dichotomous keys as field guides. In fact, I find it's much easier to introduce dichotomous keys to kids after they've been introduced to plants and animals through field guides that use straight-up photographs or illustrations for identification help. That said, I chose field guides for different ages groups by factoring four considerations: 1) the illustration method and size; 2) the order of species; 3) the amount of information provided on each species; and 4) the size and weight of the book.

1. **Illustration method.** One might argue that photos are more realistic than illustrations. But photos often contain backgrounds and other items which can detract from the subject, might capture a subject in lighting that affects the colors of the subject, during an odd pose (such as stretching), or from an odd angle (from above). Both photos and illustrations can be misleading if, say a bird is represented in only breeding plumage (which is often very different than winter plumage). So neither photographs nor illustrations are perfect. That said, I happen to prefer photos because, to my eye, they are the most realistic representations—even if the photo or the subject is flawed. But I'm a photographer and that may have something to do with my preference. There are no guidelines for choosing which books will be better for your students, but consider that the youngest of your students (K-3) are probably more accustomed to illustrations, thanks to all the illustrated children's books. I'd recommend either style for young students (K-3) and, based on my personal experience, photographic guides for students grade 4 and up (with one exception: the *Sibley Guide to Birds*—see the sidebar on page 44).

2. **The order of species**. Some field guides sort subjects by color, size, habitat. Some use dichotomous keys. Most sort by taxonomic order. Which is best for your students? I vote for taxonomic order. Even if you don't discuss taxonomic order, even if students are not ready for the concept, even if they're learning subconsciously, they are still learning groups and families.

3. **The depth of species information**. Look for a series that has the information you need without compromising the size of the photographs or the overall size of the book. For grades 4 and up, at a minimum, you'll want to know a species range, whether or not it is a native, its habitat needs, and how it reproduces.

4. **The size and weight of the book.** Just like binoculars, if the field guides are too cumbersome or heavy to take into the field, kids won't take them. When choosing your guides, consider whether or not they will travel with you in the field. If so, choose guides that are easy for students to carry—in their pockets, backpacks, or even in your traveling equipment lab.

****Caution****
**Field Guides Divided**

Many field guides separate images from information, putting all images in one section and all species information in another. In some field guides, images of a single species might be located in three different sections of the book and the species information in yet a fourth. This works for some people (I like the National Audubon Society's Field Guide to Trees, divided by barks, leaves, and so forth) but for K-5 students (or anyone new to field guides) I recommend books where the information and images are on the same page or adjacent pages.

Box Turtle

You can find the information you need (size, publisher, weight, page count, price, and so forth) on most books in print at **www.amazon.com.** You'll find additional booksellers in Chapter Six, *Resources and Recommendations.*

### My Field Guide Recommendations

I use different field guides with different ages of students for different reasons. Here's my short list of which, when, and why.

When I want illustrated guides for K-3 students, I use the ***Golden Guides*** from St. Martin's Press or the ***Peterson's First Field Guides*** by Houghton Mifflin. For photographic introductory guides for grades K-5, I like the ***Stokes Beginner Guides* and the National Audubon Society's *Pocket Guides.*** These series are compact and easy for small hands to carry. They cover the most common of plants and animals and the amount of information on each species is limited. Depending on the depth of your FGP, you might need a bigger book for your buck.

For a greater variety—or even coverage of all species of birds, insects, butterflies and mammals, I like the ***Kaufman Focus Guides*** by Houghton Mifflin. In this series the subjects are photographed, then cropped from their background and digitally edited to give you the best possible image. Keep in mind, however, that the photos are small and not well suited for the youngest of readers. I would recommend this series for grades 4 and up.

If you need comprehensive species information, consider the ***National Audubon*** series, which is a photographic series of guides. You'll find a guide to almost all groups of plants and animals in North America.

Of all of my personal field guides, the ones I don't leave home without are the ***Stokes Field Guide to Birds*** (Little, Brown, and Company) and the ***Sibley Field Guide to Birds*** (published by Knopf). The Stokes book has large photos with the species information right under the photo and it includes behavior and nesting information, It works well with any K-12 student. The Sibley Guide is the "bible" of the birding world and the multiple images of each species are very helpful in the field. It's great for middle and high school students and experienced birders. For a list of popular field guides see Chapter Five, *Resources and Recommendations.*

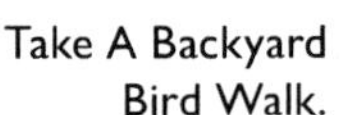

Take A Backyard Bird Walk.

## Step Three: Master Nature Observation Skills

Take A Tree Walk.

The key to successful nature observation is to start with modest expectations and make your first observation long enough for students to get acclimated to looking around and listening but not so long that they lose interest. There are two ways to approach a short nature walk:

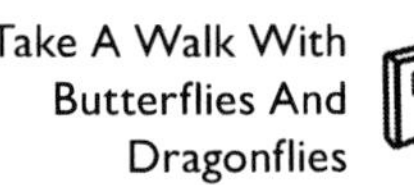

Take A Walk With Butterflies And Dragonflies

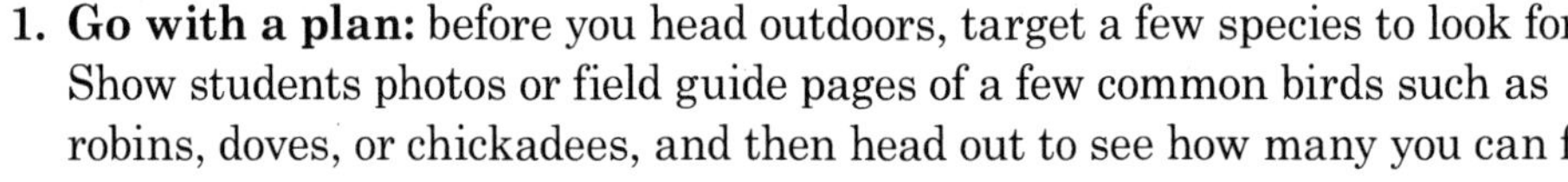

1. **Go with a plan:** before you head outdoors, target a few species to look for. Show students photos or field guide pages of a few common birds such as robins, doves, or chickadees, and then head out to see how many you can find.

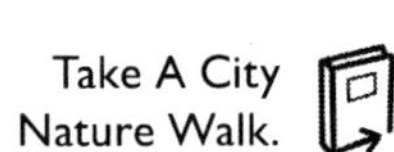

Take A City Nature Walk.

2. **Go without a plan**: simply head out and see what you find—gathering just enough information so that you can look up the plant or animal in a field guide when you return to the classroom.

I like method number two because having little or no expectations, students can't possibly fall short or be disappointed. On the other hand, if you have a group of students that works best when focused, plan first.

I've suggested several times now that you start with birds and I'm sticking to that. If you've hung a bird feeder, that's the spot to make your first nature observations. Take a field guide to birds with you so it is available when you need it. Don't position the students too close to the bird feeder or the birds will stay away. If you're observing a bird feeding station you might not need binoculars. Whether you think you'll need them or not, be sure to teach the students how to use them *before* you head outdoors.

However and whenever you take your students for their first observations, continue your nature lessons when you return to the classroom. Talk about the birds you saw. Discuss how you found the birds in your field guide—if you did. If you couldn't find the birds in your guide, why not? How is your field guide organized? By color? In taxonomic order? Discuss this with your students. Explain the importance of the field guide as a tool. Ask students what was it about the birds that they are most likely to remember? Can they describe the physical characteristics of the birds they saw? Discuss the advantages to taking field notes and make a list of things one might include in their field notes to help them remember or identify a species at a later time. One of the best methods for preparing students to take field notes, write journals, and collect data is to show them the need and the value of such. By discussing field notes after they've observed without taking field notes, your students will be more receptive to taking field notes on their next excursion.

**Using GISS**

When observing birds, quite often you get only a brief look before the bird is out of view. To help with identification in this situation, many birdwatchers use a method of observation called GISS, or General Impression, Size, and Shape. A brief look at a bird gives us a mental picture of the bird and, even when it is merely a dark silhouette against a bright sky, we can assess the general size and shape. We can also see obvious unique physical characteristics such as the size of the head, sometimes the size and shape of the beak, the size and shape of the wings and the flight pattern. GISS skills are developed over time and might be too difficult for young students. To use this skill one must first have experience identifying bird species. But teaching middle and high school students bird identification by using bird silhouettes is a good way to help them develop their GISS skills. GISS is a military term that's been around since WWII when soldiers used silhouettes of airplanes to determine if the occupants of the plane were friend or foe.

### Observing Birds

When observing birds, take notice of the size, shape, beak, and color. Color can be misleading because some birds are different colors and patterns during breeding season than they are the rest of the year. Where I live, it's a common myth that American Goldfinches migrate south in the winter. But they don't. What most people don't know is that the colorful male looks so different in the winter that people don't realize he's the same bird. You'll need your other observations (size, shape, beak) to help you in your identification. Also note the birds' behavior and location—clues to identifying the species.

To find birds in the schoolyard, start at the easiest location—the bird feeder. Then look in the following locations:

- **Near food and water sources.** If you haven't hung a bird feeder and you want to see birds, you'll need to be where the birds are—near a source of food or water. You could create your own food source by dispersing seed on the ground far enough away that the birds will feel safe taking it when you are outdoors. The best place to throw seed is near a bush or low tree that birds can use as a staging area while moving to and from the food. If you can't put down bird seed, position yourself where there is a natural food source such as insects (found in or on trees or on the ground), berries, seeds, or shallow water or puddles.

Take A Backyard Bird Walk,Identifying Birds, page 13.

**Keeping an Online Life List**

Introduce your students to the concept of life lists by creating individual or team wildlife lists at **www.enature.com**. Every time someone in the class discovers a new species of wildlife in your schoolyard, add it to your list. It's a fun, easy, and free way to incorporate the Internet and technology into your project. ENature also has online field guides to help you identify plants and wildlife.

- **In parking lots**. Scan parking lots for gulls, sparrows, starlings, killdeer, and crows. Why might they be there? The surface of parking lots gets warm from the sun and street lights provide high places for perching. Parking lots are often good places for birds to find food—particularly remnants and trash from human fast-food diets.

- **On buildings and man-made structures.** Tall signs and streetlights give birds a "birds-eye view" of their surroundings. Signs on buildings make good roosting places as well as nesting sites.

- **On wires and telephone poles.** Hawks often perch to look for small animals grazing and moving in fields or on grassy shoulders of the roads.

Understand and explain to your students that you'll see different birds at different times of the day and in different seasons. If they should find themselves very close to a bird during observation periods, advise them to avoid making eye contact with the bird. Making eye contact is a sure way to scare the bird away. Be prepared for a huge reaction from students (of any age) when they discover a "new" (new to them) species; and don't be too surprised when they discover three or four new species.

## *Observing Trees*

Take A Tree Walk. *Recording Your Observations*, page 24.

Like birds, trees offer something year-round. In the spring trees come alive with buds and blossoms and they can be just as exciting as they are in autumn when the leaves are alive with color. In summer, trees are not only fun to identify, they are home to birds, mammals and insects. In the winter, trees offer an identification challenge, requiring students to inspect the bark, shape, and size. I find one of the best ways to get kids excited about tree identification is to view the tree in terms of its worth to humans and to wildlife. For example, is a tree one we are likely to cut down for materials, what kinds of animals might live in the tree; how is the tree a food source to wildlife or humans; and so forth. View each tree for what it is: a natural, living resource.

When observing trees look at the color and texture of the bark, the overall shape of the tree, the color and shape of the leaves, and note any thorns, berries, acorns, seeds, or flowers. Trees are good subjects for kids because: they don't move; they aren't threatening; you won't find as many bees as you will in a flower garden; and unlike animals and some other plants, generally speaking, it's safe for kids to touch trees.

## *Observing Butterflies*

Take A Walk With Butterflies And Dragonflies, *Identifying Butterflies*, page 16.

In the southern parts of North America, butterflies can be seen year-round. It's a pity that most people in North American can't see butterflies during more of the school months. But we can see them as early as March and as late as November.

The best place for find butterflies is near their biggest food source—nectar. Even clover has flowers, so look beyond the cultivated garden to wildflowers and ground cover. The best time of day to see butterflies is between 11 AM and 3 PM, when the sun is at its highest. The best way to get close to butterflies is to not cast a shadow upon them for, if you do, they'll be sure to move to a sunnier spot. There are woodland butterflies, but even they will be found in the sunny spots during midday. Butterflies (particularly males) are fond of "puddling" so look where there are very shallow puddles or mud after a spring rain.

**Caution**
**Raising Butterflies**

Before you raise butterflies in your classroom, please be sure to research the proper time for releasing them into the wild. Adult butterflies eat (sip) only nectar—without a nectar source, they will die. I've seen too many schools release adult butterflies at the wrong time of year when there is no natural nectar source. Why go to the trouble of rearing and caring if you're going to release them to their certain death?

### *Observation Tips for Urban Schools*

The city is a great place to explore nature in all seasons. It is rich with food, water, and space. Food sources include our leftovers, but trash isn't the only food source for wild animals. Most cities have plenty of plants like flowers, grasses, and trees and, of course, lots of insects and small mammals. Water sources, like rivers, streams, creeks, fountains, and puddles, provide drinking and bathing water. Plants, trees, and man-made structures such as bridges and buildings provide places for wildlife to rest, nest, and seek shelter. And the urban ecology provides some additional benefits: streets and buildings act like heat collectors, making cities warmer than their surrounding areas. The warmer climate allows some species to thrive because they can bloom or lay eggs earlier than in surrounding areas.

Take A City Nature Walk, *Go Find Nature, pages 4-21.*

Pigeons nest on bridges and overpasses and, while a nuisance, they are still interesting and beautiful birds. Did you know that there are seven morphs of pigeons? The next time you see a group of pigeons in the city, see how many you can find: white; spread (almost all black); blue-bar (the most easily recognized with gray wings and two blue or blackish stripes on its wings); checkered (has a checkered pattern on it's wings); pied (lots of white blotches, particularly on the head), red-bar (looks like the blue-bar but has reddish stripes); and red (gray with red or reddish-brown coloring). Pigeons are the favorite food of Peregrine Falcons so keep your eyes open for falcons!

Take A City Nature Walk, *Will You Find Pigeons Everywhere? Pages 6-7.*

Yes, there is indeed nature in the city! Cities are very interesting ecosystems alive with nature, just waiting for you to discover it. One time while conducting a nature walk in a small city park I discovered three species of woodpeckers where I expected to find nothing more than pigeons, house sparrows, and starlings. At a train station one night my husband and I heard toads calling. More than one female and about ten males were gathered in a large puddle near the tracks, and the puddle was filled with strings of eggs. One of my favorite nature-in-the-city discoveries was one summer night when I was in Philadelphia to do a radio show. After the show we stood outside of the building to chat when I noticed a Praying Mantis on the wall of the building where there wasn't a blade of grass, a bush, or anything green within 2 blocks of that building! I can't stress enough that *nature is not a destination.*

Milkweed

## Meet the Hartford University School for Urban Exploration

Several years ago when we launched ***Take A City Nature Walk***, the good folks at the Urban Ecology Center of Milwaukee put me in touch with Robin Denison Squier, a Milwaukee teacher who studies and teaches her students about nature in the city. Robin's students at the Hartford University School for Urban Explorations submitted entries to a contest we sponsored. Several of Robin's students poems appear in our book, *Take A City Nature Walk*. Today Robin continues her important work and she sent us this note to share with you as you embark on your field guide project.

*The Hartford University School for Urban Explorations is a Milwaukee Public School serving grades K-8. It is a city-wide school with students from all over the city of Milwaukee. For many of the students, our birding walks are their first opportunity to observe nature. Students very quickly learn that there are many opportunities to observe birds around their homes, and often get other family members involved.*

*Urban students often miss out on the greatest educator there is—nature. Every week in the fall and the spring, my class and I walk a transect down a city street and into a small remaining wood lot to explore and record what we see. In September, the excitement of seeing the rock pigeons leap straight into the air from the hospital roof, or seeing the straight steady flight of the American Crow helps the students learn to question and observe.*

*We've had the thrill of seeing a small tree in the hospital parking lot beaded with thirty Cedar Waxwings, and this spring we got to watch a Cooper's Hawk build a nest and raise three nestlings. The children have learned to look around them, and have gained a skill and interest that will last their entire lives.*

## Prepare for Damage Control

Just as in the classroom and any time you are dealing with children, things can go wrong—from accidents to sensitive and seemingly unanswerable questions. I'm not going to advise you on student injuries in the field. I'm sure you have a school policy and a school nurse to help you there. But even if you don't, for obvious legal reasons, I'll keep my advice to myself!

Having said that, however, my first topic here is the law. Many people are not familiar with the laws that protect our wildlife and natural resources and I'm compelled to tell you that, unless you have the proper licensing, your collection of bird nests and feathers is probably illegal. As we look at damage control, let's start with the law.

### Do You Know the Laws?

You know that your students shouldn't drive a car without a license. You know that there are litter laws. You know that there are laws protecting your students from harmful substances being brought into the school. But do you know that there are laws that protect our plants and wildlife—and that you might have broken those laws? Of course, not knowing about the laws is no

The Cornell Laboratory of Ornithology is launching a new initiative called "Celebrate Urban Birds" and they need your help! They're asking people to observe and record urban bird species anytime between Thursday May 10 and Sunday May 13th 2007.

You can spend one hour or up to 4 whole days participating! This will likely follow the path of other Cornell Citizen Scientists programs and become an annual event.

For more information and kits (bilingual kits available) visit

**www.birds.org/celebration**

excuse for breaking them. I once visited a school where a teacher proudly displayed her collection bird nests, feathers, and even bones. She didn't know that removing bird nests from "the wild" (even her own backyard) is illegal—even if the nests are not active. She could have obtained a licence or permit to allow her to have these found treasures for educational use, but she didn't know that (see sidebar).

**Wildlife Salvage Permits**

Wildlife salvage permits authorize holders to take and possess birds, mammals, amphibians, nests, bones, and so forth for education purposes. To learn more about these permits and to apply, visit your official state Website. Or search the internet for "wildlife salvage permit [your state name]".

Here are the highlights of a few of the Federal laws protecting our plants, wildlife, and habitats. To learn more about laws in your state as well as threatened and endangered species in your state, search a phrase such as "laws that protect wildlife in Pennsylvania", replacing your state for "Pennsylvania". Know these laws and teach these laws not only in the course of your Field Guide Project, but as a citizen.

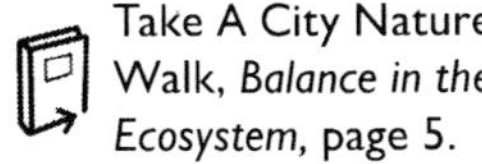

Take A City Nature Walk, *Balance in the Ecosystem*, page 5.

- **The Migratory Bird Treaty Act of 1918** is administered by the U.S. Fish and Wildlife Service. It protects all migratory birds (except for the non-native Rock Pigeon, European Starling, and English Sparrow (also called House Sparrow). It basically renders hunting, pursuing, killing, capturing, possessing, selling, buying, purchasing, bartering, or capturing migratory bird products or birds illegal and punishable by law unless you have a license or a permit. Bird products include bird parts, their feathers, eggs, nests, young, and even dead birds. By the way, many if not most of your local and native species of birds are migratory.

- **The Endangered Species Act** is administrated by the U.S. Fish and Wildlife Service. It protects our endangered and threatened species as well as their habitats. Under this law no individual (including landowners), organization or company can "jeopardize the continued existence of any threatened or endangered species or result in the destruction of adverse modification of (critical) habitat of such species." Under this law all individuals are prohibited from harassing, harming, pursuing, hunting, shooting, wounding, killing, trapping, capturing, or collecting endangered and threatened plants and animals.

- **The Clean Water Act** protects our waters, water supplies, shellfish beds, fishery areas, wildlife, and recreation areas by making it illegal to discharge any pollutant into our nation's waters without a Federal license or permit. Permits are also required to dispose of dredged or fill material into navigable waters.

Investigate these laws as well as the laws of your state so that you have, at the very least, a cursory understanding of all State and Federal laws that protect our plants, wildlife, habitats, and natural resources.

## Finding Injured Animals

Kids and well-meaning adults often find "injured" animals that aren't injured at all. There are animal behaviors we don't always understand. Sometimes we see animals that we think need our help when, in fact, they are only going about the business of being animals. Where do you think we got the expression *playing possum*? Even birds have strange behaviors; some species

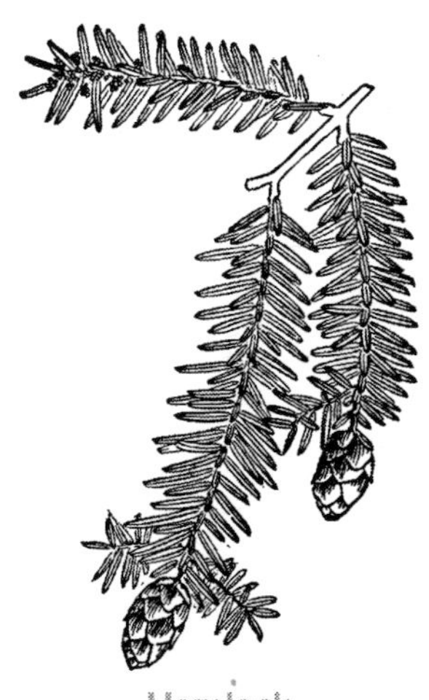

Hemlock

sunbathe and others are into anting (lying on an anthill to allow the ants to crawl through their feathers). In both of these cases the birds look dead or near dead as they lie motionless, splayed out on the ground. Young, down-covered fledglings may travel on the ground as they learn to find food, while their parents, often some distance away, forage for food. When people see the fledglings, they assume the solo flightless birds need help.

When you see an animal you think is injured, the first rule of thumb is to wait and observe for a few minutes. If the animal has not been hit by a car, if you did not witness its injury, if you don't see blood or obvious broken limbs, there's a chance the animal doesn't need assistance. If after 10 minutes' time you are convinced the animal needs help, call a wildlife rehabilitator and ask how to safely handle and transport the injured animal. Until you talk to a rehabber, avoid handling the animal and, whatever you do, don't feed a rescued animal. Would you even know what to feed wild animals? Neither do I. Call for help and realize that, by making the call, you are making a commitment to transporting the animal to the rehabber. Most wildlife rehabilitators exist on contributions from the public and simply can't leave the office (or the patients) to collect injured wildlife. If you do take an animal to a rehabber, do your best to leave a contribution, too. It's very expensive to treat injured wildlife; and, as I indicated, most rehabilitation operations exist on contributions.

Make a list of your local licensed wildlife rehabilitators *before* you actually need them; and keep the list in a central location in the school, such as the front office. I would avoid posting it in a classroom because the very words "injured animal" can conjure up all kinds of desires to help in your young students' heads and result in them looking for opportunities to help injured animals.

For more information on what to do when you find injured animals, see Appendix C, *When You Find Injured Animals.*

**My Favorite Seasonal Guide**

One of my favorite nature book series is called *The Seasonal Guide to the Natural Year.* The books in the series are a month-by-month guide to what's happening in nature a given region during a given month. They aren't designed for field identification, they're more of a travel guide to natural events.

The guide to my area (Mid Atlantic states) taught me about several nearby wintering bald eagle sites, a wildlife management area where migrating snow geese and tundra swans gather in the tens of thousands for about a week in February, and a great place for viewing blooming Trilliums in April. Before I read the book, I hadn't ever heard of those places (let alone Trilliums), and all were easy day trips from my home.

A Seasonal Guide would be helpful to you if you want to plan a nature-based field trip. But it can help you in the schoolyard, too. By learning what's happening in your region in nature, you will know which migrating birds to look and listen for in the skies, what plants to what for and when, what time of the year you can expect to see frogs and toads, and where some of the animals go when they migrate from your area.

Check Chapter Six, *Resources and Recommendations*, for information on this series.

## Controlling the Urge to Touch

The conservationist and naturalist in me want to tell you that we shouldn't disturb or touch any living thing in the outdoors. But the teacher and the realist in me know that experience is the best teacher and our children need to enjoy nature if they are to care enough to preserve it. Most kids are excited if a butterfly or a Lady Bird Beetle (aka Lady Bug but it isn't a bug at all) lands on them. Such an experience is exactly the kind that gets kids hooked on nature. So, where do you draw the line between what's OK to touch and what's not ?

Start by protecting young students as well as wildlife by telling your students not to touch anything when you are not with them. Teach *all* students what poison ivy looks like *(leaves of three, let it be)* even if there isn't any in your schoolyard; and discuss and show photos of local poisonous plants and animals to all students. Researching poisonous plants and animals is a great project for older students.

When students bring things to the classroom from outdoors, your first response should be "Put it back where you found it". There are consequences of interacting with even the seemingly benign wild animals—such as turtles. At a school visit in the fall of 2006, I took a teacher aside to ask her to return the newly-claimed classroom mascot, a box turtle, to the place it was found. Recent discoveries have taught us that many turtles, when moved from their habitat, will not eat and, of course, then die. Whether they are a food source to other animals, a pollinator, or a provider of another service, animals play an important role in nature. Besides, isn't "pet wild turtle" an oxymoron?

Under no circumstances should you allow students to feed any wild animals. Bird feeders containing wild bird seed, suet, or nectar are the exception to the rule. In most places, feeding wild animals is against the law—even feeding the geese and ducks at your local park. Don't offer "human" food to birds, because it offers little or no valuable calories or nutrition. Explain this to your students as well as the fact that feeding wild mammals puts the students at risk for ticks, rabies, parasites, and dangerous bacteria.

Take A Backyard Bird Walk, *Leave Only Footprints*, page 8.

## Addressing Field Etiquette

Take A Tree Walk, *Leave Only Footprints*, page 7.

Young students are taught to use their "indoor" and "outdoor" voices appropriately. They're taught that we have "indoor" activities and "outdoor" activities. Before you take young students outdoors, make certain they know to use their indoor voices and activities in the outdoors when doing nature observation.

Take A Walk With Butterflies and Dragonflies, *No Insects Were Injured*, page 7, *Shhh*, pg 17.

Make a list of the Rules of Field Etiquette and post it in your classroom. Suggest that all teachers post the rules and maybe you should get together to create the rules so you are consistent in teaching your students. Make the list simple:

Take A City Nature Walk, *Staying Safe In the City*, page 3.

- **Wildlife**: don't harass, chase, or scare animals. Don't interfere with animal activities. Don't assist injured animals—ask an adult for help.
- **Binoculars**: keep them around your neck and don't look at the sun through binoculars or other magnifying lenses.
- **Plants**: don't touch plants unless you ask an adult first.
- **Behavior**: Stay on school property and on trails (if you have nature trails) at all times. Leave only footprints. Observe quietly. Share resources and sightings.

Poison Ivy

You might need to explain to students what "share resources and sightings" means. Younger students tend to blurt out what they see—they want others to see things with them. Older students might be more competitive in the field and, as a result, keep sightings to themselves until students return to the classroom. This can result in a missed opportunity for others. Make certain that students understand the Field Guide Project is not a competition and the objective isn't to try to see and identify more species than others. Explain, too, that every student deserves the opportunity to view nature—even if they aren't the one who made the initial sighting.

## Data Collection: Notes and Journals

Take A Backyard Bird Walk
*Recording Observations,* page 17.
*Bird Notes,* page 19.

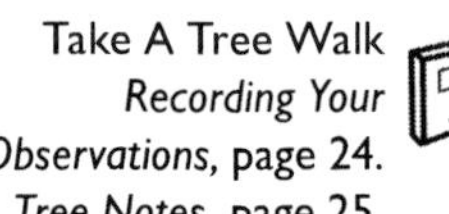

Take A Tree Walk
*Recording Your Observations,* page 24.
*Tree Notes,* page 25.

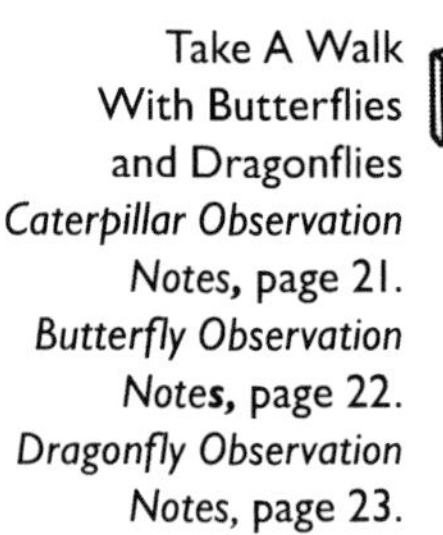

Take A Walk With Butterflies and Dragonflies
*Caterpillar Observation Notes,* page 21.
*Butterfly Observation Notes,* page 22.
*Dragonfly Observation Notes,* page 23.

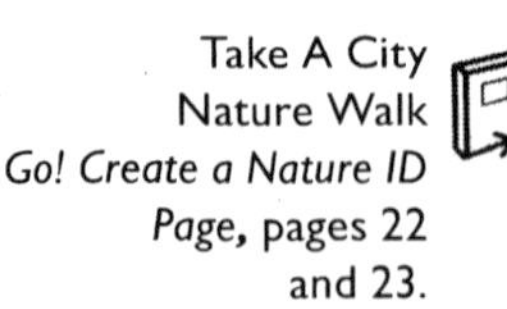

Take A City Nature Walk
*Go! Create a Nature ID Page,* pages 22 and 23.

*Field notes* are a written record of events and observations made by a researcher. A *journal* is a diary. These two types of records aren't necessarily exclusive; but for my purposes they are. I think of field notes as a place to record a particular amount of required data and a journal as a blank canvas to write and draw freely.

I always introduce young students (K-4) to the field note concept before I introduce them to journaling by providing them with pre-printed forms containing a list of the data they should collect. Even when the form is blank, it is a road map that demonstrates the benefits of collecting data in an organized, concise, clear, and consistent manner. Each of the books in my series contains field notes pages for readers to fill in or make copies of. Figure 3.1 shows an example of a filled-in *Bird Notes* page from *Take A Backyard Bird Walk.*

| | Bird #1 | Bird #2 |
|---|---|---|
| Location of bird | On birdbath | In bushes |
| Overall colors | Dark Gray with white spots and some blue | Brown |
| Wing bars (yes or no) | No | Couldn't see |
| Color of wing bars | None | None |
| Color on head | Blue | Brown with white eye stripe |
| Color on chest | Mottled gray/black and white | Buff |
| Color on Back | Blue, grey and white spots | Brown |
| Other physical characteristics | White eye ring, blue wing tips | Short tail, bobbing up and down |
| Approximate size and shape | About 7" shaped like a robin | Smaller than the bluebird |
| Behavior notes | Begging for food from parents | Loud 3 syllable call |
| Identification? | Eastern Bluebird (juvenile) | Carolina Wren |

**Figure 3.1. Example of a competed bird field notes page from *Take A Backyard Bird Walk,* ©2001, Stillwater publishing. Find a blank form in Chapter Five, *Exercises, Lessons, and Forms.***

You'll find blank field notes pages you can reproduce for your students in Chapter Five, *Exercises, Forms, and Lessons* from our books, *Take A Backyard Bird Walk, Take A Tree Walk, Take A Walk With Butterflies and Dragonflies, and Take A City Nature Walk.*

When I introduce older students (8-12) and even adults to nature observation, I like to do nature journaling exercises on blank pages—letting the students determine on their own what they want to write. We discuss the possibilities for those blank pages, such as collecting data for the purpose of species identification, illustrating a plant or animal, writing to express feelings evoked by nature, writing about and illustrating landscapes, habitats, and so forth. Figure 3.2 shows an example of nature journaling from my personal favorite book on nature journaling.

## Look for Nature Everywhere

Even in urban spaces, you can note signs of the season: sky condition, position of the sun, type of vegetation and stage of growth, animal evidence and survival. Clare made this drawing during a forty-five-minute session with a group of elementary schoolchildren in Cambridge, Massachusetts. All were amazed at how much nature could be found right around the school yard. Journaling is a great way to confront unfounded fears about nature, as well. Once the children spent time drawing and learning about earthworms, they were no longer afraid of them.

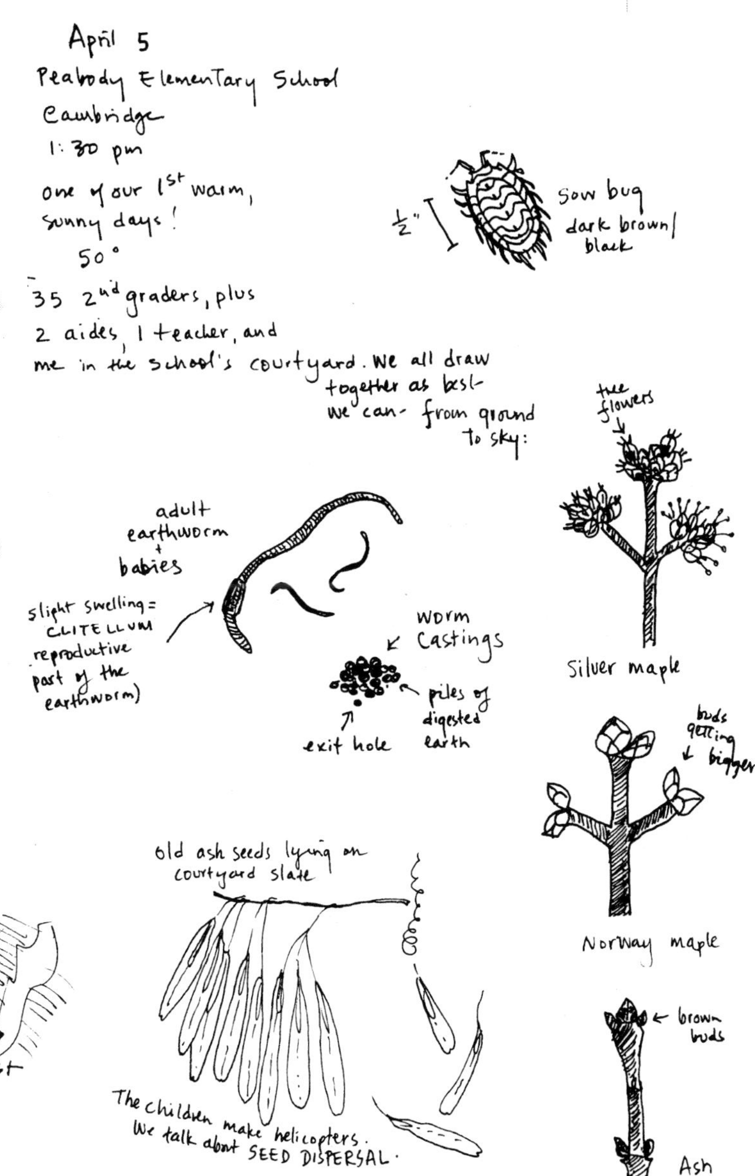


**Figure 3.2. This example of journaling in an urban schoolyard demonstrates the variety of species found in a short time spent outdoors. Excerpted from** ***Keeping a Nature Journal*** **by Claire Walker Leslie. Copyright ©2005 By Claire Walker Leslie. Used with permission from Storey Publishing, LLC, North Adams, MA.**

At Park Forest Elementary School students at every grade level begin their nature record-keeping with journals. Each student is provided with an individual journal to be kept in their classrooms. Students take their journals with them on the observation dates, to add to their journals independently, or in pairs. Students share observation information from their journals to complete a school-wide observation sheet. School-wide observation sheets are added to binders; one for each of four observation sites. Teachers are required to complete one sheet for each of the 4 sites on the one day per month they are scheduled to do an observation at that site.

Integrate technology into your FGP for middle and high school students by creating a database for your field data. You can do this in Microsoft Word (use data forms), Microsoft Excel, or any number of inexpensive database managers. By entering your data into a database, you can sort the data by species, sighting dates, season, location, or key on any of the fields in your database. You can even create individual life lists for students. If you do create a database or spreadsheet, consider sharing it with other readers by sending it to me in an email addressed to our editor (editor@takeawalk.com).

You'll decide what works best for your students. Both journaling and field notes are good methods for collecting data in the field. If you don't like any of the forms you find in this book, create your own. Or better yet, let students design field note and journal pages from the criteria you indicated on your Planning Workbook. As you collect data keep in mind that you are creating your book content.

## In Conclusion

Congratulations! You've set your FGP goals and prepared yourself, your team, and your students for the project. If you haven't started already, you'll soon begin your regular schoolyard explorations and data collection.

I thank you for providing your students with this opportunity to discover nature "up close and personal". Analytically or anecdotally, they will eventually come see their schoolyard and themselves as a part of the larger, more ecologically diverse community known as planet Earth. It is at that very moment that they will begin to grow as global citizens and caretakers. I envy you. I wish I could be witness to your students' journey.

In Chapter Four you'll learn about designing, assembling and distributing your book. Just as I've always felt that "nature is not a destination", I feel that your field guide book is not the final destination of your Field Guide Project. Your book is a small but tangible representation of your investment in your students and your community from which we will all reap the benefits.

House Finch

www.istockphoto.com/ScottDunlap

**In This Chapter**

- Creating Hand-drawn Templates
- Creating PowerPoint Templates
- Getting the Most From Your Scanner
- Sourcing and Placing Images
- Creating PDF Files

CHAPTER FOUR

# Creating Your Book

When does a collection of pages become a book? When the collection of pages tells a story or acts as a resource or reference with a beginning, middle, and end. When the pages have a consistent look and feel. And when they are bound in some way with a cover displaying a name for that collection of pages (a book title).

Your book is the culmination of the hard work and dedication of all its participants and contributors and it should do justice to those efforts in both design and function. We addressed the function in previous chapters and your book is now a collection of related pages. Now, you'll organize your book (to give it a beginning, middle, and end) and design the layout to give your pages a consistent look and feel.

The organization part isn't difficult. The easiest, most straightforward approach is to break your content into sections. At the top level, you might have three sections:

1. Front section. This is optional. If you have front matter it would be those pages discussed in Chapter Two such a an *About Our School* page, a *School Map* page, or any of the other bonus pages.

2. Middle section. The middle section is the story or—in your case—the plant and animal pages. You'll need to determine how to organize this section. You might group by subcategories such as trees, wildflowers,

**Worth Repeating**

*It is clear to me that unless we connect directly with the earth, we will not have the faintest clue why we should save it.*

**Helen Caldicott**

mammals, insects, and so forth. Within those groups you could sort by taxonomic or alphabetical order. Alternatively, organize this section by season. Seasonal organization helps readers to know which species they can expect to see during a given season. Include year-round species in each season and emphasize any seasonal changes. And if all this organization sounds too bothersome, then organize this section alphabetically, by the common name of the subject. But be careful. Otherwise, students might not know to look for "Robin" under "American Robin" or "Chickadee" under "Black-capped Chickadee".

3. Back matter. Most elementary school field guides won't have any back matter. Typically the back section of a book contains appendices and an index. But if your project is being conducted by middle or high school students, and if they are creating the book using desktop publishing software, then I suggest that at the very least, you include an index.

Once you have your content organized you're ready to design the layout. Most books are designed and laid out using desktop publishing software (this book was laid out in Adobe InDesign). But not many schools have desktop publishing software. So I'm going to show you how to create a template by hand and how to create one in Microsoft PowerPoint—a software program commonly used in schools and one of the first software programs students learn to use. Whichever method you choose, you'll begin with the first step in book design best practices—a *template.* A template is a design element. It's a container that:

1. Provides a consistent look and feel for the pages of your book—such as: page size and orientation, colors, margins, page numbers, font style (if you're using a computer) and so forth.

2. Helps students to place their images and text in the same position on each page.

When you use a template to construct individual pages of related content and then bind your book it will indeed, become—a book!

You can create the template *for* your students, *with* your students, or by assigning the task *to* your students. They may not know what a template is or does, but they'll catch on quickly. Even the youngest of students understands the concept of staying within the lines in their coloring books; and that's really all that a template is—a framework for them to use so they can stay within the lines. Whether your book pages will be handwritten or computer-generated, a template is your key to a finished look. Let's begin with a hand-drawn template.

**Worth Repeating**

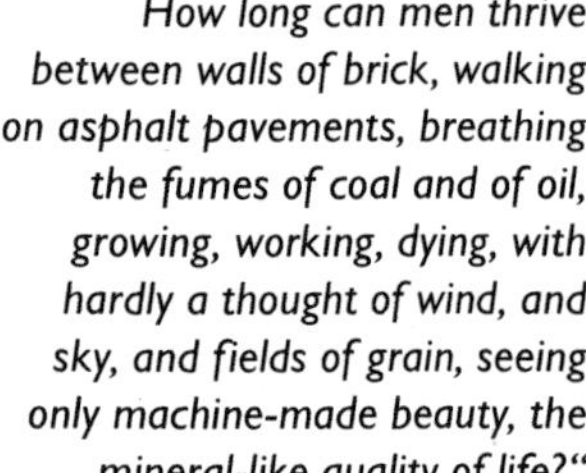

*How long can men thrive between walls of brick, walking on asphalt pavements, breathing the fumes of coal and of oil, growing, working, dying, with hardly a thought of wind, and sky, and fields of grain, seeing only machine-made beauty, the mineral-like quality of life?"*

**Charles Lindbergh**

## Creating Hand-drawn Page Templates

It only takes a few minutes to create a hand-drawn template. That is, unless your name is Jane Kirkland, in which case you'll change your mind several times before you settle on the final look of your pages. You can create a template for your pages in four easy steps:

1. **Choose your paper**—white is best if you're going to make paper copies of your book, colors are good for the Web as long as they provide sufficient contrast between the text and background. You could also use a paper with a pale pattern or watermark.

2. **Set the margins.** Determine your right and left margins. Leave ample room on the left for your binding. At a minimum, the inside margin should be 1". If you are planning for more that 20 pages or you're going to punch holes in your pages, you should allow 1.5" for the inside margin.

3. **Create a left and right page template**. If your inside and outside margins are the same size, you can skip this step. If your inside margin is wider than your outside margin, you'll need to create a mirror template for the facing page. Place the left and right pages next to one another on a table and you have what's called a *spread*.

4. **Choose your layout.** If you plan for one page per species, you need only one layout. But if you are going to do a spread-per-species, you'll need a right page layout and a left page layout. Whether or not they are exactly the same is up to you. Divide your page up into sections (columns and rows, as many as you wish). Draw boxes within those sections to act as placeholders for images and text. Put labels on the boxes so students know what goes where. Later they'll cover the labels with their artwork. If you want students to write in the text box, don't put a label on it but you can label the photo boxes because students drawings or pictures will be pasted over the label. Decide if you want one image or more per species, if you want one column or more for text, where you want the page number to go, and if and where you want the student's name placed on the page. Figure 4.1 illustrates some page layout suggestions.

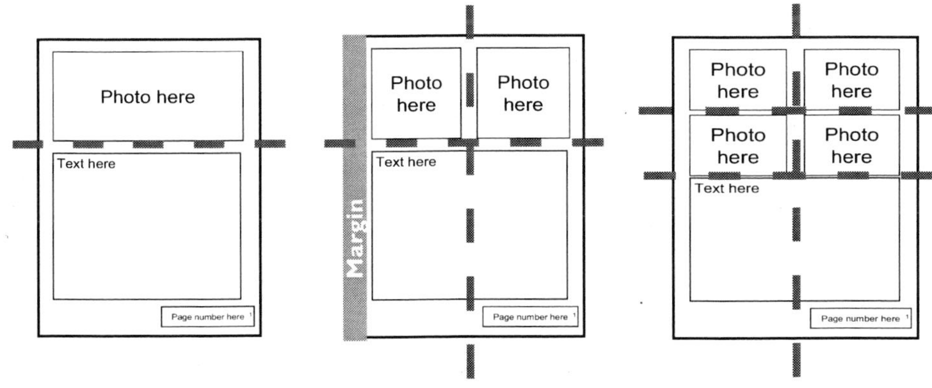


**Figure 4.1. Divide your paper into equal rows and columns. Be sure to leave ample room for binding as shown in gray in the middle page, above. Draw borders to act as placeholders for photos and text. In this example, the page on the left is designed for one photo or image, the middle page for two, and the right page for four.**

After you sketch your template, make copies for your students. They'll cut and paste images onto the pages and write their text in the appropriate

**Worth Repeating**

*The habitats in our schoolyard give homes to many interesting animals. At the pond you see frogs and spiders. At the playground you see worms and wasps. In the woods you see deer, birds, and squirrels. At the meadow you see butterflies. Our schoolyard has the best habitats!*

**Colin Ayres**
**Grade 3**

space. Figure 4.2 shows a hand-drawn page based on a hand-drawn template.

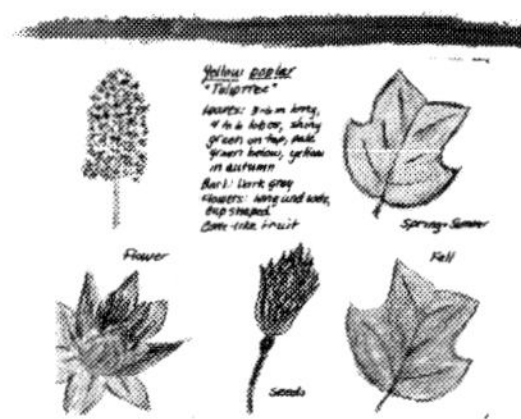


**Figure 4.2. This example uses three placeholders: one at the top for the title, one in the center for the image and one at the bottom for text.**

If you're a crafty type, you might want more artistic pages. Figure 4.3 shows three papers which make up a page: a white page glued onto a slightly larger black paper with scalloped edges, then onto an even larger paper with a printed pattern. You can use colored or patterned paper for the second and third papers. Remember that each page of your book will have a front and a back, so in this example, you need one patterned paper (assuming it does not have a right side and wrong side, two black papers, and two white papers (a total of 5 papers). This method will certainly make your book pages very strong but they probably won't fold open well so I recommend this method for books that will be hole-punched and put in a three ring binder. This method also requires a lot of paper cutting—the largest paper should not be larger than 8.5" x 11" to fit in a standard binder. Therefore, the other two papers will have to be cut smaller than 8.5" x 11". This is a good opportunity to use recycled paper—each page in your book can be different papers—paper bags and old book covers, wrapping paper, newspapers, pages from magazines, and used construction paper are all good examples of papers you can recycle and use for your middle sheet. They'll add a lot of color and pattern to your book. If it's heavy enough, used writing paper can be turned over and glued as the top sheet.

**Figure 4.3. Glue together several sheets of paper with to add interest to your field guide pages.**

## Creating PowerPoint Page Templates

Both desktop publishing and word processing are the software of choice for creating books. The good news is that they give you a lot of control over the look and feel of a publication. The bad news is that in order to have that amount of control one must have a huge amount of product knowledge. Complicated equipment, machinery, and software require knowledgeable operators. Unless you or your students are masters of either of those types of software, I recommend you use PowerPoint. For elementary students in particular, PowerPoint offers several advantages for your FGP. They are:

**Recycled Materials**

Encourage your students to use as many recycled materials as possible in their book.Use recycled paper—or recycle used paper. This very book is printed on 100% recycled laser paper.

- **Automatic font size adjustment.** PowerPoint has a huge advantage when you are creating a template for pages. If you use one of the PowerPoint layouts for your slide (page), the software will compensate the font size according to the amount of information you want to put on the page. In other words, the more you type, the smaller the font becomes—automatically. This means that if you have a page with more information on it than other pages, the font will be smaller on that page. Normally, a publisher wouldn't want that to happen—they'd want the same font sizes throughout the book. But you're not a publisher and it will be so much easier for you to let the software fit your information on your pages than to have to muck with font sizes or editing text to fit within a predefined space.

- **Ease of use**. PowerPoint is easy for students to use. It's more of a graphical interface than a word processing program and more intuitive for youngsters.
- **Pre-defined layouts**. PowerPoint comes with loads of templates—or layouts—from which you can choose the best for your pages. You can change the layout with the click of a mouse and you can download even more templates from Microsoft and other sources.
- **Loads of designs.** If you want to apply backgrounds and graphics to your pages, Power Point has a huge number to choose from.
- **Flexibility**. You can create Web pages and Adobe PDF files of your book from within PowerPoint.

Figure 4.4 shows some pages created in PowerPoint, using PowerPoint slide design templates.

**Figure 4.4 Four different PowerPoint design templates were applied to one page. The names of the templates are from left: Contport.pot, Artsy.pot, Poetic.pot, and Expeditn.pot.**

**Strut Your Stuff**

Want to show off your field guide to the world? Send a copy to me. If possible send a PDF file on a CD along with a cover letter explaining what is on the CD. Otherwise, send a hard copy. With your permission, I'll post pages from your guide (not the entire book) at our Website as an example for other teachers and students. Please include all of your contact information, including how to reach you at home.

How easy is it to create these pages in PowerPoint? Very easy—if you have a basic knowledge of the program. If you've never used PowerPoint, consult with the PowerPoint teacher or media specialist in your school to help you get up and running.

To create pages, you'll create a custom paper size (which also sets your margins), select a design (choose your paper color and style), and finally, choose your layout. To make this task as easy as possible, you should set all page margins the same and not try to create a left and right page. Of course, if you know your way around PowerPoint, you probably can figure out how to create a different left and right page.

The steps to creating book pages in PowerPoint are similar to those you take when creating a template by hand. Three steps will get you up and running: 1) create a custom paper size; 2) choose your background color and pattern; and 3) choose your layout. It should take you just a few minutes to do this but if you're like me, you'll want to see all the design choices PowerPoint has to offer, so budget at least one half hour to set this up. Following are the step-by-step instructions for creating your page template(s) in PowerPoint 2003.

## Creating a Custom Paper Size

Start Microsoft PowerPoint. A new, blank slide should open automatically. If it does not, click File, New, and on the right of your screen choose Blank Presentation. You should now see a blank slide as shown in Figure 4.5.

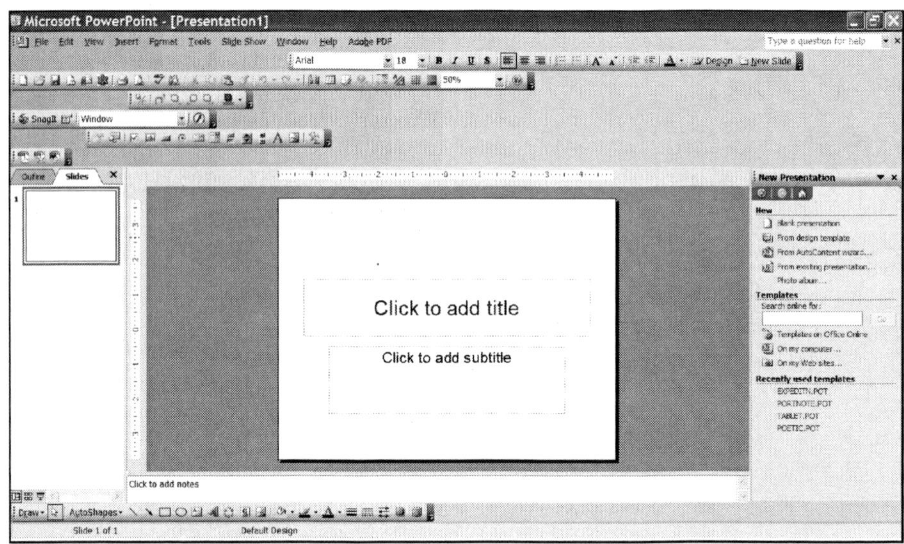


**Figure 4.5 The pane on the right of the screen is called the *Task Pane.* If you do not see the Task Pane in PowerPoint, click View, Toolbars on the PowerPoint menu and select Task Pane from the list.**

By default, PowerPoint presents a slide in *landscape* format. That is, the slide is set up so the page is wider than it is tall. For your book, you'll most likely want *portrait* set-up, or a page that is taller than it is wide. The first step is to change the page orientation. To do this:

****Caution****
**Save Your Files**

As you make changes to your Power Point file—page orientation, layout, design templates and so forth—don't forget to save your changes by saving your file frequently. If you think you might want to preserve a version so you can revert to it later, do a **Save As.**

1. Choose **File, Page Setup.** The Page Setup dialog box appears as shown in Figure 4.6. Change the orientation from **Landscape** to **Portrait**. If necessary, change the paper size to **Letter Paper.** Click **OK** to close the dialog box and return to your newly-formatted page.

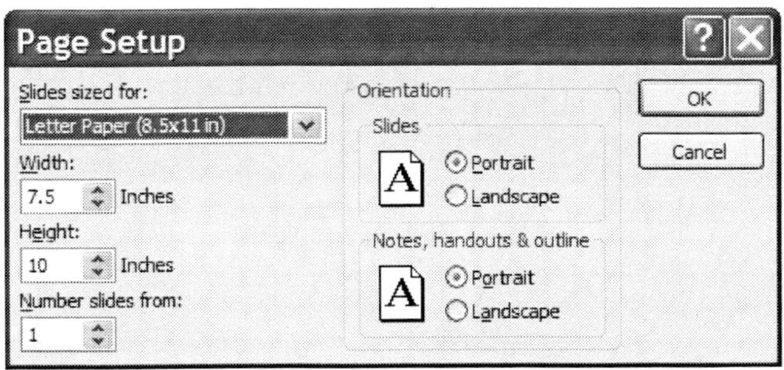


**Figure 4.6. PowerPoint does not have a margin setting but when you choose letter paper, it sets the width and height one inch shorter than a letter-size paper. This effectively gives you a one inch margin if you print your slides on letter-size paper.**

2. To add pages to your book, click New Slide on the toolbar as shown in Figure 4.7.

**Figure 4.7 To insert a new slide, click the New Slide button on the toolbar.**

## Choosing a Slide Design

With your file open choose your background color and design using PowerPoint's *slide design* in the task pane. If you don't see the Task Pane, choose **View**, **Task Pane** on the menu bar. Choose a slide design from the Task Pane.

1. To view the available designs, click the drop down triangle in the Task Pane and choose **Slide Design** as shown in Figure 4.8.

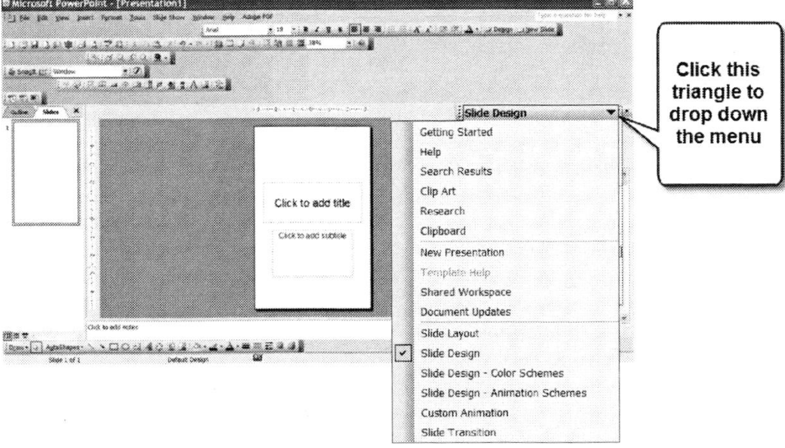


**Figure 4.8 The drop-down menu of the Task Pane helps you to navigate through PowerPoint.**

**Worth Repeating**

*I really enjoy the nature in my schoolyard. My favorite thing is a bush with tiny red berries because it brightens up the playground. The colorful berries are fun to step on when they fall to the ground. I love to hear them crunch under my feet!*

**Adam Tankus**
**Grade 4**

2. Scroll down in the Task Pane until you see the title *Available for Use.* Under that title you'll find many different designs to choose from. As you click on one design in the task pane, your choice will be displayed on your page as shown in Figure 4.9

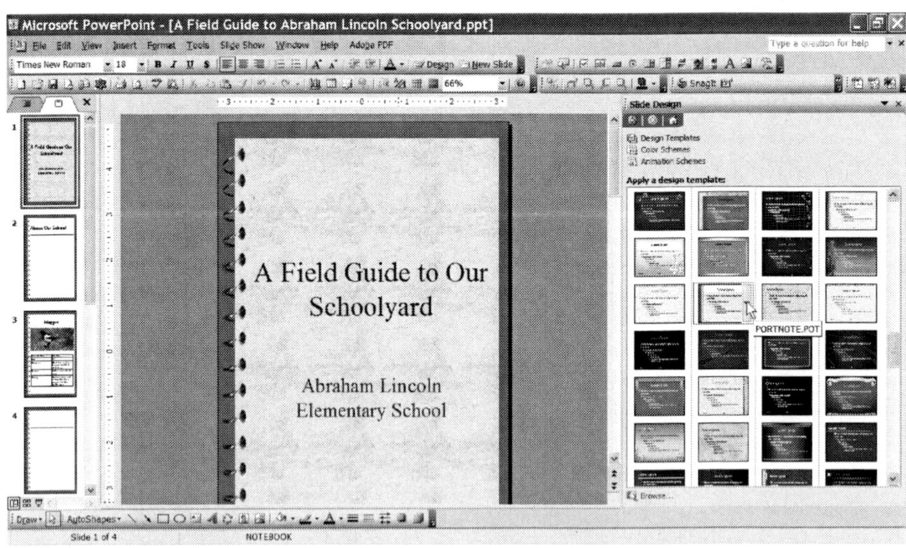


**Figure 4.9 PowerPoint templates are designed for landscape slides and some won't work well on a portrait page. You'll need to scroll through the choices to find the ones best suited for your pages such as this one called *Portnote.pot.* (Hint: "port" is short for "portrait").**

3. By default, when you click on a design in the Task Pane, PowerPoint applies it to all of the slides in your presentation (or, in your case, all of the pages in your book). If you want to use different designs for different pages, select the pages and right click the desired design in the Task pane. Then choose **Apply to Selected Slides** as shown in Figure 4.10.

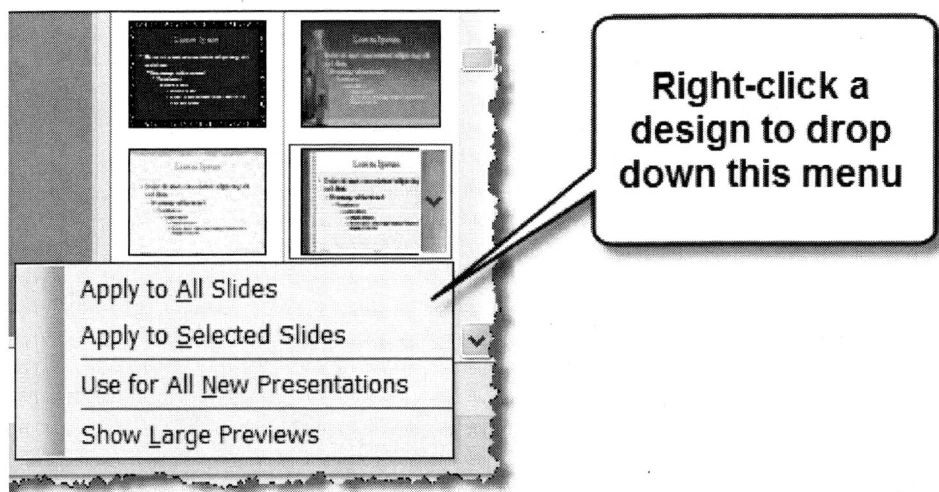


**Figure 4.10. Right-click a slide design and choose how you want to apply it to your slides.**

**Worth Repeating**

*When one tugs at a single thing in nature, he finds it attached to the rest of the world.*

**John Muir**

4. If you want to change the text color of your design, change the *color scheme.* This feature changes your text color, not your slide color. You might want to do this if you've chosen a slide design you like, but you feel the text color in the design doesn't provide enough contrast to the background. To view available schemes, click the drop-down menu in the Task Pane and choose **Slide Design—color schemes.** The Task Pane then displays available color schemes as shown in Figure 4.11.

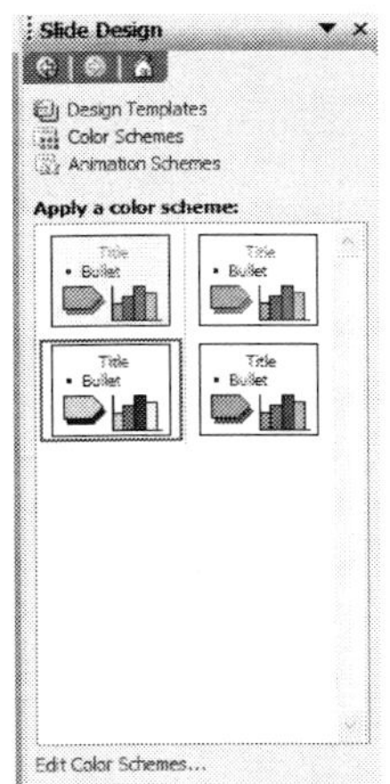


**Figure 4.11. Color schemes affect your text colors.**

Once you settle on a slide design, you're ready to choose the layout for your slides.

## Choosing a Slide Layout

PowerPoint slide layouts offer many choices for placing text and pictures (graphics) on your pages (slides). You might want one layout for your book cover, one for your species pages, and one for those "bonus" pages of your book such as the "About Our School" page. To choose slide layouts:

1. Click the drop-down menu on the Task Pane (as shown in Figure 4.12) and select **Slide Layout.**

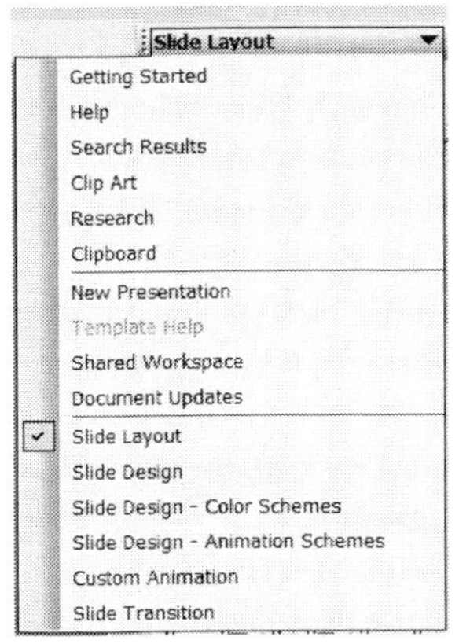


**Figure 4.12 Select Slide Layout from the drop-down menu of the Task Pane to view choices.**

2. The available slide layouts appear in the Task Pane as shown in Figure 4.13. They are shown in four categories: **Text Content Layouts** (text only pages—a suitable choice for your book cover), **Content Layouts** (for pages that contain images only), **Text and Content Layouts** (a perfect selection for your species pages) and **Other Layouts** (a collection of everything-else layouts). As you move your mouse over each layout, the layout name will appear.

Once you choose a layout, insert text on your page by clicking in the text box and typing or pasting.

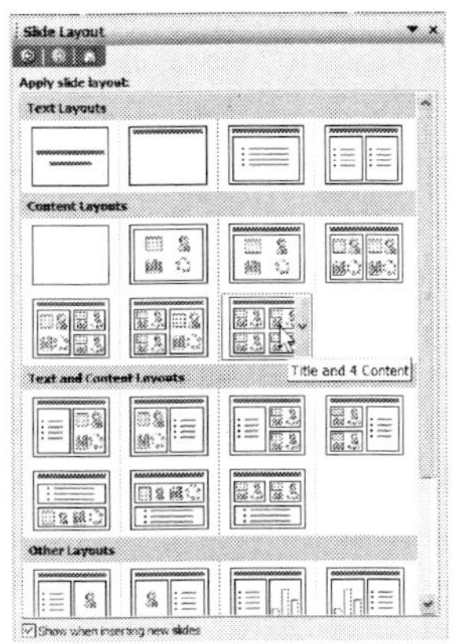


**Figure 4.13. Choose Title and Content for most of your pages.**

**Worth Repeating**

*The best thing one can do when it's raining is to let it rain.*

**Henry Wadsworth Longfellow**

Figure 4.14 Illustrates some book pages that are all based on the *Portnote.pot* design template and each has a different slide layout applied to the page. On the third (right) page I applied a layout template which I'll use for most of the pages of my book. That layout is called "fit content over text".

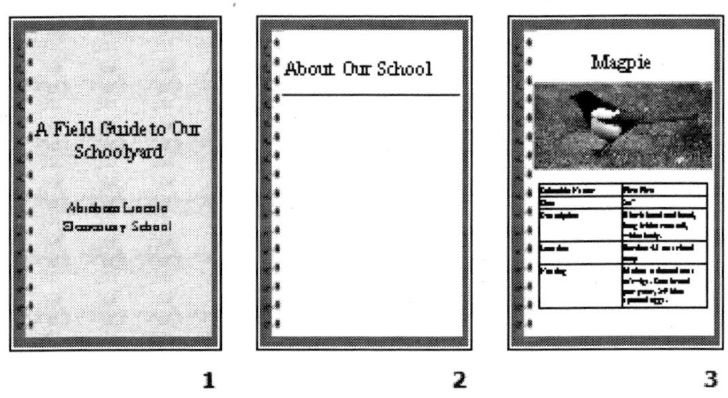


**Figure 4.14 One design and three layouts give us a cover, title**

## Inserting Images

Whatever type of illustrations you use for your book: photos or drawings, they'll need to be in electronic format in order to place them in your PowerPoint book. Unless you use a digital camera or purchase electronic images, you'll need to scan your images to create electronic files.

Placing an image into a PowerPoint slide is very easy. Make certain the pictures or scanned images are on your computer, network, CD or DVD and that you have access to the directory in which they are stored. If you are using a PowerPoint design layout, simply click the picture icon in the "click icon to add content" box on your layout page as shown in Figure 4.13. The **Insert Picture** dialog box appears. Select the the file you want to insert, and choose **Insert.** It's that easy—PowerPoint will size the image appropriately.

**Figure 4.13. Click the picture icon to add your image.**

## Getting the Most From Your Scanner

You can create electronic files from your students' artwork, incorporate non-digital photographs, and capture items you collect in the field (leaves, flowers, and such) to your PDF, PowerPoint, or Web files by using a scanner. But much like binoculars, lots of people have scanners and they don't really know how to make the best use of the equipment because they don't bother to read (or don't have access to) the instructions.

You can scan all kinds of things—not just pictures. You can scan flowers, acorns, leaves, books, artwork, hands, and, well, you get the picture. You can

**Worth Repeating**

*A worm squirmed around on the ground. I didn't step on it because it would kill nature. I tried to catch it but I failed. I heard the birds cooing like a choir of angels. It was beautiful, that's why I love my schoolyard.*

**Lina Ruth Duiker**
**Grade 3**

capture the growth cycle or seasonal changes of an item by scanning it in different forms.

Most scanners today are *flat-bed* scanners. They have a flat glass surface on which you lay the item you want to scan. To get the best results from a flat-bed scanner you need to keep the glass clean—smudges and scratches will show up in your final image. You also want to keep the inside of the lid clean.

When you scan with the lid closed, if your image or object is smaller than the lid, the backside of the lid becomes the white background of your image as shown in figure 4.14. If you scan with the lid up and your image or object is smaller than the glass, your image will have a black background, as show in Figure 4.15.

**Figure 4.14. These acorns were scanned with the scanner lid down, resulting in a white background. Dirt or smudges on the inside of the lid would show as black marks on this white background.**

**Figure 4.15. These leaves and seeds were scanned with the scanner lid open, resulting in a black background.**

## Scanner4 Resolution

Think of a picture as a series of dots. The more dots per inch (DPI) the picture contains, the greater the quality and detail of the picture. This is called *resolution*. When you scan an item, you need to set your scanner to your desired resolution.

The higher your resolution, the larger your file will be, too, so don't set the resolution larger than is really necessary. What's the best resolution to use? It depends on how you will be using the scanned image—whether you'll be printing your final book on paper or creating files for the Web. 300 DPI is a good resolution if you plan on printing your book from an Adobe PDF or PowerPoint file (more on that later) and 72 DPI is a good resolution if you're planning to put your book on a Website. Now, there are really a lot of scenarios when it comes to your book and scanning at the right resolution. And

**Worth Repeating**

*All my life through, the new sights of nature made me rejoice like a child.*

**Marie Curie**

there is software, such as Adobe Photoshop, that can change image resolution for you without losing quality. But, you know, entire books are written on this subject and I'd really rather take the fast lane with the fewest turns to get you to your destination. So I'm addressing three scenarios here to give you a guideline. Scan at the following resolutions for the following situations:

1. **You plan to create your book in PowerPoint.** Scan your images at 300 DPI. That way, they'll be at a good resolution if you print your book from PowerPoint. Should you use PowerPoint to create Web pages of your book, PowerPoint will take care of converting your images to the best resolution for the Web. Use the same resolution if you are creating your book in a word processing or desktop publishing program.

2. **You plan to create your book manually, then scan it to print it.** You might want to send an electronic file of your book to a printer or copy service company that will print copies of the book for you. Scan your pages at 300 DPI.

3. **You plan to create your book manually, then scan it for the Web.** If you need scanned images of your book for the Web only, scan at 72 DPI or 100 DPI, whichever is the lowest available to you in your scanning software.

If your scenario is not addressed here, or your questions not answered, consult with your media specialist, computer software expert, or Web developer at your school or district or, as my husband likes to say, "ask a thirteen-year-old". If you're still in doubt, scan at 300 DPI. You can always reduce the resolution with computer software but you can't increase it without chancing the loss of quality.

In addition to resolution, you can set the image size before scanning. There is no sense in scanning an image and saving it as 8 x 10 inches, when you are only going to print it or display it at 4 x 5 inches. Scan it as close to the size you are going to use as possible by telling your scanning software to reduce the image size to your preferences. Most scanners come with software in which you can preview your scan. You can then adjust how the image will look before you save the file.

**Worth Repeating**

*Our schoolyard has an apple tree that makes me happy. In the spring, the apple tree has pretty pink flowers that smell sweet and delicious. There is a special shady spot under the apple tree where I like to play with my friends on hot days.*

**Megan Stone**
**Grade 4**

In addition to resolution and image size, you can also crop your pictures. Cropping lets you remove any part of the picture you don't want to save (like a lot of white space around the picture) by selecting the part that you do want to save. You could also just capture the faces of a group instead of their bodies.

To get some additional tips on scanning, read your scanner manual, visit the Web site of the scanner manufacturer, or visit **www.scantips.com.**

## Sourcing Images

Do you want photos, illustrations, scanned images, clipart, or a combination of each? Will students create all the images or will you need to get some from other sources? Some subjects, such as trees, will warrant multiple images—one of the entire tree, at least one of a leaf (two if you want to show fall colors), and one each of the seeds, fruit, flowers, and bark.

When you need to go beyond your students' artwork and photographs for illustrations and photographs in black and white or color, there are numerous sources for images. You're probably familiar with sources specifically for school use. Some of these Websites are free, others charge a subscription price—most are reasonably priced. To find these Websites, Google *"images for school use","* *"photos for school use," "pictures for school use," "clipart for school use"* and so forth

Other royalty-free and copyright-free sources are available in both hard copy and electronic form. Dover Publications (**www.dover.com**) has a has a book series of black and white illustrations that you can cut and paste into your field guide book as well as CDs of electronic images in color. Clipart.com is a subscription service that charges an annual (and very affordable) subscription service with unlimited downloads of royalty-free images. Many of the illustrations in this book came from Clipart.com. There are numerous Websites where you can purchase royalty-free photographs such Istock.com where you can find beautiful photographs for as little as $1.00. Many of the photographs used in this book came from **www.Istock.com**, .

Copyright is an important legal consideration—even for school use. At some point in your Field Guide Project you'll be gathering information and images from the Internet. Most of what you find on the Internet is copyrighted. This might be a good time to teach your students about copyrights and to brush up on copyright laws yourself. Teach your students about copyright with this handy online interactive lesson: **www.cyberbee/com/cb_copyright.** Also check out **www.copyrightkids.org.** Learn how copyrights apply to teachers in Circular 21 *"Reproduction of copyrighted Works by Educators and Librarians"* at the Library of Congress Website: **www.copyright.gov.**

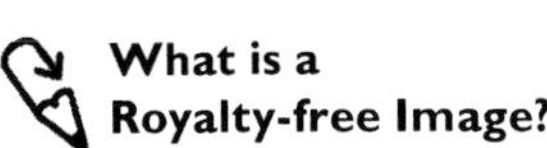

**What is a Royalty-free Image?**

A royalty-free image is typically a "rented" image—one for which you pay a licensing fee. You don't own the photo or copyright, you don't have exclusive rights to the photo, and you can use the photo only as many times as (and for the purposes) the licensing agreement indicates. Sidebar images in this book are royalty-free images licensed by JupiterImages at: **www.clipart.com.**

## Copies and Distribution

How many original field guides will you create? Will each student create their own field guide or will students collaborate to create one field guide? How many copies of each will you need to distribute? If you create one collaborative field guide, will each student want their own copy? You'll probably want to make these decisions before you determine how you'll bind your book (just in case you have to take it apart to make copies). Here are five scenarios to handle your copying and distribution needs:

1. **You want multiple hardcopy originals, no reproduction or distribution.** Each student creates his or her own field guide. This might be a good option for lower grades (K-2) and students who are not ready to work

in teams. But if you really want to make the FGP a collaborative project, you'll want to make one book by many contributors.

2. **You want one hardcopy original, no reproduction or distribution.** Just because this is an option doesn't mean it's a *good choice*. Won't students want a copy? Where will you keep the original? Won't you need at least one additional copy for your school library?

3. **You want one original (hardcopy or electronic) reproduced and distributed in hardcopy**. This is the best option *if* you can afford color copies. But color copies are very expensive.

4. **You want one original (hardcopy or electronic) and you plan to sell color copies.** If you decide to sell your field guide to school families, don't print "production" copies until you've sold them. You'll need to put some effort into selling, too. Run a "media blitz" to generate interest in your book. This would be a fun project for upper grades. Ask your local newspaper to write a feature article about your project. Write articles about your field guide for your school yearbook, newsletter, or Website. Invite your local TV news crew or morning show hosts to take a nature walk with your students in your schoolyard.

5. **You want one original (electronic) posted at your school Website and no reproduction or distribution. You do—yes—this is the one you really want!** This might just be your best option, saving you on reproduction costs and allowing students to have their own copies if they print them from home. In this scenario, depending on your software, you create Web pages, a photo album, an online PowerPoint show, or Adobe PDF file from your original field guide and post the file on your school Website. Students, their families, friends, and even distant relatives can view the file online or download it and print their own copy. Imagine your Field Guide on the Internet for the entire world to see!

## Choosing Binding

When all of your pages are finished, your book is ready for binding. If you have a spiral binding machine at school, then spiral binding will no doubt be your best choice. Staple binding and saddle stitching (sewing) will only work well if you have a very small book. Putting your pages in page protectors and into a three-ring binder has advantages over spiral binding, stapling, or saddle stitching. First, you can easily update, replace, or remove (for copying purposes) the pages from a three-ring binder. Second, a three-ring binder allows readers to browse your book without having to bend the pages. The downside to a three-ring binder is the cost. If you intend to distribute or sell your book, you'll have to add in the cost of the binder. Otherwise, a three-ring binder is probably the best choice for your field guide book.

**Worth Repeating**

*Nature does nothing uselessly.*

**Aristotle**

## Creating Files for the Web

There are several ways you can prepare your book for the Web. Here are three common methods which don't require you to be an HTML editor or Web page designer.

1. **Use the software in which you created your book**. Many software programs have a feature that saves your work for the Web. If you can't find that feature, look in the help file for your software and search for "Web" or "HTML" or "Saving for the Web" or some such search terms. In PowerPoint click the **File** menu and choose **Save as Web Page**. PowerPoint will make an album from your pages for the Web.

2. **Use photo management software**. Most photo management programs provide an option to create a photo album for the Web; and your book is (or can be) essentially a photo album. Once you have your pages saved in an electronic image form (such as JPEG or GIF) your photo management software will do the rest. Keep in mind that you need to be working with finished pages; this is not software that will construct your pages with a mixture of text and images like PowerPoint. Figure 4.16 shows an example of a Web album created in photo management software.

3. **Create Adobe PDF files and post the PDF files on the Web.**

Just because you create Web files from your book doesn't (of course) make them available on the Web. You'll need to get together with your Website guru and make arrangements to have your book posted at your school's Website. Figure 4.16 shows a field guide page created in PowerPoint while viewed through a Web browser.

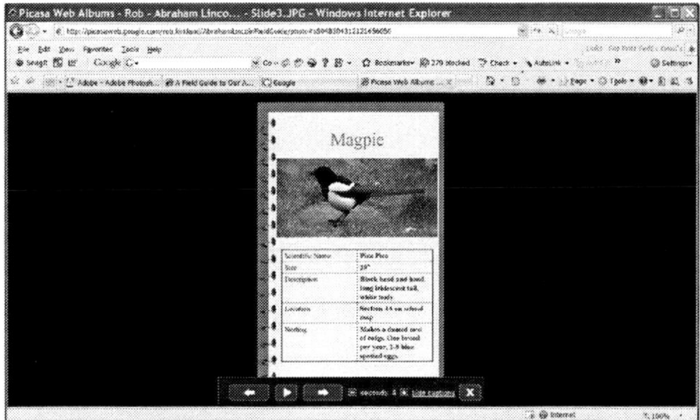


**Figure 4.16 Many Websites offer free photo management software such as Picasa, from www.google.com and Photo Story 3 from www.microsoft.com. Here you see one of our field guide pages viewed in Picasa on the Web. The guide was created from scanned images saved as JPEGs.**

**Worth Repeating**

*My school is so fortunate. We have a marsh and woods right by our school playground. One day my friend looked out the window and saw a blue heron standing on top of a small cedar tree! it was awesome. It was just standing there, not a care in the world.*

**Will Mullins**
**Grade 6**

## In Conclusion

As you can see, you don't need to be particularly artistic or have advanced computer skills to assemble your book. A good part of its charm is the fact that it's handmade and that it represents the adventures and discoveries of your students. Your book doesn't have to look ready for prime-time—it simply needs to represent it's many contributors.

**Worth Repeating**

*Autumn is a second spring when every leaf is a flower.*

**Albert Camus**

Your Field Guide Book is a book of hope. It represents an awakening to the nature that surrounds us. Nature that we have the power to destroy. Nature that we destroy daily and often without knowledge of that destruction. We cannot appreciate what we do not know. Your book of hope and memories is a reminder to all that we should stop, look, and listen to our world. Teach your students to cherish their book and you teach them to cherish their world.

www.istockphoto.com/filo

## In This Chapter

FGP Planning Workbook

Field Notes Pages for Students

Habitat House Hunt Lesson Plan

Glorious Weeds Lesson Plan

Bird Sleuth Lesson Plan

Dichotomous Key Lesson Plan

Making Maps Exercise

Quick Quadrat Exercise

Reflections Exercise

CHAPTER FIVE

# Exercises, Lessons, and Forms

This chapter is a collection of works from many sources. In addition to the *Planning Workbook* and forms from Take A Walk® books, the collection represents the contributions of many authors, educators, and publications.

I selected these works for a variety of reasons: how well they fit into a *Field Guide Project™*, how easily they can be adapted for various grade levels, and how useful their source (magazine, book, Website, etc.) can be to you in your project. If you are not familiar with the sources, please take the time to visit the Websites listed in the permissions statements at the bottom of the pages. I know you'll find a wealth of information and materials you can use.

The inclusion of works from other publishers, authors, magazines, and so forth does not automatically grant you permission to copy those pages. Please do not copy and distribute any pages in this book unless permission to do so is granted on the page.

As our *Field Guide Project* efforts grow at Stillwater, we'll be adding new information for teachers at our Website. Watch for our new teacher Website to launch in 2008, where you'll find more exercises, lessons and forms for your project.

**Worth Repeating**

*In every walk with nature one receives far more than he seeks.*

**John Muir**

## Field Guide Planning Workbook



| Item | Qty | *Description | Price Each | Supplier | Total |
|---|---|---|---|---|---|
| Binoculars | | | | | |
| Binoculars | | | | | |
| Binoculars | | | | | |
| Books | | | | | |
| Books | | | | | |
| Books | | | | | |
| Books | | | | | |
| Books | | | | | |
| Books | | | | | |
| Books | | | | | |
| Books | | | | | |
| Books | | | | | |
| Camera | | | | | |
| Compass | | | | | |
| GPS Unit | | | | | |
| Magnifying Lens | | | | | |
| Rain Ponchos | | | | | |
| Tape Measure | | | | | |
| | | | | | |
| | | | | | |
| | | | | | |
| | | | | | |
| | | | | | |
| | | | | | |
| | | | | | |
| | | | | | |
| | | | | | |
| | | | | | |
| | | | | | |
| Total | | | | | |

*Description: Part number, ISBN, etc.

Supplier Information

*Use this area to list teachers participating in the study. Include number of students per teacher if you are going to distribute copies of the field guide to each student. If you are assigning the field guide by task, list the tasks assignments for each class under "contribution".*

| Teacher | # of Students | Contribution or Task | Observation Dates | | | | | | | | |
|---|---|---|---|---|---|---|---|---|---|---|---|
| | | | | | | | | | | | |
| | | | | | | | | | | | |
| | | | | | | | | | | | |
| | | | | | | | | | | | |
| | | | | | | | | | | | |
| | | | | | | | | | | | |
| | | | | | | | | | | | |
| | | | | | | | | | | | |
| | | | | | | | | | | | |
| | | | | | | | | | | | |
| | | | | | | | | | | | |
| | | | | | | | | | | | |
| | | | | | | | | | | | |
| | | | | | | | | | | | |
| | | | | | | | | | | | |
| | | | | | | | | | | | |
| | | | | | | | | | | | |
| | | | | | | | | | | | |
| | | | | | | | | | | | |
| | | | | | | | | | | | |
| | | | | | | | | | | | |
| | | | | | | | | | | | |
| | | | | | | | | | | | |
| | | | | | | | | | | | |

*Total

* This number represents the total number of student participants. This is useful if you plant to distribute copies of your field guide.

## Field Guide Planning Workbook Page 2 of 4

**Subjects**

**Field Guide Subjects**

Number of pages per species:

| | Check here | **Notes** |
|---|---|---|
| Birds | | |
| Mammals | | |
| Insects | | |
| Plants | | |
| Other | | |

**Subject Data**

| | | ***Check here*** | **Comments** | *Format | See Note |
|---|---|---|---|---|---|
| **Name** | Scientific name | | | L | |
| | Pronunciation key | | | L | |
| | Common name | | | L | |
| **Description** | Size | | | L | |
| | Physical description | | | P | |
| | Observed behavior. | | | | |
| | Field marks | | | I | |
| **Range** | Range. | | | I OR P | A |
| **Illustrations** | Illustration | | | I | |
| | Photograph | | | I | |
| **Seasonal Changes** | Growing season | | | C | |
| **Other** | The habitat and food needs. | | | | |
| | Status | | | L | B |
| | Reproduction Info | | | P | |
| | Value | | | P | C |
| | Location | | | C, L or P | D |
| | Origination | | | P | E |
| | A natural history of the species. | | | P | |
| | Known conservation issues. | | | P | |
| | Property Improvements | | | P | F |
| | Nuisance | | | P | G |
| | Value | | | P | |

*** Format Key: L=List or checklist, P=paragraph format, I=illustration or Photograph, C=Chart, M=Map**

*** Indicate number if you intend to include more than one**

**B: Whether the species is native, non-native, endemic, invasive, threatened, or endangered.**

**C: The value of the plant to wildlife, or the value of wildlife to the plant (pollinators) and any synergistic relationships with like kind or others.**

**D: The time, date, and a map or written description of the plant's location.**

**E: Origination—A theory or speculation about why the plant or wildlife is in your schoolyard. Was it planted there by someone? Is the animal a year-round resident? How does the schoolyard meet the survival needs of the species?**

**F: Property improvements—Whether or not improvements to the schoolyard can help plants and animals survive and, if so, what improvements are needed.**

**G: Nuisance—Whether or not the presence of a species is harmful, dangerous, or in any way a problem or nuisance.**

**H: Value—Its value to humans, other wildlife and plants and/or its habitat.**

**Bonus Content**

| **Page Name** | ***Check here*** | **Est. # Pages** |
|---|---|---|
| Foreword | | |
| About Our Students | | |
| About Our School | | |
| About Our Schoolyard | | |
| Our Watershed | | |
| Project History | | |
| Map of Our Schoolyard | | |
| Total Additional Pages | | |
| Number Pages per species | | |
| * Number of Species | | |
| Total Est. Pages | | |

* When you finish your study and know the number of species you are including in your book, place that number here to calculate the total number of book pages.

## Bird Observation *from* Take A Backyard Bird Walk



# Bird Notes

| | Bird #1 | Bird #2 |
|---|---|---|
| Location of bird | | |
| Overall colors | | |
| Wing bars (yes or no) | | |
| Color of wing bars | | |
| Color on head | | |
| Color on chest | | |
| Color on Back | | |
| Other physical characteristics | | |
| Approximate size and shape | | |
| Behavior notes | | |
| Identification? | | |

**Use this area to draw or paste a photo of the bird**

### For You

There are lots of books about birds for kids. Here's one you might enjoy:

***Backyard Bird Watching for Kids*** written by George H. Harrison, published by Willow Creek Press. This book covers the better known backyard birds. It recommends plants for the birds, gives ideas on how to feed birds, and teaches you about birdhouses to build or buy.

*Need more room to draw or write? Use blank paper or download free forms at www.takeawalk.com.*

## Caterpillar Observation *from* Take A Walk With Butterflies and Dragonflies

# Caterpillar Observation Notes

If you find a caterpillar but don't see its picture on the opposite page, use this form to write down a description of it. Be sure to include the date that you saw the caterpillar. If possible, go back to see your caterpillar a few days later to see how it has changed. When you observe your caterpillar, record the following information about it:

☑ **Habitat and location.**

☑ **Color and pattern.** If you draw the pattern, this can help you to remember later.

☑ **Description of spikes or hair** (if it has any).

☑ **The name of the plant**. Write down the name of the plant on which you find your caterpillar. If you don't recognize the plant, describe it in writing and draw a picture of the leaf. You might recognize the leaf from one of the photos of a caterpillar in a field guide.

### Caterpillar Ouch!

It's a good idea not to disturb insects. But if a good idea isn't good enough for you then at least take my word of caution.

Some moth caterpillars can sting.

You will not recognize every caterpillar you see and, therefore, you won't be able to tell if the caterpillar is a butterfly or moth. The moth caterpillars that sting are usually those with long bristles, or spines. Really—don't pick them up—*really*!

Need more room to draw or write? Download more forms at www.takeawalk.com.

## Butterfly Observation *from* Take A Walk With Butterflies And Dragonflies

Butterfly Observation *from* Take A Walk With Butterflies and Dragonflies.

# Butterfly Observation Notes

### What Bird did That?

Birds eat caterpillars. But they don't eat bird droppings. So some caterpillars have adapted to look like bird droppings!

### Butterfly Factoids

Butterflies can see red, green, and yellow.

Some can fly as fast as 30 MPH. The Skippers are our fastest.

Non-poisonous butterflies fly faster than poisonous ones.

Butterfly sizes range from as tiny as 1/8" to as large as 12".

If you see a butterfly but don't find its picture in this book, use this form to record information. The list below is a guideline to help you in your observation and notes. Use these notes to help you identify the butterfly with the help of a field guide. For a description of the items in this list, turn to page 18. You can record information about several butterflies on this page.

☑ **Habitat and location.**

☑ **Size.**

☑ **Posture.**

☑ **Colors and pattern.**

☑ **Shape**

☑ **Flight Pattern.**

You can sketch your butterfly on this form.

22 Go!

Need more room to draw or write? Download more forms at www.takeawalk.com.

## Nature Observation *from* Take A City Nature Walk

# Nature ID Page.

Circle one (if you know it)

This is a Plant Bird Mammal Amphibian Reptile Insect Spider

Habitat and location.

Size and physical description.

Behavior Observation (if it is an animal).

Additional Notes.

Species Name.

(Optional) Make a drawing here:

Need more room to draw or write? Use blank paper or download free forms at www.takeawalk.com.

**Nature Observation Notes *from* Take A City Nature Walk**

### Key Word Search

If you like to use your computer to do research and learn more about nature in the city, try searching for these words and phrases:

**Urban Ecology**

**Nature in the City**

**Urban Wildlife**

**Environment**

**Urban Parks**

### Jalen's Crows

*Dark black*<br>*Sharp, pointed beak.*<br>*Beady eyes.*<br>*Wings as black as its belly.*<br>*Intelligent enough to fly away from predators.*<br>*Caw Caw Caw!*<br>*Call of the Crow.*

*Jalen Perry*<br>*Age 9,*<br>*Milkwaukee,*<br>*Wisconsin.*

**Go! 23**

## Field Notes *from* Take A City Nature Walk



# Field Notes

### Your Field Notes Page:

You can use this form or you can use blank paper for your Field Notes. If you need more forms you can download them for free at our website. Your field notes should include today's date and your location (the name of the city, the street, or the park you are exploring). Fill in the time of day you are walking. Write about today's weather: the temperature, what the sky looks like, and so forth. You can also use this form to list the plants and wildlife you see. Write what you can now, and then add more during and after your walk.

Need more room to draw or write? Use blank paper or download free forms at www.takeawalk.com.

## Tree Observation *from* Take A Tree Walk

# Tree Notes

Date:

Tree location:

Tree shape:

Circle one: Broadleaf or conifer

Bark color and texture:

Leaf Type:

Leaf color:

Flower or seed description:

Tree Name:

### As Good as a Photo

Our friend Lauren Frail (age 11) wrote this about a tree she observed on her tree walk:

*"The tree doesn't have many leaves but the leaves are a jungle green. The bark is grayish brown in color. The flowers are a clean white and they're soft like silk. In the centers of the flowers are green balls."*

Lauren's description of the tree's flowers was so good, I knew which tree she was describing. Lauren found her tree in a field guide and identified it as a flowering dogwood. She was right!

Tree Observation Notes *from* Take A Tree Walk

25

## Habitat House Hunt *from* Green Teacher Magazine

Photographs by Kristin Mack-Hammer

# Habitat House Hunt

*In this activity, students play real estate agents who must find suitable homes for their urban animal clients*

by **Kristin Mack-Hammer** and **Janice Denney**

ALL LIVING CREATURES NEED a habitat that provides them with the essentials of survival — food, water, shelter, and space — and investigating the unique ways that animals meet these needs can be fascinating. While out-of-classroom experiences in natural settings afford many opportunities for students to learn first hand about the components of habitats, learning about habitats in an urban setting can be challenging. This challenge was the inspiration for Habitat House Hunt, a multidisciplinary activity in which students work in cooperative learning groups to investigate the habitat needs of urban animals.

Habitat House Hunt combines classroom work with outdoor explorations in the schoolyard and incorporates activities that accommodate a variety of learning styles. In the first part of the activity, students play the role of real estate agents who must find suitable homes for animals in the schoolyard or a nearby park. They research the animals' preferred habitats and demonstrate their understanding of habitat components by identifying appropriate habitats outdoors and creating a property guide for their animal "clients." In the second part of the activity, the groups exchange property guides and the students switch into the roles of animals who use the guides to find suitable homes for themselves. Here, students integrate their knowledge and understanding in order to evaluate "habitat homes" and predict which one would best suit a particular animal.

Drawing strategies from the best practices in education, we have crafted Habitat House Hunt to suit our objectives and our students' needs. We hope that others will be able to adapt this lesson to suit their needs and environment.

**Grade level:** Grades 5–8

**Time required:** Two class periods

**Materials:** For each group of 3 or 4 students, pictures of four urban animals native to the area (or stuffed toys that represent the animals); field guides with information on the animals; four Animal Description Worksheets (see page 35); various craft materials (construction paper, pencils, markers, crayons, Popsicle sticks, glue, scissors); compasses; sample real estate listings.

**Objectives:**

- Students will identify the habitat needs of four urban animals.
- Students will demonstrate their understanding of urban animals' habitat needs by creating a habitat home description.
- Students will evaluate other students' habitat home descriptions.
- Students will predict which home is most suitable for their assigned urban animal.

## Introduction to habitats

1. Begin with background information or a brief activity such as "Habitat Lap Sit" from Project WILD, which introduces the topic of habitats.

2. Have the students begin thinking of what animals need from a habitat. Ask them questions such as the following:

- What determines where animals build homes?
- What causes animals to abandon their homes?
- What are some things that can interfere with animals' homes?
- Why do some animals use the home built by another animal?

## Researching habitat needs

1. Tell the students that in this part of the activity, they will play the role of real estate agents. Discuss what is involved in buying and selling a home: real estate agents look for and find properties (e.g., houses, apartments, acreages, farms, cottages) for clients; and people who are looking for homes browse through real estate listings and visit homes.

2. Divide the class into groups of three or four students.
Assign four urban animals to each group (you may provide pictures or stuffed toys). Provide each group with four Animal Description Worksheets (see page 35) and a variety of field guides or other references useful for researching habitats.

3. Explain that, as real estate agents, they must find suitable homes for the animal "clients" assigned to them. To do this, they must first get acquainted with each animal's habitat needs. Have each group work together to find this information and complete an Animal Description Worksheet for each of their assigned animals.

## Finding property for animal "clients"

4. Once the students are familiar with the habitat needs of their assigned animals, go to the schoolyard or to a nearby park and have the groups look for areas that would make good homes for their "clients." They may use their completed Animal Description Worksheets as references. As they find homes, a member of the group should take detailed notes on the characteristics of the habitat.

*Beautiful weedy lot boasts excellent insect populations.*

*Secluded island getaway features plenty of bushes.*

5. Back in the classroom, have students make "For Sale" signs, numbered 1 through 4, that feature creative written descriptions of the four homes they found. The signs should describe the properties, but should not state what animal the property is for. The notes that students recorded outside may be used in their descriptions. Read aloud some examples of real estate listings from the newspaper so that students have an idea of the type of wording used. Also read an example or two of a "habitat home" description. For example:

*For Sale: Luxurious studio apartment. Well-constructed brush heap overlooking a beautiful vegetable garden filled with berries and greens. Plenty of room for a rapidly growing family. Immediate occupancy.*

*For Sale: Perfect aquatic community located in beautiful scenic area. Plenty of food markets. Great schools just a swim away. Call 555-SWIM.*

## Creating property guides

6. Ask each group to organize their property listings in the form of a property guide that will direct prospective buyers from home to home. The students must determine the format for their guide and can use a variety of methods such as maps, compass bearings, riddles, clues, puzzles, landmarks, or a scavenger hunt. As examples, "Go to the playground. Look around, both up and down, to find a place where this

## Animal Description Worksheet

| How big is your animal? | Where does your animal find food? What does your animal eat? |
| --- | --- |
| What type of home does your animal live in? How is it made? What materials are needed? | What features make your animal unique? Does it have any unusual habits? When is your animal active? |
| Does your animal sometimes use the homes of other animals? Will offspring need to use the home too? | Does your animal live alone or in a group? |

creature could call home base," or "Take 15 paces toward the flag pole; turn left and hop 22 times; look down and you will see home number 2."

7. After they have completed their "For Sale" signs and property guides, have students return to the schoolyard to post the signs. They should place the signs near the homes they have identified, but hidden so that they are not easily seen.

## House hunting

8. Have the groups trade animal lists and property guides (e.g., Group 1 gets Group 2's animal list and property guide and vice versa). Explain to students that they are now going to assume the role of animals who are looking for new homes. Their property guide will lead them to the homes that are available, and they must work together to determine which of the homes is best suited to each animal. Designate a place for the groups to meet when they have finished.

9. When all of the animals and habitats have been matched, ask each group to verify whether the correct matches were made by the students who were following their property guide. They should also explain why each home is appropriate for the animal (this is an opportunity for students to teach the group about the animals).

## Wrap-up

10. End the activity with a group discussion. Questions and discussion points may include the following:

- What important information did you learn about habitats or specific animals?
- Compare your habitat needs with those of two urban animals.
- Predict the effects of a depletion of one habitat component on one of the urban animals studied.
- Humans have adapted to a variety of habitats; where in North America would be your preferred habitat?

Kristin Mack-Hammer is a preschool teacher and environmental educator in Rockford, Illinois.

**Resources**

Knapp, Clifford E. *Just Beyond the Classroom: Community Adventures in Interdisciplinary Learning*. Charleston, WV: Clearinghouse on Rural Education and Small Schools, 1996

Peterson, Roger Tory (Ed.). *First Guide to Urban Wildlife* (Reissue edition). Houghton Mifflin, 1988.

Project WILD. Council for Environmental Education. Houston, TX. <www.projectwild.org>

Swan, Malcolm D. (Ed.). *Tips and Tricks in Outdoor Education*. 5th ed. Danville, IL: Interstate Publishers, 1995.

## Glorious Weeds! *from* Green Teacher Magazine

Photographs by Gail Littlejohn (left and right), Will Munger (centre)

# Glorious Weeds!

by **Jack Greene**

OF ALL THE TOOLS I'VE USED in many years of teaching, I've found plants to be the most exciting, if not transformative. Wherever my travels have taken me — to the inner city of Los Angeles, along the urban trails of Anchorage, to a camp for wayward youth in Michigan, a park in Atlanta, or a campus in Nova Scotia — familiar plants have been there to greet me. Certain plants that we often refer to as "weeds" are ubiquitous, many species being common to virtually all regions of North America. They are free for the picking and often found on or near school grounds. And if you're hungry, they are rich in nutrients, have minimal packaging, and grow organically. Following are a few stories to whet your appetite.

I was invited to accompany a group of inner city youth from Los Angeles on a weeklong backpacking trip in the Sierra Nevada of California. Many of the youth had never experienced the wilds outside of Los Angeles. Once we were on the trail it became apparent that we would have a major challenge to help them enjoy their experience in this strange if not seemingly hostile environment. Along with the unfamiliarity of their surroundings was the added discomfort of carrying a heavy backpack up several miles of steep trail. Although I had never visited the area, many of the plants were common to the mountains of northern Utah where I live, so I began introducing some of my favorites. As always, I found a bit of nibbling on some gastronomic delights to be highly engaging. Within a few hours the complaining had largely subsided as the students' interest in the virtues of nearly every new plant we encountered overshadowed their fear and discomfort. As the week progressed, many of them became amateur ethnobotanists as their interest and excitement grew along with their taxonomic skills. They were soon teaching one another and constantly discovering new plants to key out.

*Within a few hours the complaining had largely subsided as the students' interest in the virtues of nearly every new plant we encountered overshadowed their fear and discomfort.*

On another occasion, my teacher son-in-law coaxed me into leading a fifth grade class on a botany hike on the school grounds — a daunting assignment in a schoolyard covered with asphalt and concrete and surrounded by chain link fencing and busy urban streets. But thanks to numerous cracks and holes wrought by nature's weathering processes, there was an abundance of delightful, delectable "weeds" to collect for study and stories, and later to serve as treats. The children's favorites were pineapple weed and wood sorrel, followed by clover and sour dock. Once again, "weeds" saved the day by generating considerable excitement and adding a new dimension to the schoolyard experience.

As our lives become increasing urban and we drift further from our natural underpinnings, it becomes imperative that we find ways to help our students reconnect to the broader community of life. Richard Louv's recent book *Last Child in the Woods* presents strong evidence of the relationship between academic performance and outdoor experiences in natural settings. Plant studies offer wonderful segues into the natural realm and "natural" connections between subject areas. If a study of plants includes ethnobotany (the study of how different cultures use plants), it slides easily into the social sciences. If it includes plant population studies, mapping, and other forms of measurement, it is easily incorporated into math activities. Even physical education and technology make the list of related curricular areas, as the location and identification of plants can be integrated into a plethora of exciting and challenging orienteering activities using compass or Global Positioning System (GPS) tools.

I often introduce plants by stating that Native Americans had no word in their vocabulary for "weeds," as all plants had uses. Even poisonous species were often utilized medicinally, or for hunting and warfare. I challenge my students to choose any plant they consider a weed and to find some human use for it or learn its ecological significance, especially in its place of origin. The further they look, the longer their lists grow. They often discover that different Native tribes had different uses for the same plant. Further, I mention that great mystery awaits explorers of the plant world, as new plants continue to be discovered. Perhaps only ten percent have been listed in botanical literature, and of those less than one percent have been researched for medicinal application. Finally, I emphasize that many "weeds" that we attempt to remove from our lawns and gardens have greater nutrient value than our cultivated plants.

## Plant identi□cation

There are many excellent resources for identifying plants, including field guides and other books with dichotomous keys, websites, plant collections, and knowledgeable individuals. If your students are from gardening families, they or their parents may be helpful. Master gardeners, greenhouse operators, nature center staff, members of native plant societies, and land management agencies are good resources as well. I have found slides and flash cards of plants to be very effective for teaching my students. In addition, students can use plant identification websites to enhance their skills, and, with a color printer, can make their own flash cards. I concentrate on identifying the most common plants found in the immediate area and group them according to habitat type (e.g., wetland, forest, field, disturbed area).

## Collecting and ingesting plants safely

*For the plants' safety:*

1. Take care not to over-harvest, especially if you find only a few of a particular species in the area.

2. If you are not going to use the root, leave it in the ground to reduce the impact on soil and allow for the plant's regeneration.

3. If the plant is an aggressive invasive species, avoid transporting its seeds.

*For the humans' safety:*

1. Never eat a plant unless you are certain of its identity.

2. Know which part of the plant is safe to use.

3. Eat only small quantities to avoid possible allergic reactions.

4. If the area has been sprayed, or is an industrialized area, wash plants before eating them and avoid eating large quantities unless they have been tested and are known to be safe.

## Other activities

Following is a brief description of some of my favorite activities.

**Plant collection:** Have students make a plant collection to use as a reference at school or at home.

**Food preparation:** Research the nutrient values of "weed" plants and compare to the nutrient values of similar cultivated plants (see chart). Try out recipes using native plants and weeds. This can be done as a homework assignment or in a homemaking lab at school. My students bring in their preparations for the class to sample — a potpourri of wildness!

## Eat Your Weeds!

Harvesting and preparing dishes of "weed greens" is one of the most enjoyable aspects of a study of wild plants. Most edible weeds and wild plants are low in fat and higher in vitamins than store-bought produce. Compare the Vitamin A and C in wild plants and common garden plants in the chart.

| Plant | Vitamin A Units/100 g | Vitamin C Mg/100 g |
|---|---|---|
| Dandelion greens | 4,931 | 35 |
| Lamb's quarter | 15,000 | 130 |
| Plantain | 10,000 | 19 |
| Purslane | 8,300 | 26 |
| Prickly lettuce | 9,700 | 44 |
| Shepherd's purse | 5,000 | 91 |
| Broccoli | 660 | 89 |
| Celery | 240 | 9 |
| Leaf lettuce | 330 | 6 |
| Green onions | 2,000 | 32 |
| Spinach | 8,100 | 51 |

Data on wild and domestic plants are from T.M. Zennie and C.D. Ogzewalla, "Ascorbic Acid and Vitamin A Content of Edible Wild Plants of Ohio and Kentucky," *Journal of Economic Botany*, vol. 31, 1977, pp. 76-79. Additional data on domestic plants are from Nutrition in Foods, <www.nutritioninfoods.com>.

**Ethnobotan research:** Research the ways in which plants have been used by people of different cultures.

**Weed garden:** Till an area and observe the new plants that grow there naturally. "Weeds" are often the first to become established. Identify them and research their uses.

**Biotic communities:** Observe and list the plant types associated with different biotic communities (e.g., forests, fields, wetlands, shrublands) and with different environmental factors (e.g., sandy soil and clay soil, south-facing and north-facing slopes).

**Weed transects:** Establish transects and measure and compare native and exotic species of weeds. Track their changes over time.

**Plant orienteering:** Establish an orienteering course in which students navigate to various GPS or compass points to locate and identify specific trees, shrubs, and other plants.

Lisa Moore

*Using a hand lens for close observation of ower parts.*

**Weeds in art:** Draw or paint your favorite weed. Use weeds for nature crafts.

## Plants in your neighborhood

A host of common plants can be found in almost all regions of North America. Considered weeds, many of these plants are loaded with nutrients, have very exciting histories, and ripen well before garden varieties. The following are brief descriptions of five favorites that have wide distribution.[1]

**Chickweed** *(Stellaria media)*: Other names include satin flower, stitchwort, starwort, adder's mouth, and skirt buttons. Harvest time is from early spring through autumn. Chickweed is a tender, mild-tasting plant that can be used in a wide variety of dishes. The greens are low in calories and packed with copper, iron, phosphorous, calcium, potassium, and vitamin C. As its name implies, chickweed is well liked by chickens and other poultry. The seeds have been used for centuries as feed for caged birds. Rabbits and pigs also thrive on the greens and seeds. Ancient Romans regarded chickweed as "the elixir of life."

**Dandelion** *(Taraxacum officinale)*: Other names include lion's tooth, priest's crown, blowball, swine snout, and cankerwort. Different parts of this amazing plant can be harvested throughout the year. Harvest the leaves before flowers appear. Many foragers cut dandelions about one inch below the surface of the ground in order to harvest the tasty dandelion "heart." Spring and autumn are the best times to harvest dandelion roots. Dandelion buds are good pickled and added to omelettes. The flowers are rich in vitamin D. The greens are exceptionally high in vitamins A, B, and C, and the minerals copper, phosphorus, potassium, iron, calcium, and magnesium. During World War Two, the Russians cultivated a species of dandelion for its "milk," which was high in latex and could be used as a rubber substitute.

**Lamb's Quarter** *(Chenopodium album)*: Other names include pigweed, wild spinach, fat hen, hog's delight, strawberry blite, and Indian spinach. The best harvest time is spring to early summer. The greens are rich in protein, vitamins A and C, the B vitamins thiamine, riboflavin, and niacin, and the minerals iron, calcium, phosphorus, and potassium. The seeds are used like poppy seed and are suitable as seasoning or as a grain or coffee substitute. They can even be harvested after a heavy frost. Lamb's quarter was a famine plant during times of warfare. Napoleon relied on the ground seeds for making a black bread to feed his troops. During World War Two, the greens were frequently harvested as a food source.

**Shepherd's Purse** *(Capsella bursa-pastoris)*: Other names include lady's purse, pickpocket, mother's heart, poor man's pharmacetty, and pepper and salt. The leaves are best when harvested in spring, the seeds in summer and fall, and the roots in spring or fall. A member of the mustard family, this highly nutritious plant provides lots of calcium, iron, potassium, phosphorous, and vitamins A, B, and C. The flower buds are high in protein. It is extremely high in vitamin K, the blood-clotting vitamin. Shepherd's purse was brought to North America with the pilgrims and sold at markets in Philadelphia into the 1800s. It is still grown commercially in China. The seeds are sometimes scattered over water to control mosquitoes, as they produce a gummy substance that binds to the mouths of larvae and kills them.

**Plantain** *(Plantago major)*: Other names include white man's footstep, waybread, cart-track plant, and soldier's herb. Early spring is the best time to harvest common plantain greens, while early fall is best for seeds. Seeds make a good, unleavened bread. Plantain provides beta-carotene, calcium, and mucilage, which reduces both LDL cholesterol and triglycerides, helping to prevent heart disease. Scots called plantain the "plant of healing" for its many medicinal properties. On St. John's Eve (summer solstice) during the Middle Ages, plantain was smoked and then hung in barns and homes as protection against evil. It has been reported that cobra-stricken mongooses neutralize the venom with plantain and that toads have done the same when bitten by spiders.

## Giving thanks

While teaching a nature crafts course at Central Michigan University, I had the great honor and pleasure of accompanying Chief Little Elk and his son Little Bear of the Saginaw Chippewa Indian Reservation on an outing to collect black ash trees for a basket weaving project he was assisting me with. While we were bushwhacking our way into a swamp in mid-Michigan a heavy rain began pummeling us. The Chief instructed us to gather any dry material we could find in order to build a fire. In spite of the deluge, we soon had a dandy little blaze going. Assuming the purpose was for warmth, I was puzzled when Little Elk began sprinkling tobacco on the flames and emitting a mysterious, unsolicited chant. He went on for several minutes after which he explained this was common practice — to thank the Earth Mother and Grandfather for the gifts we were about to receive. "We always give thanks whenever we go out to pick berries, hunt deer, catch fish, or gather plants," he said. It is a statement I will never forget. How far we have strayed from this ancient wisdom of paying our respect and gratitude for the daily gifts we enjoy from our miracle planet!

When harvesting plants, consider performing one of the following harvest rituals,[2] or create your own ritual with your students.

- Before gathering plants, turn to the seven directions — East, South, West, North, Father Sky, Mother Earth, and Sister Moon — while scattering cornmeal and thanking all for the gifts.
- Seek the elder of the plant community — the oldest tree or strongest plant in the community. Take a moment to meditate. Leave a gift. Mentally ask permission to gather.
- Plant something each time you harvest. Plant seeds where you harvest a root.
- Offer a prayer of thanks for the harvest.

**Jack Greene** is a teacher, naturalist, activist, writer, and artist who recently retired from 30 years of teaching environmental science and outdoor education in various institutions, organi□ations, and agencies throughout North America. He lives in Logan, Utah.

**Notes**

1. Plant descriptions are paraphrased from Janice F. Schofield, *Discovering Wild Plants: Alaska, Western Canada, the Northwest*. Oregon: Graphic Arts Center Publishing, 2000, pp. 288-311.

2. Schofield, 2000, p. 323.

**References**

Look for field guides and other plant identification resources that cover edible and useful plants in your bioregion. A local native plant society may be helpful in finding such resources. The following books have made the top of my list for detail, accuracy, illustration, and enjoyable reading.

Brill, S., and Dean, E. *Identifying and Harvesting Edible and Medicinal Plants.* New York: Hearst Books, 1994.

Dowden, Anne Ophelia. *Wild Green Things in the City.* New York: Thomas Y. Crowell Co., 1972.

Jones, Pamela. *Just Weeds.* Vermont: Chapters Publishing, 1994.

Schofield, Janice F. Discovering *Wild Plants, Alaska, Western Canada, the Northwest.* Oregon: Graphic Arts Center Publishing Co., 2000.

**Websites**

<www.nutritioninfoods.com>, Nutrition in Foods, nutrition data charts for a variety of foods.

<www.taoherbfarm.com/herbs>, Tao Herb Farm, information on medicinal and culinary uses of over 60 wild plants.

<www.botany.org/newsite/education/>, Botanical Society of America, Education and Teaching pages. This is an extensive and comprehensive site for educators with classroom activities and links to related resources.

<www.accessexcellence.org/RC/Ethnobotany/botlist.html> This National Health Museum site has links to ethnobotany sites all over the world

# Bird Sleuth *from* Cornell Laboratory of Ornithology



**Sleuthing for Science**
**Become a Citizen Scientist through eBird**
**(adapted from BirdSleuth, Cornell Lab of Ornithology)**

***Goal***

Students will observe and identify birds during a stationary or traveling count and enter count data into the eBird database.

***Learning Objectives***

1. Students will be able to describe and implement a bird count protocol.
2. Students will be able to enter data into the eBird database.

***Background***

Our scientists would love to have your assistance in the field! At the Lab of Ornithology, "citizen scientists" are the eyes and ears of Lab scientists. Citizen scientists throughout the country submit their bird count data online into a database such as eBird, our newest and largest project. Biologists can use this data in reports and conservation plans. Students enjoy learning to identify birds, and they find helping scientists and birds through citizen science especially rewarding and motivating. By observing birds and collecting data in their schoolyard, students explore how science works, their schoolyard habitat, bird identification, data collection and interpretation, and research design. The eBird database is easy to use- check it out- and become a citizen scientist!

***In Advance***

- Teach students to identify birds, and conduct practice counts. You may wish to use "BirdSleuth: Most Wanted Birds" (www.birds.cornell.edu/birdsleuth), which is focused learning to count and identify birds and comes with bird ID focus cards and CD-Rom. Another suggested resource is the All About Birds "Birding 1-2-3" web site for help (http://www.birds.cornell.edu/AllAboutBirds/birding123/).
- Important! Run through the entire eBird data entry process on your own. Observe a bird and enter it on the web site as a casual observation.

**1. Prepare to Conduct a Count**

a. Refer students to the Bird Count Tally Sheet. Point out the information that they need to record while in the field (count site name, date, start time, total birding time, number of people in the group, bird species, and number of individuals seen for each species). All of this information must be gathered each time students count birds.

b. Tell the students it is very important that they identify birds correctly, and get an accurate count of the birds they can identify (See Teacher Tip Box, "Bird ID is Important"). Brainstorm a plan to conduct a class stationary or traveling count and develop guidelines to ensure that bird identification and counting are done accurately.

***Discuss these issues by asking:***

- *Where will we count birds? Where will we stand? What path will we take?*
- *How do you think we'll have to behave to make sure we see as many birds as possible? (quiet, still, careful watching.)*
- *How can we be sure we don't misidentify a bird?*
- *How can we avoid counting the same bird more than once?*

For example, in early counts, guidelines might include that for a bird to be officially counted; at least two students must see or hear and positively identify the bird.

c. Explain to students that they should count all the birds that they see and hear from the count area or along the count route.

d. Establish any expectations you have for outdoor bird watching.

e. If you wish to collect weather and habitat data, you might consider creating a new data collection sheet with specific information you or your students wish to collect about the site.

**Count Your Birds**

a. Take students outside to count birds for at least 15–20 minutes.

**Summarize the Class Count**

a. When you return to the classroom, list the names of birds the students have seen, and how many individuals of each species they saw. See the It Happened in Class Box, "Summarizing Bird Counts," for details and advice about compiling a class list. Transfer this master (class) list to a new bird count tally sheet that will serve as the master tally sheet for the class. You can make extra copies of the Bird Count Tally Sheet for this purpose. The summarized count will be entered into the eBird database during the next session.

**Register for eBird**

a. Go to www.ebird.org and explore the eBird web site. Create a class account by entering a username, password, and your email address. You may do this step in advance of the investigation because the user name and password are created only once.

b. Give students a quick overview of the three basic steps to registering and entering data in the eBird database:

1) Log onto <www.ebird.org >
2) Enter date and effort information, as required by the observation type
   a) Casual observation: enter date
   b) Stationary count: enter date, start time, and duration
   c) Traveling count: enter date, start time, duration, and distance
3) Indicate the species and numbers of birds you saw.

c. Project the eBird web site to demonstrate for students how to enter eBird data. Each student needs to become familiar with entering bird count data so they can continue to enter class data working in pairs or groups.

d. Enter and submit bird count data.

**5. Make a Plan to Continue Citizen Science**

a. Tell the students that they will continue to regularly observe and count birds and enter their data.

b. Create a class plan for data collection with your students, deciding

- What kind of count to do (i.e., stationary, traveling)
- Where counts will take place
- How long each count will last (recommended: 10 minutes to 1 class period)
- How often you will conduct counts (i.e., twice a week, weekly, every other week, monthly)
- Who will enter data (you may want to develop a class schedule, with pairs or triads entering data)

**Teacher Tip**
**Bird ID is Important!**

**Some teachers express concern that their students' data are not good enough to be included in the eBird database. Birding skills are critical to entering accurate data, and students need skills and practice in identifying birds. Let students know why their data are important and need to be reliable, and encourage your students to enter only data they are confident about. You might wish to consider how you'll respond if students report seeing birds you know are unlikely. For example, one field test teacher stated,**

"As a serious birder, I feel uneasy about submitting data that is inaccurate. I also don't want to tell students "No, you couldn't have seen that." As an example, Lesser Goldfinches are an uncommon bird here in December, and the park we visited is not a likely place to find them. Yet I had one group who insisted they saw five of them. I questioned them about how they knew they were Lesser Goldfinches, and they gave an appropriate answer. I still doubt it, but we entered it. How do I handle situations such as this?"

**We'd like to offer these possible responses if you are concerned about a student's identification of a species:**

- What makes you think it was that species? Do the field marks match?
- Is that species found here at this time of year?
- Is that species found in this habitat?
- What other species could it have been? What makes you confident that it was that species?
- Let's not enter that bird this time, since we aren't sure about it. But next time you see that kind of bird, point it out to the class so we can figure it out together!

**Note that improbable data might be "flagged," and our regional editors might contact you to ask if your report could be a mistake. For example, if Lesser Goldfinches are never found in a certain state, the eBird editor might later email you to ask, "Are you sure it wasn't an American Goldfinch that you saw?"**

### *It Happened in Class*
#### *Summarizing Class Counts*

This conversation was overheard when Mrs. Toth's class summarized their bird data for the first time:

**Mrs. Toth:** What birds did you see when we were outside?

**James:** I saw three American Crows.

**Mrs. Toth:** Yes, I actually counted two crows. Are you pretty sure you saw three different birds?

**James:** Yes. Two were flying together and later I saw another one perched in a tree in another area. I don't think they were the same birds.

**Mrs. Toth:** Did anyone see more than three?

**Resana:** Katie and I wrote down five on our list. I think we saw the two flying ones that James saw, and we saw three that were perched in trees. I think they were all different birds too.

**Mrs. Toth:** We'll write down five then. What other birds did you see?

**Katie:** We also saw two seagulls.

**Mrs. Toth:** What kind of gulls? Aren't there several species of gulls around here?

**Katie:** I don't know what kind they were, I just wrote down "seagull."

**Mrs. Toth:** Did anyone who saw the gulls look them up in a field guide or sketch them?

**Students:** No.

**Mrs. Toth:** Well, we can't count those gulls since we need to know what species they are. Let's look in our field guides. Next time we see gulls, what should we look for?

**Students:** The size of the gull…whether it has a ring around its beak…whether it has a red spot on its beak…what color its wings are.

**Mrs. Toth:** In this area, what are the common gulls we might see?

**Stephen:** The Herring Gull and the Ring-billed Gull. It says both are common. But the Herring Gull looks a lot bigger and has a different beak.

**Mrs. Toth:** Next time we see gulls, we should look for those field marks. Maybe we can figure it out during another count!

**Graem:** Could we write down "gull" in the notes section, to remind us that we saw them?

**Mrs. Toth:** That's a great idea! I'll add "two unknown gulls" to the notes section.

Note: The Cornell Lab of Ornithology (CLO) develops programs combining research, education, and citizen science that focus on birds and their conservation needs. Education projects, courses, and citizen-science projects developed at CLO provide many excellent resources for learning and teaching about birds. Their new curriculum, BirdSleuth, brings the Lab's largest Citizen-Science project—eBird—to students in both formal and informal educational settings. Through citizen science, students submit the data they collect on their local birds to scientists who study bird populations and develop bird conservation programs. Students enjoy learning to identify birds, and they find helping scientists and birds through citizen science especially rewarding and motivating. By observing birds and collecting data in their schoolyard, students explore how science works, their schoolyard habitat, bird identification, data collection and interpretation, research design. They can publish their findings in our BirdSleuth Reports online student research magazine. Tools to help educators guide student groups in bird study include a Teacher's Guide, a student Investigator's Journal, and a Reference Guide and kit. You can find out more, view BirdSleuth Reports, and order the curriculum at **www.birds.cornell.edu/birdsleuth.**

Name: Date:

# Sleuthing for Science

**Scientists at the Cornell Lab of Ornithology are bird sleuths too!**

## Citizens Helping Scientists

Answer the following questions after watching the "Urban Bird Studies—Citizens Helping Scientists" video.

1. What kinds of questions are Lab scientists trying to answer?

2. Why is it useful to have students help scientists?

Bird Sleuth *from* Cornell Laboratory of Ornithology

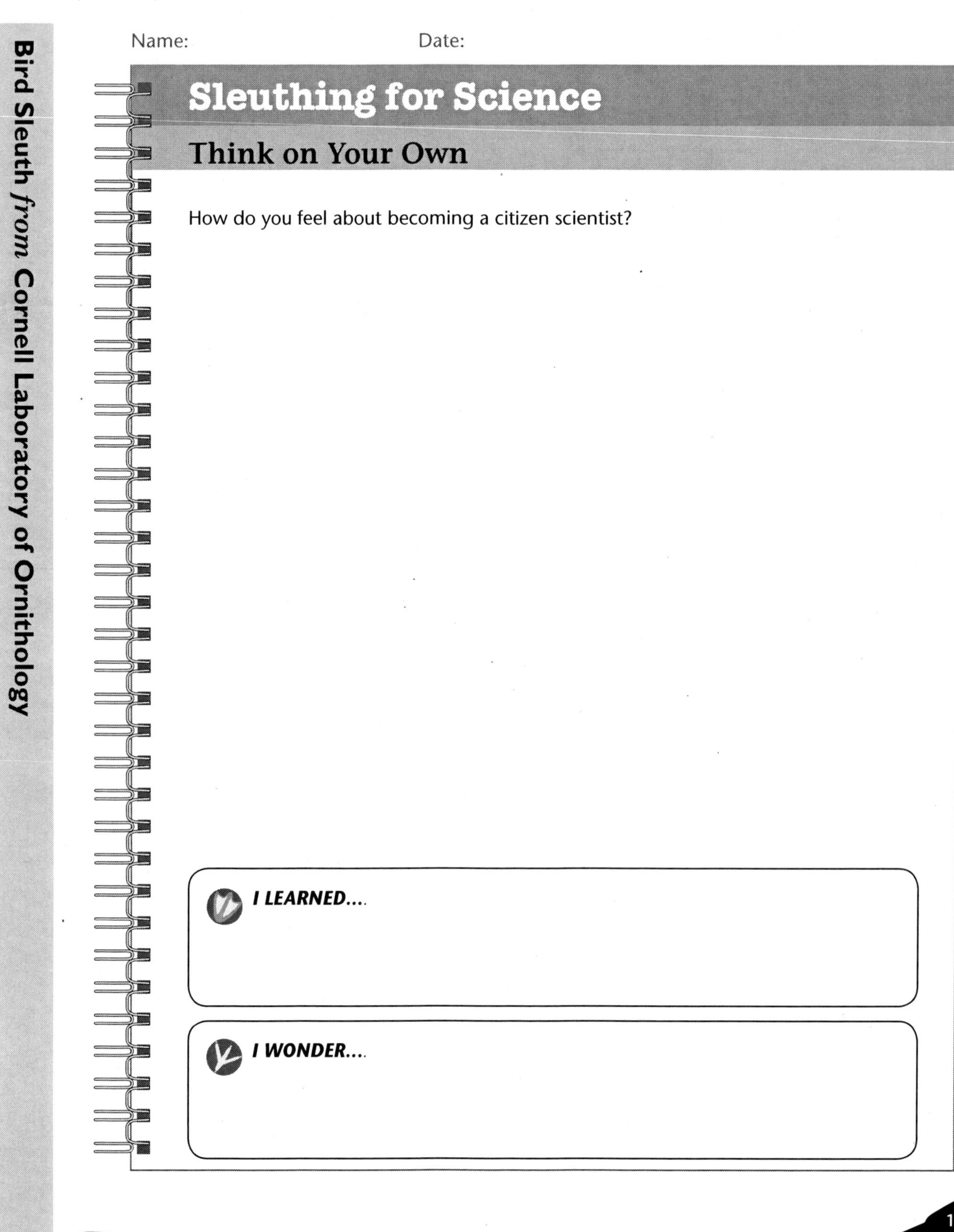

# Creating a Dichotomous Key *from* Bridges to the Natural World

## CREATING A DICHOTOMOUS KEY

GRADE LEVELS
1 - 6

OBJECTIVE
**To classify objects by distinctive characteristics.**

BACKGROUND INFORMATION
A dichotomous key provides a method for distinguishing between species of animals or plants. An observer creates a dichotomous key by separating species initially into two all-inclusive categories according to distinctive characteristics. These categories are then repeatedly subdivided so as to more specifically describe the initial categories.

MATERIALS
- chalkboard
- chalk
- Making A Dichotomous Key (Figure 13)*

PREPLANNING
1. Assemble the class in an area where they can all stand in a large group.

2. Tell the students they will be learning how to create a dichotomous key, which is a tool that people use to help organize scientific information so it can be identified more easily.

3. Lead the students through this process in the following way:
   A. Ask the students to divide themselves into two groups. The two groups must include all students. (For example: boys and girls, or people with shoelaces and no shoelaces.) The categories must always be observable. Qualities such as age, virtues, etc., do not apply.
   B. Ask each group to divide itself into two subgroups. Each subgroup must include all members of the main group. Let the students decide on the criteria. (For example: boys with brown eyes and boys with different eye color or girls with slacks and girls with dresses.) Call on each group to define themselves by the criteria.

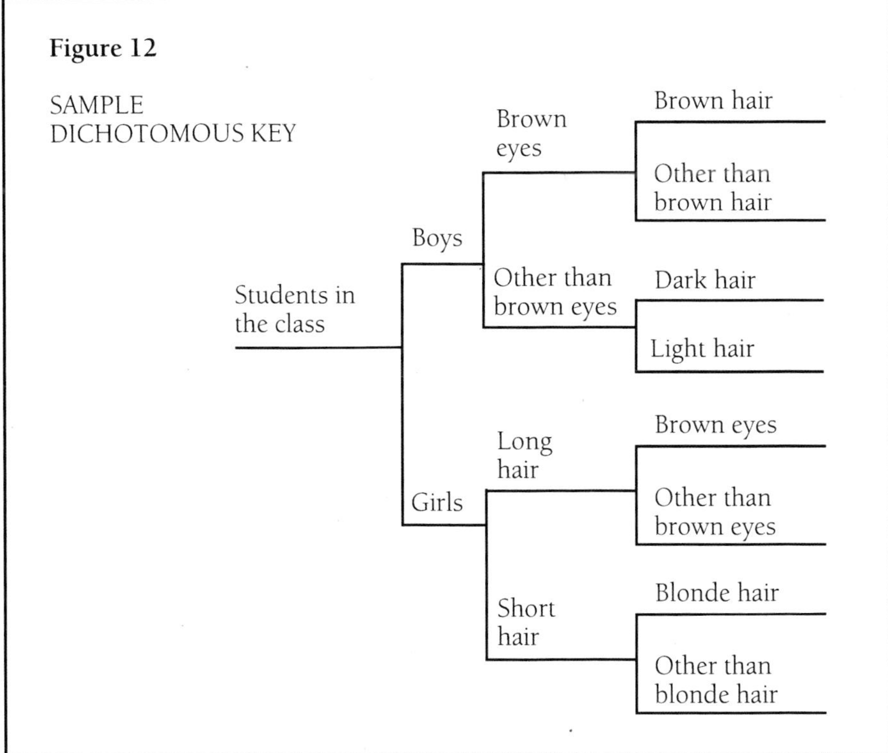


**Figure 12**

SAMPLE DICHOTOMOUS KEY

Bridges to the Natural World

C. Each of these subgroups must divide into two more subgroups. As before, these smaller groups must contain all members. (For example: brown-eyed boys with button shirts and those with no-button shirts.) Again, have the groups define themselves by the criteria they have chosen.

4. On the chalkboard, create the dichotomous key using the divisions that the students made.

5. To practice further, divide the students again by a different observable characteristic. Allow the groups to divide themselves again and have the opposite teams try to determine the physical feature that divides them. Continue with one or two more divisions.

(See Figure 12 for a sample dichotomous key for this activity.)

FOLLOW-UP
LEAF KEY

1. Have each student collect eight different leaves from the ground. (This activity works well in autumn.)

2. Provide each student with a blank dichotomous key (Figure 13).

3. Guide the students into creating a key for their leaves in the following way:

A. Divide your eight leaves into two categories of your choice. Base your decision on the leaves' characteristics. (E.g., leaves may be divided into groups by color, shape, texture, size, etc.) Write a simple description of each category on the lines marked #1.

B. Look at each of your main groups of leaves separately. Take each group and divide it into two subgroups. Write these descriptions on the lines marked #2.

C. If possible, divide each of these subgroups one more time. Write these descriptions on the lines marked #3.

SCHOOL YARD IDENTIFICATION KEY

Challenge the students to create a dichotomous key for the school grounds. Ask them to follow these steps:

1. Collect a sample leaf from the different trees on the property.

2. Identify each leaf using a tree identification guide.

3. Create a key using the categories suggested in the activity Leaves on Parade (p. 165).

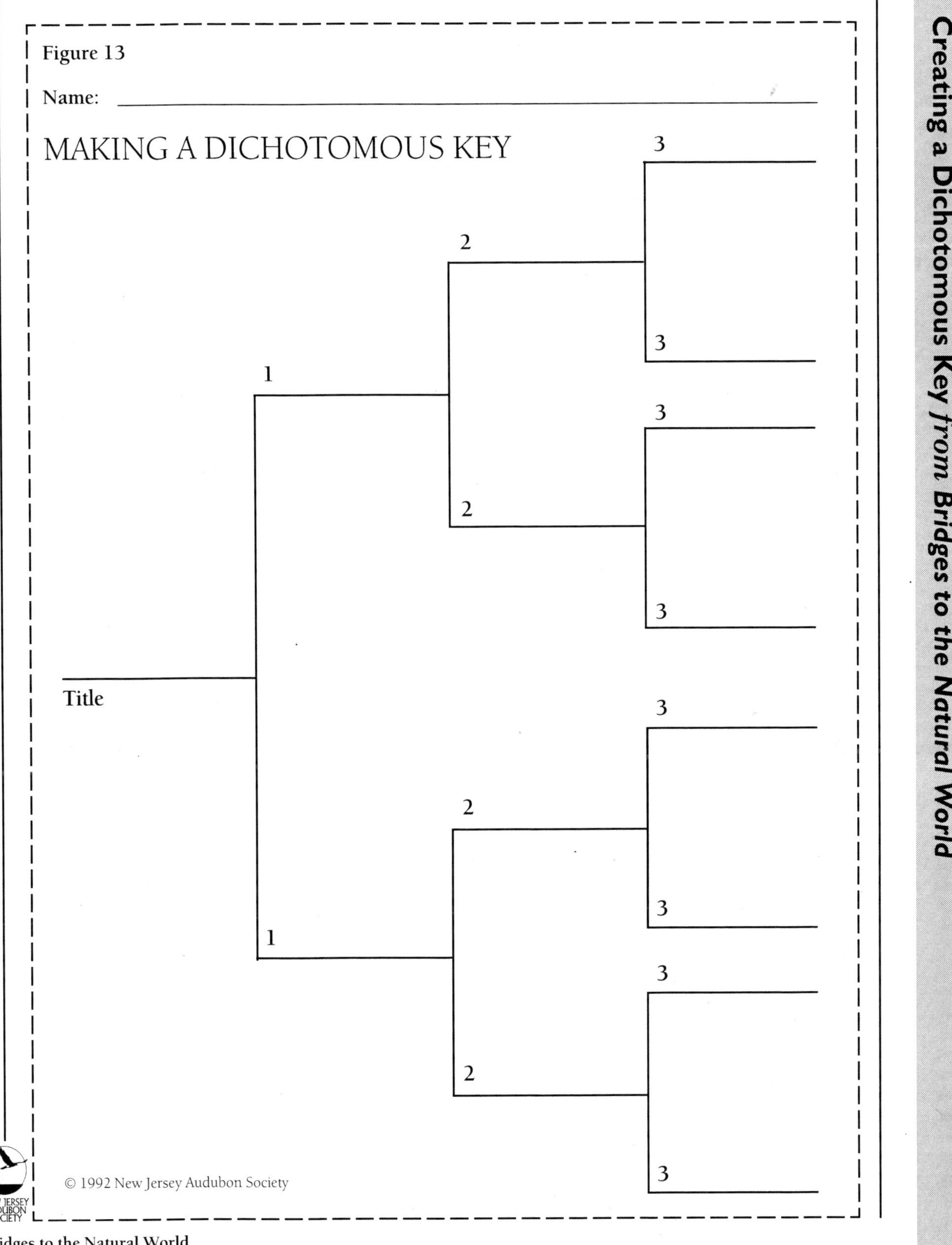


Bridges to the Natural World

# Making Maps—A Different Point of View *from* Discovering Barnegat Bay



**Author**: Christine R. Raabe, Education Consultant

**Affiliation:** Ocean County Soil Conservation District

**Objectives:** Students will be able to:

- Examine the layout of their community by drawing a map of the route from their house to the school.
- Identify features and landmarks within their community
- Practice using scale, direction, and distance measurements.

**Materials:** Large drawing paper, color pencils, ruler, and a pencil. Also several copies of your township map (available from your municipal hall)

**Subject Areas:** Social Studies, Mathematics, and Art.

**Duration:** One or two class periods.

**Setting:** Indoors or out.

**Making Connections**: Having an understanding of maps as models of the land can be a powerful tool in gaining an understanding of your watershed and your place in it. As a visual representation of a specific land area and its features, maps provide a critical link to helping students interpret their surroundings. Having students create their own maps, even at a very young age, can teach the necessary skills for reading and interpreting maps. Showing students a variety of maps from all different sources can be a lead-in discussion on how maps are made, what types of information is included on maps, how can students prepare a map of their school grounds or classroom, the route from school to home, a map of their town, etc.

**Warm Up:** Ask your students the following to prompt some thoughtful considerations regarding their community. It may be helpful to first have the class define "community." Think about our community for a moment. Let's make a list of some of the things that make it special or unique. What does it look like? What is your neighborhood like? Do the number of people in your community make a difference? What makes a community a good one? What types of things would you find on your way from home to school?

**Background:** Mapping provides a tangible way for students to interpret their surroundings. While creating maps, students become engaged in details and exercise their observation skills. Even very young students have an understanding of what maps are and how they are used. Basic understanding of maps, directions, scale, and distance, perspectives, etc., can be powerful tools for future activities related to the watershed.

Making Maps is from *Discovering Barnegat Bay, An Interdisciplinary Guide for the Historical, Cultural, and Natural Resources of the Barnegat Bay Watershed.* Produced by the Ocean County Soil Conservation District and the Barnegat Bay Watershed Environmental Education Roundtable Steering Committee. Reprinted with permission from the Ocean County Soil Conservation District.

## Activity One
## For Grades 1-4 and older as an Introduction to Map Making

- Tabletop maps are a simple way to introduce even very young children to maps and map making. Children tend to see the world from eye level and will draw things from a landscape or pictorial perspective. Use a table and a very large piece of paper so that all the children can gather around and participate in making this map. A good subject for the first map is the classroom itself. The teacher may start by asking, "How would our room look from the doorway?" A simple pictorial map showing two or three walls of the classroom will be drawn, with important furnishings (i.e. desks, chalkboard, book shelves, etc.) in their proper positions. Have students help identify items that should be included. When the teacher wants to move to the next step and introduce aerial perspective, he/she may say, "Our picture map is a good one, but we can't show everything on it, can we?" Let's make a map that shows everything in the classroom. Where do we need to be to see everything? Eventually, the students come to the conclusion that they have to be up high - on the ceiling.

- At this point, the teacher places four large (8.5 x 11) letter signs (N. S. E. & W.) in the appropriate places on the classrooms walls. The teacher then draws the classroom walls on the map to establish the shape of the room and labels the walls appropriately. The teacher tells the students that labeling the map will help to keep it turned the "right" way. From this point on, fill in the details by asking the students prompt questions such as: "Where should the doors go? The windows? Why should we put them there? Where is the teacher's desk? How should we show the bookshelf? Along the way, ask the children about their location in the room. Have them show their location on the map by pointing at it. How do they know? (Introduce the concept of landmarks.)

- Now that the room map is finished, many activities can be done with the students to utilize their maps to "navigate" the classroom. Use some items to represent each child and the teacher. : a small school photo, or their name on a small piece of paper. Let's play a travel game with the map. This is a game where everyone gets to take a trip." The teacher determines the "trip" by having the students show their current location on the map. The teacher then moves each student's nametag to a new location. The student then "travels" to that new location. Repeat for all students.

- Another way to utilize the classroom maps is to have a "treasure hunt." The teacher places an item - a sticker, piece of candy, etc., throughout the room. Their locations are marked on the map with a circle. Students find the items using the map. The same process can be repeated on the school grounds. The boundaries may need to be set by the teacher and the directional signs may need to be taped to chairs along the edge of the property.

The above description of table-top maps is from *Orienteering and Map Games for Teachers* by Mary E. Garrett, United States Orienteering Federation.

## Activity Two - For Grades 4 and up

In order to complete this activity, you will need to:

- Familiarize yourself with all of the landmarks and street names on the route between your home and school. Whether you are driven to school in a car or take a bus, have someone help you to record the names of the streets and directions that you turn on the way to school.

- You will need to take notes and pay attention to the things you see along the way. Although the ride to school is probably familiar, students often do not notice details. The purpose here is to have students pay particular attention to things that may otherwise go unnoticed.

- Gather your materials for the activity.

- Take your time and work carefully and neatly to compete the assigned map.

**Directions:** Introduce students to their hometown by showing them a map. Township and municipality maps are usually available from the municipal offices. Discuss and point-out some of the main features and their locations for the students. (Note: For younger students, you may want to complete this as a class project.)

**Option One: Assign to each student:**

1. Create a map of the route you take from home to school.
2. Your map should include a compass rose/ directional indicator, scale, roads, and landmarks found on the route.
3. Represent these items by symbols and reference them in a legend on the map.
4. Be sure to provide a key for your symbols. You should have at least 3 items in your key.
5. Your map should be drawn on a grid.
6. Your map should also include labels for all of the roads and many landmarks.
7. Your street address should be included in the appropriate spot on the map.

**Option Two: As a Class – for younger students and to save time:**

1. Using the town map, have students highlight the route they take from home to school.
2. When the class has completed the highlighting, all of their routes will come together at the school.
3. Next, have groups of students that are from the same area, name some of the things they pass along their routes (i.e., malls, office buildings, banks, other schools, playgrounds, parks, etc.) Have each group place a marker on the map to symbolize the feature. Use a different color marker or symbol for each item.
4. Repeat for all groups.

**Wrap Up**

- Have students calculate/approximate the amount of land that they travel over to get to their school each day.
- What are some of the impacts on the waterways of the Barnegat Bay watershed from your town?

**Action**

- *For Option One map*
  Examine the maps as a class and discuss their proximity to each other. Can they be connected, with the school as the focal point?
- *Using the Town map:*
  Have the class begin a discussion of their connection to the nearest body of water. Can they name the body of water? Is it a stream, a river, a creek, the Barnegat Bay? Explain to the class the term watershed (all of the land area that drains into a particular body of water.) Provide a visual tour of the water traveling from your town or school and eventually ending up in the Barnegat Bay.

**Assessment:** Completion of the maps and participation in the discussions.

**Extensions:** Have students use their maps as a basis for determining which areas of their communities could be improved through projects. Possible projects to consider include: litter pick-up, adopt-a-spot beautification, tree planting, etc. In small groups, students can mark such locations on the maps and describe how these projects would improve the watershed.

## Resources Referenced

Although there are numerous books and teaching manuals available on maps and mapping, this one is very comprehensive and presents, in simple terms with complete explanations, directions for each activity. A must have reference for a teacher wishing to incorporate meaningful mapping into their curriculum.

*Orienteering and Map Games for Teachers*, Mary E. Garrett, United States Orienteering Foundation (USOF), P.O. Box 1444, Forest Park, Georgia 30051. 404-363-2110. 1996.

## Additional Resources on this Topic

- 1-800-USA-MAPS
- Ocean County Planning Department
- Barnegat Bay Estuary program Website: **www.bbep.org.**
- New Jersey Geological Survey (NJGS) **www.state.nj.us/dep/njgs/index/htm.**
- US Geological Survey – NJ District – nj.usgs.gov

## Joining the Global Green Map System

By registering with the Green Map System (GMS), teachers and students become part of a growing global network of green mapmakers. Teachers can receive an activity guide and a set of map icons that are available on disk as a digitalized font for PC or Mac. Participating groups agree to allow their maps to be posted on the GMS Website or published in green map compilations, and to provide feedback about their mapmaking experience that might be useful to others.

Contact: Green Map System, c/o Modern World Design, P.O. Box 249, New York City, NY 10002, e-mail info@greenmap.com, telephone (212) 674-1631. (E-mail gets the quickest response.) Additional information and resources are posted on the Green Map System Web site at **www.greenmap.org**.

## Stewardship Project Ideas Related to this Topic

Create maps of the schoolyard and utilize them as the basis for creating outdoor classrooms, habitat enhancements projects, rain gardens, and other environmental projects on the school grounds.

## To Purchase Discovering Barnegat Bay:

Discovering Barnegat Bay is available through professional development opportunities for a $35. The latest workshop schedule can be found at www.ocscd.org. or by contacting Christine Raabe, Education Outreach Specialist, Ocean County Soil Conservation District, 714 Lacey Road, Forked River, NJ 08731, 609-971-7002 ext.21. craabe@ocscd.org.

---

## Quick Quadrat Exercise *from* Discovering the Naturalist Intelligence



*The sun shines not on us, but in us. The rivers flow not past, but through us.*--- John Muir.

A naturalist feels connected. John Muir explains in two sentences a concept vital for the survival of all living things. We are related to everything in our environment. Understanding the naturalist intelligence and cultivating it within our students is our responsibility not only as teachers but also as human beings. Howard Gardner defines a naturalist as a person who recognizes flora and fauna plus other consequential distinctions in the natural world and uses this ability productively. In our culture the term naturalist is applied to people who have an outstanding knowledge of the living world. The importance of the naturalist intelligence is well established in evolutionary history. Gardner has mentioned Charles Darwin and E. O. Wilson as his end states. Rachel Carson, Sylvia Earl and Jane Goodall would be great end stateswomen too.

### The Novice Naturalist

I am not a science teacher. I never liked science in school. I never experienced much success. However, I am a sixth grade teacher in an elementary setting so I have to teach science. That was a problem until I was introduced to Howard Gardner's Theory of Multiple Intelligences and the GREEN network of teachers a few years ago. I now understand that students learn in a variety of ways. They have intelligence strengths and weaknesses. I now have a network of professionals I can rely on for support when I need mentoring with science facts, skills and knowledge.

GREEN stands for Global Rivers Environmental Educational Network **www.green.org**. The name is confusing but the model isn't. GREEN is a group of very dedicated science teachers working with an integrated watershed based curriculum. The network stresses watershed stewardship across the US and internationally. This collection of teachers encompasses five school districts in the watersheds of the South Sound Region of Washington State. A consortium of public and private organizations have provided funding for an education coordinator. She is the vital communication link that binds the scattered teachers together.

I'm sure Howard Gardner would consider this position a true "school - community broker". These networked teachers are true naturalists. I am not. I just sneak around in their shadows and soak in their encouragement.

I was in the audience sitting with a fellow GREEN teacher when Gardner unveiled the Naturalist Intelligence at the National ASCD Conference in Baltimore last year. (Read more about this on this Website: **www.newhorizons.org/strategies/mi/campbell.htm**. He confirmed something we already knew. Some kids just seem connected to the outdoors. We were already in the process of hooking students into integrated lessons based on an emotional connection and authentic learning. We immediately wanted to jump up and share what we were seeing in our classrooms.

Observation is a skill I have yet to develop. Even though I'm not very experienced at knowing the natural environment I'm trying desperately to provide my sixth grade class with opportunities to learn and be outside. By providing my kids with trips for field studies I personally have experienced a high learning curve. A former special needs student could identify any bird that flew over. I asked him how he knew and he gave me a five minute lesson on shapes of heads, tails, body coloring, silhouettes and bird calls. I was stunned. This kid was learning. He spent lots of time observing outside. Family members provided him with the names and information much like folklore was passed down from generation to generation. No standardized test would give him the score he deserved.

There really is a Naturalist Intelligence. I see it in my students and my friends! There is a bond that draws some to the outside to understand and enjoy the world that surrounds us. I have had little exposure to nature but that doesn't mean I can't learn when provided the opportunities. I don't have to be a science teacher to teach science. I don't need to be an expert. I just need to facilitate the learning process. The benefit for me is that I'm learning right along with the kids and developing my own intelligences.

## Educational Implications for the Naturalist Intelligence

Developing the naturalist intelligence is no different than teaching math or reading skills. Teachers must provide the opportunity for this intelligence to grow.

We need to stop and consider the implications this identified intelligence has on our educational settings. Getting on a bus and moving to an appropriate expedition site extends learning beyond walking down the hall to the gym or the art room. Doing field studies extends experiential learning beyond working with pattern blocks in math class. By observing outside we can see those same patterns in nature and understand connections. Employable success in the future requires that our children be computer literate. We have stocked our classrooms and constructed computer labs to provide this opportunity. The quality of life on this planet requires that our children have experience with nature. We must provide the best educational learning opportunities for the Naturalist Intelligence.

All teachers are facing reforms that include state essential learnings and national standards. Naturalist topics and themes make some of the best curriculum integrations that will help us reach these goals. An example would be the themes of change, cycles, and connections. Topics that help enrich curriculum could revolve around the ecosystem where the school is located. Teachers in the Pacific Northwest could establish integrated studies around marine ecology, watersheds, forests, aquatic life. The instructors in the Southwest could focus on the desert environment. After all, intelligence has been defined as solving problems and fashioning products valued in one culture or community. Knowing and understanding your community environment and using it as an extended classroom just makes sense.

One simple way to encourage the Naturalist Intelligence is to take students outside to explore their school community. Careful observation will find weeds in the cracks of almost any playground surface. The eaves of a roof provide nesting places for birds. Water from storm runoff pours down storm drains in the parking lot. Data collected can be returned to the classroom and distributed in tables, charts and graphs . One trip outside can generate enough questions for inquiry that a school's library and research lab could be utilized all year. These consistent short experiences outside on your school grounds provide a learning environment that will empower kids. Let them research solutions to problems they may identify. Allow them to make a plan of action, design a project based on certain criteria and then implement it. Invite community resource professionals to support you. Celebrate with your entire school community when the problem is solved and the project is completed. Howard Gardner defines understanding as the capacity to apply knowledge in new situations. Providing for the Naturalist Intelligence is one way to encourage true understanding.

A teacher's primary responsibility is to be sure all children experience success and learn. We must consider each child and provide the skills they need to grow. We must consider all ways to deliver curriculum. We must consider all intelligences when planning and organizing lessons. Tom Hoerr, Principal of New City School in St. Louis, states, "The Naturalist Intelligence offers one more way to help students understand and learn."

## Teaching to the Naturalist Intelligence

One of the lessons I have done with my students is called A Quick Quadrat. The goal of the lesson was to provide an experience to improve data collection and observation skills. A quadrat is a marked area that is a square. The quadrat on the school grounds can be designated by using a variety of materials such as yarn, string, or a wood frame. This lesson reinforces observation skills by getting the student to focus on one small area. That small area is then a representation of what lives in the larger area surrounding it.

Before we left the classroom we cut a piece of yarn into a forty inch length and tied the ends together. The students practiced making a square on their desk top that had sides with a length of ten inches. I explained that this was called a quadrat and it is used by scientists for data collection and observation of the area it surrounds. My sixth grade students then discussed area and perimeter from this construction. At this point, I had the class predict what kind of items they thought they would find in their quadrats when they constructed them outside on the playground. We brainstormed a list and recorded it on the classroom whiteboard for a comparison when they returned from outside.

In the field, I guided the students to a spot on the playground where I thought they would likely find a variety of natural objects. They then constructed their quadrats. If the quadrat was in dirt or grass they used pencils as posts to form their square around. On a data sheet they were to tally, count and record what they saw. I also had them draw and try to replicate their observations from the quadrat.

When they returned to the classroom they shared the results of their data with partners and then with the whole group. We discussed several questions. What kind of items did they predict they would find outside correctly? What did they find in their quadrats that they hadn't predicted would be there? Several interesting comments were made that reinforced the fact that some students saw connections. Several students were more interested in connecting the things in the quadrat and talking about why they appeared in that space together.

I was strictly interested in collecting data and recording it. Looking for connections never occurred to me. After some exchanging of views we went on to record the total classroom data of at least one object from everyone's quadrat. We discussed if they would feel comfortable making a prediction on how many of these objects could be found on the entire playground? They chose pinecones and were leery of making a prediction because they had no idea of how many square feet of playground space there was. A discussion on accurately mapping the playground followed.

There are lots of extensions for this lesson that teacher could chose at this point. The class could construct a pictograph of the data. In pairs they could write mathematical story problems using the data collected and try to stump others in their team. They could select one item from the quadrat and write a story of how it got on the playground. They could do research on an object discovered. They could recreate their quadrant for an art display.

I chose to have them reflect in their field studies journal about their experience outside by giving them several prompts:

- Today we . . .
- I saw . . .
- One thing I thought was curious was . . .
- I learned . . .
- I think . . .

For the elementary teacher, teaching for the Naturalist Intelligence provides the key to integration. All levels of students need these types of experiences. Our generation grew up riding our bikes to the nearest park or vacant lot to play and explore. Children today are not permitted this freedom. They are more easily supervised and are safer at home in front of the TV.

## Learning Strategies for the Naturalist

Teachers should provide opportunities that encourage:

- Sensory observation: feeling, smelling, listening
- Data collection from observation
- Grouping of natural objects (classification)
- Observation of animal behavior
- Growing things . . . plants, garden, butterfly garden
- Recycling projects and worm boxes
- Field studies . . . out of doors
- Observation through the microscope, telescope, binoculars, hand lens
- Drawing, sketching, photographing, video taping nature
- Manipulating outdoor equipment or kits (water testing kits or nets)
- Outdoor silent observation, reflection, journaling
- Identifying sounds in nature
- Interacting with animals (bugs) and plants
- Establishment of a nature trail, viewing deck, or outdoor classroom,
- Making scientific instruments (inventing)
- Designing experiments
- Field trips (real, electronic, video, guided imagery)
- Walks outside for fresh air, sounds of nature, and dirt underfoot
- Modeling, measurement, or scale drawings of animals, plants, or outdoor settings
- Writing poems or songs using adjectives from the outdoors
- Identifying shapes in natural setting
- Observation of plants or out of doors change over the course of the school year
- Observing a fruit, vegetable or other plant or animal material decompose overtime
- Collecting trash or other items (rocks, feathers, flowers, leaves . . . ) in the school yard and group (classify) the items by their characteristics (shape, color, etc.)

- Read aloud stories/articles relating to the out of doors, space, natural phenomena, animals, or plants
- Performing role plays of cycles in nature, animal behavior, plant growth etc.

## Naturalist Checklist

A child or adult who possesses the Naturalist Intelligence can be identified through observation. Usually a naturalist is a person who:

- Is very comfortable in the out of doors.
- Chooses to read books and watch programs about animals and ecosystems.
- Nurtures living things (plants and animals).
- Readily follows cyclic phenomena such as tides, seasons, phases of the moon, and climate.
- Recognizes patterns, colors and classifications.
- Automatically uses senses to explore environment.
- Is a patient observer.
- Feels a definite connection and relationship with nature.
- Has an affinity for natural habitats such as oceans, forests, desert, wetlands.
- Always wants to view and appreciate the aesthetics of nature.
- Favors natural settings over the human influenced environment.
- Is renewed by visiting natural settings.
- Is constantly aware of their surroundings.
- Will touch and explore "yucky things"
- Enjoys collections of rocks, minerals, leaves, flowers, shells, feathers etc.
- Seeks out music related to nature.
- Would rather go to a zoo than an amusement park.
- Sets up feeding stations for birds, small mammals and other wild life
- Participates in volunteer projects that benefit plants, animals, watersheds or the earth
- Uses binoculars, telescopes, microscopes, and hand lenses when observing
- Receives satisfaction in learning names of flowers, trees, animals, rocks and minerals, cloud types, volcanoes, etc.
- Collects articles, posters, pictures, figurines, stuffed animals related to wildlife or nature
- Grows plants (gardens, window boxes, indoor plants, herbs)
- Photographs or sketches animals, plants, habitats (places)
- Shares observations with others (enjoys showing something like a flower blooming or small insect etc.)
- Has a sense for detail and notices even the smallest of things
- Manipulates equipment to find out more about environmental water test kits, butterfly nets, plant presses, etc.
- Works with natural materials for crafts and projects (ex. dried arrangements, plant presses, shells, and wood material)
- Documents by sketching, photographing, or listing natural phenomena
- Pet stores are special places as are aquariums, wild life parks, zoos, farms etc.
- Enjoys recreations such as hiking, fishing, mountain (rock) climbing, cross-country skiing, camping, sailing, scuba diving, etc.

# A Reflection Page *from* Keeping a Nature Journal

Written prompts can be provided on a separate sheet of directions for each day's activities, or you may want to create small loose-leaf journal booklets, with prompts for each small project written at the top of each journal page. (See pages 68–69 for some examples.)

## Projects to Encourage Learning and Reflection

Make sure your student journalists reread journal entries regularly and reflect on what they have observed, and what they may have missed. Encourage them to return to a particular journaling site again and again, on different days of the week and at different times of the day, to see what has changed or what they may have missed before.

As a group activity in a classroom or club setting, journaling may be seen as merely another form of busy work. With your guidance, the students may find that journaling can be a joy when exercised as a form of self-expression, creativity, and discovery. You can instruct them in *ways to use* the journal, as well *as how to keep* it in the first place.

### A Reflection Page

Provide your students with a page every week or two that asks them to review what they have put in the journal, and to summarize on those pages what they think are the most important things they have observed or learned. They may put their thoughts into prose, poetry, or a detailed drawing that summarizes their experiences.

**REFLECTION PAGE**

Read your journal pages. Think about the questions below and write or draw your thoughts about the questions.

What were the most interesting things I observed over the time period we have been keeping this set of journal entries?

What are the big ideas that I have learned from this set of journal entries?

What skills do I plan to improve upon over the next set of entries?

Which of my observations and comments would I most like to share with others?

From the Journal of: ____________

Date: __________ Time: __________
Location: ____________________
Temp: __________ Humidity: _______
Pressure: ________
Percent cloud cover: ____________

Session task: Look around for things that are in the process of changing. Describe the object or event and indicate how it is changing.

A Reflection Page Exercise *from* Keeping a Nature Journal

## Making Connections *from* Walk on the Wild Side—Explore Your Public Lands

ACTIVITY

# Making Connections

Go outside . . . anywhere. Stop and look. What connections can you find? Chances are you can see plenty of them right in your own backyard, school yard, or local park–a bird eating some berries, perhaps, or a squirrel gathering acorns. Your backyard is a small ecosystem. But does it have connections beyond your backyard? Absolutely! The squirrel might live in a nearby forest. And who knows where the bird might have traveled? Maybe it spends winters in South America or summers in Alaska. It depends on the berries in your backyard for food. But it's also part of the "big picture" that BLM and everyone needs to be aware of.

Think about connections. Then draw pictures in the empty circles below. In the small circle, show two or more things in your backyard that are connected. In the larger circle, show some things that are connected to your backyard but are outside it.

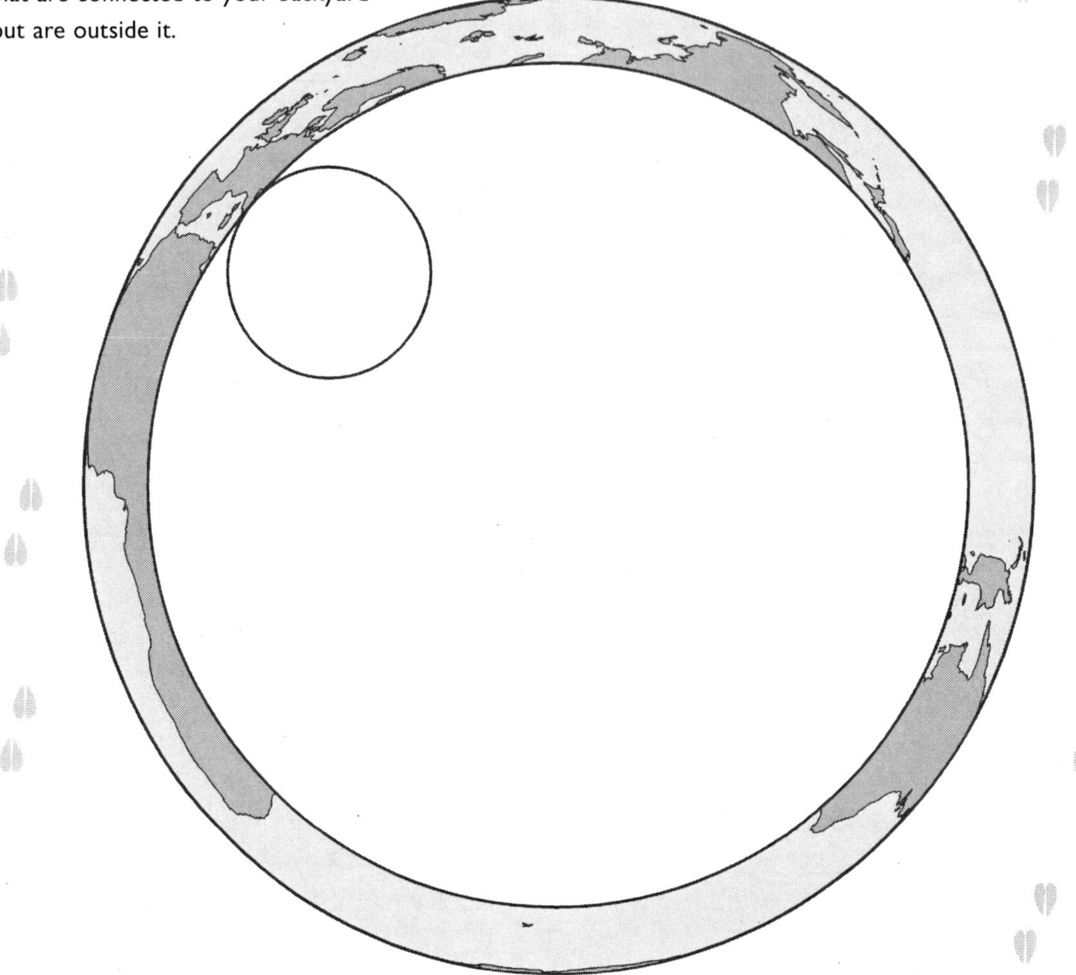

www.istockphoto.com/AnitaPatterson

**In This Chapter**

Contests

Grants and Donor Programs

Films

Websites

Books

Coupons and Special Offers

CHAPTER SIX

# Resources and Recommendations

In this chapter you'll find lists of resources for materials and supplies for your Field Guide Project. I based my selection on personal experience—these are books, materials, and websites I've read, used, and visit frequently—and on recommendations from educators. Except for field guides, I omitted the obvious and popular books about nature and the environment and listed some you might not have heard of but which deserve your attention. Websites include those that have lesson plans and other classroom resources as well as e-commerce site where you can purchase books and materials.

We categorized resources so you can locate them easily but note that the categories are not in alphabetical order. At the end of the resources and recommendations list you'll find some discount coupons for teachers.

We hope to feature more resources, recommendations, and coupons at our new educator Website scheduled to launch in 2008. If you have recommendations for books, websites, and other resources that you'd like to share with other teachers, please share them with us by sending an email to: editor@takeawalk.com.

 **Worth Repeating**

*Young people, I want to beg of you always keep your eyes open to what Mother Nature has to teach you. By doing so you will learn many valuable things every day of your life.*

**George Washington Carver**

## Contests

*Nature-related contests for students.*

Take A Walk® books. Every year we sponsor one or two writing or drawing contest for students ages 8 to 12. The works of winners are featured in our books. Check frequently for new contests to be announced.
**www.takeawalk.com**

The National Arbor Day Poster Contest. A national art contest for 5th graders.
**www.arborday.org.**

The River of Words. An annual environmental poetry & art contest Conducted in affiliation with The Library of Congress Center for the Book.
**www.riverofwords.org**

## Films

*Nature-related films for students.*

Fly Away Home.
A father and daughter attempt to lead a flock of Canada Geese on a southern migration. 1996. Sony Pictures. Rated PG.

Happy Feet.
Animated penguin film. 2006. Warner Home Video. Rated PG.

Life in the Undergrowth.
David Attenborough's ground-breaking documentary of invertebrates. 2006. BBC Warner. Two disc set. Not rated.

Life of Birds, The.
David Attenborough's detailed documentary of birds, examining a variety of species. Three disc set. 2002. BBC Video. Not rated.

Life of Mammals, The.
David Attenborough's comprehensive documentary of how a mammals evolved. Four disc set. 2003. BBC Warner. Not rated.

March of the Penguins.
Documentary following the life cycle of Emperor penguins. 2005. Warner Home Video. Rated G.

Nature—Pale Male.
A documentary about the world's most-watched resident of Central Park, New York—a Red-tailed Hawk, nicknamed Pale Male by birdwatchers. 2003. Questar Inc. PBS Nature Series. Documentary. Unrated.

Canada Goose

Planet Earth.
Originally aired on the Discovery Channel, and 11-part documentary that is, perhaps, the greatest nature series ever filmed. 2007. Five discs. BBC Warner. Not rated.

Winged Migration.
Documentary following the migration of birds throughout the world. Very little narration with mesmerizing cinematography. 2001. Sony Pictures. Rated G.

## Grants and Donor Programs

The Adopt a School Garden Program links donors with school and community programs that wish to start or rejuvenate a youth garden project. The NGA education staff works directly with recipient organizations to create effective learning plans, and to build a foundation and framework for project sustainability. Learn more and register your garden program at:
**http://assoc.garden.org/ag**. (Note: do not use WWW.)

Environmental Protection Agency (EPA). The Grants Program sponsored by EPA's Environmental Education Division (EED), Office of Children's Health Protection and Environmental Education, supports environmental education projects that enhance the public's awareness, knowledge, and skills to help people make informed decisions that affect environmental quality.
**www.epa.gov/enviroed/grants.html**

Lowe's Build an Outdoor Classroom grant.
**www.lowes.com**

National Gardening Association. Awards 400 Youth Garden Grants to schools and other community organizations. Each grant consists of an assortment of quality tools, seeds, and garden products donated by companies in the lawn and garden industry.
**www.kidsgardening.com/grants.asp**

National Science Teachers Association. Organization of science teachers committed to promoting excellence and innovation in science teaching and learning for all. Grant information available at their website.
**www.nsta.org**

National Wildlife Federation.
The Wild Seed Fund gives 50 $250 mini-grants to assist schools in establishing Schoolyard Habitat projects.
**www.nwf.org/schoolyard**

North American Association for Environmental Education (NAAEE). Organization of environmental educators. Provides a great source for EE news, jobs, and grants at:
**eelink.net/grants-generalinformation.html**

*The Bluebird carries the sky on his back.*

**Henry David Thoreau**

## Grants and Donor Programs (continued)

Wild Ones: The Lorrie Otto Seeds for Education Fund.
The Lorrie Otto Seeds for Education Fund awards small monetary grants to schools, nature centers, or other educational organizations whose projects reflect creating natural landscapes using native plants.
**www.for-wild.org/seedmony.htm.**

## Websites

Sites where you can find free resources for teachers including clipart. Also reference/learning sites and shopping sites.

Acorn Naturalists. Resources for the trail and classroom.
**www.acornnaturalists.com**

Awesome clipart for educators—free.
**www.awesomeclipartforeducators.com**

Classroom clipart—free.
**www.classroomclipart.com**

Clipart.com, subscription-based, royalty free images and photos.
**www.clipart.com**

Cornell Laboratory of Ornithology. Research, citizen science, conservation, education. If you want to learn about birds, you want to visit this site and join at least one of their citizen scientist programs, which I highly recommend.
**www.birds.cornell.edu**

Discovery School Clipart Gallery—free.
**www.school.discovery.com/clipart**

Dover Electronic Clipart, CDs and books:
**www.doverpublications.com**

Enature. National Wildlife Federation's online and regional field guides, life lists, and general information about plants and wildlife.
**www.enature.com**

Environmental Literacy Council. A non-profit organization dedicated to helping citizens develop a fundamental understanding of the systems of the world.
**www.enviroliteracy.org**

**Worth Repeating**

*Adapt or perish, now as ever, is nature's inexorable imperative.*

**H.G. Wells**

Journey North. A project that engages students in a global study of wildlife migration and seasonal change. K-12 students share their own field observations with classmates across North America. They track the coming of spring through the migration patterns of monarch butterflies, bald eagles, robins, hummingbirds, whooping cranes — and other birds and mammals; the budding of plants; changing sunlight; and other natural events. Find standards-based lesson plans, activities and information to help students make local observations and fit them into a global context.
**www.learner.org/jnorth**

Istock Photo. Royalty-free images and photos.
**www.istock.com**

KidsGardening.org. Hands-on projects and activity ideas, online courses for teachers, free curricula, and much more.
**www.kidsgardening.com**

Lady Bird Johnson Wildflower Center
**www.wildflower.org**

National Wildlife Federation. Schoolyard Habitat program, conservation programs, books, Ranger Rick magazine, shopping.
**www.nwf.org**

Plants National Database
**www.plants.usda.gov**

Plant Conservation Alliance
**www.nps.gov/plants**

Steve Spangler Science. Books, science experiment kits and more.
**www.stevespanglerscience.com**

Teacher Files. A free educational resource with lesson plans, ideas, clipart and more.
**www.teacherfiles.com**

The National Gardening Association. Gardening supplies, information, and education.
**www.garden.org**

Wild Bird Centers of America. Wild bird feeders, seed, and supplies.
**www. wildbirdcenter.com**

**Migrating Dragonflies**

In September of 2004 we were photographing in Central Park, New York for *Take A City Nature Walk*. It was a beautiful Saturday and the park was filled with thousands of people walking, playing ball, and resting on blankets on the ground. Turning a bend in a path we were suddenly surrounded by thousands of Common Green Darner dragonflies. I watched people on blankets and benches as they shooed and swatted the dragonflies. Green Darners are our largest dragonfly (4.5") and it can be a bit daunting to have them flitting around one's head. Like the butterflies, the dragonflies were migrating. For several hours we photographed nature in the park. Many people were swatting the dragonflies as they enjoyed the park but I didn't see one person to stopped to look at what they were swatting. I wondered if anyone knew they were in the path of a dragonfly migration.

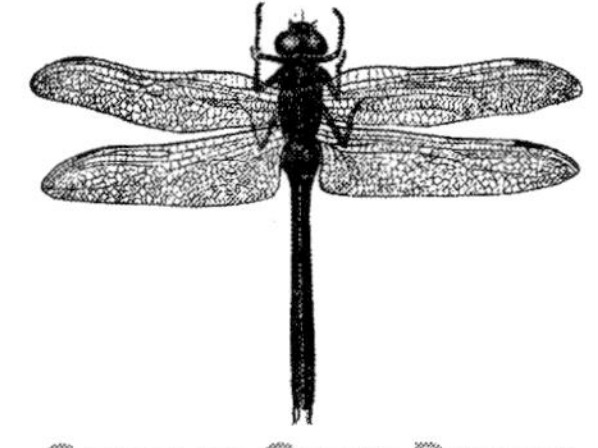

Common Green Darner

## Books: Field Guides

### Birds

A Field Guide to the Birds, 4th Edition.
Roger Tory Peterson. Houghton Mifflin Company, New York, 1980.

A Field Guide to the Birds' Nests: United States east of the Mississippi River.
Hal H. Harrison. Houghton Mifflin Company, New York, 1975.

Backyard Birds.
Roger Tory Peterson. Houghton Mifflin Company, New York, 1996.

Birds of North America.
Kenn Kaufman. Houghton Mifflin Company, New York, 2000.

Eastern Birds.
John Farrand,Jr. McGraw-Hill Book Company, New York, 1988.

Eastern Trailside Birds.
Kenn Kaufman. Houghton Mifflin Company, New York, 1996.

Familiar Birds of Sea and Shore.
Simon Perkins. Alfred A. Knopf, Inc., New York, 1994.

National Audubon Society Field Guide to North American Birds: Eastern Region.
John Bull and John Farrand,Jr. Alfred A. Knopf, Inc., New York, 1994.

National Geographic Society Field Guide to the Birds of North America, 2nd Edition.
National Geographic Society, Washington, DC, 1985.

Stokes Field Guide to Birds.
Donald and Lillian Stokes. Little, Brown & Company, New York, 1996.

The Sibley Field Guide to Birds of Eastern North America.
David Allen Sibley. Alfred A. Knopf, Inc., New York, 2003.

The Sibley Guide to Birds. (Includes all of North America and Mexico).
David Allen Sibley. Alfred A. Knopf, Inc., New York, 2000.

Western Birds.
John Farrand, Jr. McGraw-Hill Book Company, New York, 1988.

### Fish

National Audubon Society Field Guide to North American Fishes, Whales, and Dolphins.
Herbert T. Boschung, Jr., et al. Alfred A. Knopf, Inc., New York, 1983, 1995.

Hummingbird Moth

## Flowers, Plants and Weeds

Flower Finder: A Guide to Identification of Spring Wild Flowers and Flower Families East of the Rockies and North of the Smokies, Exclusive of Trees and Shrubs.
May Theilgaard Watts. Nature Study Guild, Rochester, NY, 1955.

National Audubon Society Field Guide to North American Wildflowers: Eastern Region.
William A. Niering and Nancy C. Olmstead. Alfred A. Knopf, Inc., New York, 1979, 1998.

National Audubon Society Field Guide to North American Wildflowers: Western Region.
Richard Spellenberg. Alfred A. Knopf, Inc., New York, 1979, 1996.

Roadside Wildflowers.
Roger Tory Peterson. Houghton Mifflin Company, New York, 1996.

Simon & Schuster's Guide to Garden Flowers.
Guido Moggi and Luciano Giugnolini. Simon & Schuster,Inc., New York, 1983.

Simon & Schuster's Guide to Plants and Flowers.
Francesco Bianchini and Azzurra Carrasa Pantano. Simon & Schuster, Inc., New York, 1974.

Weeds.
Alexander C. Martin, Golden Books, New York, 1987.

Wildflowers.
Media Projects Incorporated. Reader's Digest, Pleasantville, NY, 1998.

## Identification (Dichotomous Keys)

A Field Guide to Animal Tracks, 2nd Edition
Olaus J. Murie. Houghton Mifflin Company, New York, 1974.

Berry Finder: A Guide to Native Plants with Fleshy Fruits for Eastern North America.
May Theilgaard Watts, Tom Watts. Nature Study Guild, Rochester, NY, 1986.

Fern Finder: A Guide to Native Ferns of Northeastern and Central North America.
Anne C. Hallowell, Barbara G. Hallowell. Nature Study Guild, Rochester, NY, 1981.

Track Finder: A Guide to Mammal Tracks of Eastern North America.
Dorcas S. Miller, illustrated by Cherie Hunter Day. Nature Study Guild, Rochester, NY, 1981.

**Worth Repeating**

*Nature teaches more than she preaches. There are no sermons in stones. It is easier to get a spark out of a stone than a moral.*

**John Burroughs**

## Books: Field Guides (continued)

Tree Finder: A Manual for the Identification of Trees by Their Leaves.
May Theilgaard Watts. Nature Study Guild, Rochester, NY, 1991.

Winter Tree Finder: A Manual for Identifying Deciduous Trees in Winter.
May Theilgaard Watts, Tom Watts. Nature Study Guild, Rochester, NY, 1970.

### Insects and Spiders

A Field Guide to Eastern Butterflies.
Paul A. Opler, Vichai Malikul, Roger Tory Peterson. Houghton Mifflin Company, New York, 1992.

A Field Guide to Moths of Eastern North America.
Charles V. Covell, Jr. Virginia Museum of Natural History, Martinsburg, VA, 1984, 2005.

Butterflies.
Paul Opler and Amy Bartlett Wright. Houghton Mifflin Company, New York, 1996.

Butterflies and Moths: A Guide to the More Common North American Species.
Robert T. Mitchell and Herbert S. Zim. St. Martin's Press, New York, 2002.

Butterflies of North America.
Jim P. Brock and Kenn Kaufman. Houghton Mifflin Company, NY, 2003.

Butterflies Through Binoculars: A Field Guide to the Butterflies of Western North America. (There is also an Eastern North America version—same author and publisher)
Jeffrey Glassberg. Oxford University Press, Oxford, 2001.

Caterpillars.
Jonathan P. Latimer and Karen Stray Nolting. Houghton Mifflin Company, New York, 2000.

Caterpillars in the Field and Garden: A Field Guide to the Butterfly Caterpillars of North America.
Jeffrey Glassberg, et al. Oxford University Press, Oxford; 2005.

Dragonflies.
Cynthia Berger. Stackpole Books, Mechanicsburg, PA, 2004.

Dragonflies through Binoculars: A Field Guide to Dragonflies of North America.
Sidney W. Dunkle. Oxford University Press, Oxford, 2000.

**Worth Repeating** 

*My favorite habitat at school is the stream. The stream is very shallow and narrow with mini waterfalls that help keep the water clean. I like the stream because it's peaceful and home to animals. I like having it in our schoolyard because it's fun to go study the real thing.*

**Daniel Famiglietti**
**Grade 5**

Kaufman Field Guide to Insects of North America,
Kenn Kaufman. Houghton Mifflin Company, NY, 2007

National Audubon Society Field Guide to North American Insects and Spiders.
Lorus and Margery Milne. Alfred A. Knopf, Inc., New York, 1980, 1996.

Peterson First Guide to Caterpillars of North America.
Amy Bartlett Wright. Houghton Mifflin Company, New York, 1993.

Stokes Beginner's Guide to Dragonflies and Damselflies.
Blair Nikula and Jackie Sones. Little, Brown & Company. NY, 2002.

## Mammals

A Field Guide to Cows.
John Pukite. Falcon Press, Helena, MT, 1996.

National Audubon Society Field Guide to North American Mammals.
John O. Whitaker; Jr. Alfred A. Knopf, Inc., New York, 1996, 1997.

## Mushrooms and Fungi

Simon & Schuster's Guide to Mushrooms.
Giovanni Pacioni. Simon & Schuster,Inc., New York, 1981.

## Regional, Regions and Habitats

A Field Guide to North Atlantic Wildlife: Marine Mammals, Seabirds, Fish, and Other Sea Life.
Noble S. Proctor and Patrick J. Lynch. Yale University Press, New Haven, CN, 2005.

A Field Guide to Your Own Back Yard.
John Hanson Mitchell. The Countryman Press, Woodstock, VT, 1985, 1999.

National Audubon Society Field Guide to California.
Peter Aldin and Fred Heath. Alfred A. Knopf, Inc., New York, 1998.

National Audubon Society Field Guide to the Mid-Atlantic States.
Peter Alden et al. Alfred A. Knopf, Inc., New York, 1999.

National Audubon Society Field Guide to the Pacific Northwest.
Peter Alden and Dennis Paulson. Alfred A. Knopf, Inc., New York, 1998.

National Audubon Society Field Guide to the Southeastern States.
Peter Alden and Gil Nelson. Alfred A. Knopf, Inc., New York, 1999.

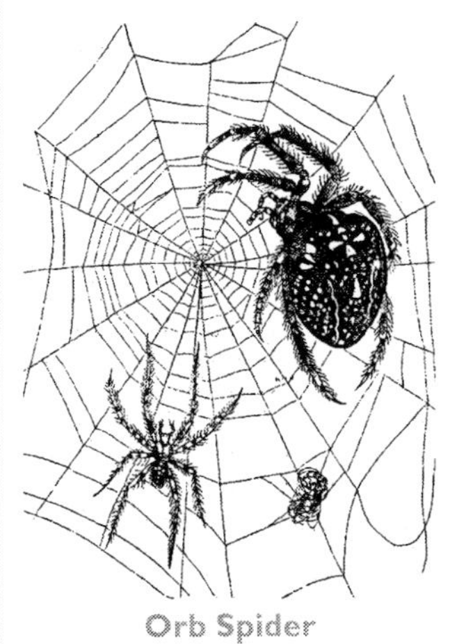
Orb Spider

## Books: Field Guides (continued)

National Audubon Society Field Guide to North American Seashore Creatures.
Norman A. Meinkoth. Alfred A. Knopf, Inc., New York, 1981.

Peterson First Guide to Seashores.
John Kricher. Houghton Mifflin Company, New York, 1992.

Peterson First Guide to Urban Wildlife.
Sarah Landry. Houghton Mifflin Company, New York, 1994.

Pocket Naturalist: Urban Wildlife: An Introduction to Familiar Species.
James Kavanagh, Raymond Leung. Waterford Press, Inc., Phoeniz, AZ, 2001.

Pond Life: A Guide to Common Plants and Animals of North American Ponds and Lakes.
Gregory K. Reid. St. Martin's Press, New York, 2001.

*Seasonal Guide to the Natural Year: A Month by Month Guide to Natural Events (CO, NM, AZ, UT).
Ben Guterson. Fulcrum Publishing, Golden, CO, 1994.

*Note: some of the Seasonal Guides by Fulcrum Publishing are out of print and might be difficult to purchase. Check your local or city library for these books—they are still a treasure!

Seasonal Guide to the Natural Year: A Month by Month Guide to Natural Events (FL, GA, AL).
Timothy O'Keefe. Fulcrum Publishing, Golden, CO, 1996.

Seasonal Guide to the Natural Year: A Month by Month Guide to Natural Events (IL, MO, AR).
Barbara Perry Lawton. Fulcrum Publishing, Golden, CO, 1994.

Seasonal Guide to the Natural Year: A Month by Month Guide to Natural Events (MN, MI, WI).
John Bates. Fulcrum Publishing, Golden, CO, 1997.

Seasonal Guide to the Natural Year: A Month by Month Guide to Natural Events (NC, SC, TN).
John Rucker, Fulcrum Publishing, Golden, CO, 1996.

Seasonal Guide to the Natural Year: A Month by Month Guide to Natural Events (New England, New York).
Scott Weidensaul. Fulcrum Publishing, Golden, CO, 1993.

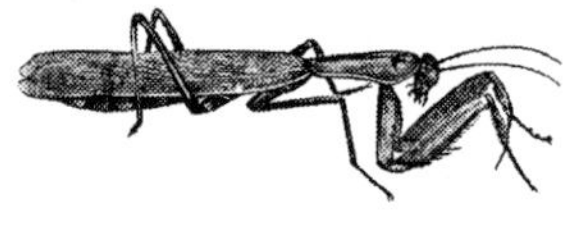
Praying Mantis

Seasonal Guide to the Natural Year: A Month by Month Guide to Natural Events (Northern CA).
Bill McMillon. Fulcrum Publishing, Golden, CO, 1995.

Seasonal Guide to the Natural Year: A Month by Month Guide to Natural Events (PA, NJ, MD, DE, VA, WV, DC).
Scott Weidensaul. Fulcrum Publishing, Golden, CO, 1992

Seasonal Guide to the Natural Year: A Month by Month Guide to Natural Events (Southern CA and Baja California).
Judy Wade. Fulcrum Publishing, Golden, CO, 1997.

Seasonal Guide to the Natural Year: A Month by Month Guide to Natural Events (Texas).
Steve Price. Fulcrum Publishing, Golden, CO, 1996.

Seasonal Guide to the Natural Year: A Month by Month Guide to Natural Events (OR, WA, BC).
James Luther Davis. Fulcrum Publishing, Golden, CO, 1996.

Urban Wildlife: An Introduction to Familiar Species.
James Kavanaugh and Raymond Leung. Waterford Press, Inc., Phoenix, AZ, 2001.

Wildlife of Pennsylvania and the Northeast.
Charles Fergus. Stackpole Books, Mechanicsburg, PA, 2000.

## Reptiles and Amphibians

A Field Guide to Reptiles and Amphibians: Eastern and Central North America.
Roger Conant and Joseph T. Collins. Houghton Mifflin Company, New York, 1958, 1978.

## Rocks and Minerals

National Audubon Society Field Guide to North American Rocks and Minerals.
National Audubon Society. Alfred A. Knopf,Inc., 1978.

Peterson First Guide to Rocks and Minerals.
Frederick H. Pough. Houghton Mifflin Company, 1991.

Rocks and Minerals: A Guide to Field Identification.
Charles A. Sorrell. Golden Books, New York, 1973.

## Shells

National Audubon Society Field Guide to North American Seashells.
Harold A. Rehder. Alfred A. Knopf, Inc., New York, 1981, 1996.

Peterson First Guide to Shells of North America.
Jack Leatherbury Douglass. Houghton Mifflin Company, NY, 1989.

*One touch of nature makes the whole world kin.*

**William Shakespeare**

## Books: Field Guides (continued)

Seashells of the Northeast Coast from Cape Hatteras to Newfoundland. Julius Gordon and Townsend E. Weeks. Hancock House Publishers, Blaine, WA; 1982.

### Sky and Weather

National Audubon Society Field Guide to North American Weather. David M. Ludlum. Alfred A. Knopf, Inc., New York, 1991.

National Audubon Society Field Guide to the Night Sky. Mark R. Chartrand. Alfred A. Knopf, Inc., New York, 1991.

### Sounds and Calls

A Guide to Night Sounds: The Nighttime Sounds of 60 Mammals, Birds, Amphibians, and Insects.
Lang Elliott. Stackpole Books, Mechanicsburg, PA, 2004.

Birding by Ear: Eastern and Central North America. Richard K. Walton, et al. Peterson Field Guides, 2002.

Why Do Whales and Children Sing: A Guide to Listening in Nature. David Dunn. Earth Ear, Santa Fe, NM, 1999.

### Trees

Familiar Trees of North America, Eastern Region. Ann H. Whitman, Ed. Alfred A. Knopf, Inc., New York, 1986.

National Audubon Society Field Guide to North American Trees: Eastern Region.
Elbert L. Little. Alfred A. Knopf, Inc., New York, 1980, 1996.

National Audubon Society Field Guide to North American Trees: Western Region.
Elbert L. Little. Alfred A. Knopf, Inc., New York, 1980.

Trees
George A. Petrides, et al. Houghton Mifflin Company, New York, 1996.

**Worth Repeating** 

*Earth and sky, woods and fields, lakes and rivers, the mountain and the sea, are excellent schoolmasters, and teach some of us more than we can ever learn from books.*

**Sir John Lubbock**

## Books: Journals

A Kid's Fall EcoJournal, with Nature Activities for Exploring the Season. Toni Albert and Margaret Brandt. Trickle Creek Books, Mechanicsburg, PA, 1997.

A Kid's Spring EcoJournal, with Nature Activities for Exploring the Season.
Toni Albert. Trickle Creek Books, Mechanicsburg, PA, 1997.

A Kid's Summer EcoJournal, with Nature Activities for Exploring the Season.
Toni Albert. Trickle Creek Books, Mechanicsburg, PA, 1998.

A Kid's Winter EcoJournal, with Nature Activities for Exploring the Season.
Toni Albert. Trickle Creek Books, Mechanicsburg, PA, 1998.

Keeping a Nature Journal: Discover a Whole New Way of Seeing the World Around You.
Clare Walker Leslie and Charles E. Roth. Storey Publishing, North Adams, MA, 2005.

## Books: Recommended Reading (Grades 9 to adult)

100 Birds and How They Got Their Names.
Diana Wells. Algonquin Books of Chapel Hill, Chapel Hill, NC, 2002.

101 Ways to Help Birds.
Laura Erickson and Roger Hall. Stackpole Books, Mechanicsburg, PA, 2006.

Advice from a Tree.
Ilan Shamir. Better World Press, Inc., Fort Collins, CO, 2000.

Curious Naturalist: Guide to Understanding and Exploring Nature, The
Mary B. Dickinson, et al. National Geographic Society, Washington, DC, 1991.

Ghost with Trembling Wings: Science, Wishful Thinking, and the Search for Lost Species, The
Scott Weidensaul. North Point Press, NY, 2002.

Legacy of Luna: The Story of a Tree, a Woman, and the Struggle to Save the Redwoods, The
Julia Butterfly Hill. HarperCollins, NY, 2000.

Mind of the Raven.
Bernd Heinrich. Harper Collins Publishers, Inc., New York, 1999.

On the Wing: To the Edge of the Earth with the Peregrine Falcon.
Alan Tennant. Alfred A. Knopf, Inc., NY, 2004.

Silent Spring.
Rachel Carson. Houghton Mifflin Company, NY, 1962.

**Worth Repeating**

*In nature there is no effect without cause; understand the cause and you will have no need of the experiment.*

**Leonardo Da Vinci**

## Books: Recommend Reading (Grade 9 to adult) (continued)

Sense of Wonder, The
Rachel Carson. Harper & Row Publishers, NY, 1965.

Thermal Warriors: Strategies of Insect Survival, The
Bernd Heinrich. Harvard University Press, Cambridge, MA, 1996.

Trees in My Forest, The
Bernd Heinrich. Harper Collins Publishers, Inc., New York, 1997.

Urban Naturalist, The
Steven D. Garber. Dover Publications, Inc., Mineola, NY, 1987.

Winter World: The Ingenuity of Animal Survival.
Bernd Heinrich. Harper Collins Publishers, Inc., New York, 2003.

## Books: Recommended Reading or Activity (Students)

Everybody Needs a Rock.
Describes the qualities to consider in selecting the perfect rock for play and pleasure. Byrd Baylor. Aladdin Paperbacks, NY, 1974. Recommended for ages 4-8.

Growing Flowers Series: Flowers, Leaves, Seeds, and Stems.
The series explains the growing process. Labeled photographs clearly identify parts of plants. Gail Saunders Smith. Capstone Press, 1998. Recommended for grades K-2.

Look What I Did with a Leaf.
Demonstrates how to create fanciful animals from leaves. Morteza E. Sohi. Walker & Company, NY, 1995. Ages 4-8, 32 pages.

Look What I Did with a Shell.
Demonstrates how to create fanciful animals from shells. Morteza E. Sohi. Walker & Company, NY, 2000. Ages 4-8, 32 pages.

Lorax, The.
A classic Suess story book about mindless progress and the danger it poses to the earth's natural beauty. Dr. Seuss, Random House, NY, 1971. Recommended for ages 4-8, 64 pages.

Man Who Planted Trees, The.
A timeless eco-fable about what one person can do to restore the earth. T. Jean Giono. Chelsea Green Publishing Company, 1987. Recommended for ages 9-12, 180 pages.

**Worth Repeating**

*Study nature, love nature, stay close to nature. It will never fail you.*

**Frank Lloyd Wright**

One for Sorrow, Two for Joy.
An owl befriends a robin to help forge an alliance between raptors and seabirds against their enemies, magpies and crows. Clive Woodall, Ziji Publishing, London, 2003. School Library Journal recommends this book for grade 9 and up, 320 pages.

Peterson Field Guide Color-In Book Series: Birds, Butterflies, Mammals, Reptiles and Amphibians, and Wildflowers. Houghton Mifflin. Elementary, 64 pages.

Red-Tails in Love: A Wildlife Drama in Central Park.
(The story of Pale Male). Marie Winn. Vintage Departures, 1999. Recommended ages 15 to adult, 352 pages.

That Quail, Robert.
The acclaimed story of a family who adopts a helpless quail which prefers human companionship to other quail. Margaret Stanger. Harper Collins Paperbacks. Reissued 1992, 128 pages. Harper recommends this for ages 18 and up. I would recommend it for readers as young as 13.

Stranger in the Woods.
Photographic illustration of forest animals, awakened by a birds' warning that there is a stranger in the woods. They set out to discover if there is danger and find, instead, a wonderful surprise. Carl R. Sams II and Jean Stoick. Carl R. Sams Photography, 2000. Ages 9-12, 48 pages.

## Books: Recommended Reading (Educators)

GrowLab: A Complete Guide to Gardening in the Classroom.
National Gardening Association. Knox Parks Foundation and National Gardening Association, 1988. Intelligence Reframed: Multiple Intelligences for the 21st Century.
Howard Gardner. Basic Books, NY, 1999.

Last Child in the Woods: Saving Our Children from Nature-Deficit Disorder.
Richard Louv. Algonquin Books of Chapel Hill, Chapel Hill, NC, 2005.

Learning about Spring with Children's Literature.
Margaret A. Bryant, et al. 2006. No publisher listed.

Learning from the Land: Teaching Ecology through Stories and Activities.
Brian "Fox" Ellis. Teacher Ideas Press, Englewood, CO, 1997.

Math in the Garden: Hands-On Activities That Bring Math to Life.
Jennifer M. White, et al. National Gardening Association, Burlington, VT, 2006.

Nature at Your Doorstep: Real World Investigations for Primary Students.
Carol G. Basile, et al. Teacher Ideas Press, Englewood, CO, 1997.

Canada Goldenrod

Schoolyard Mosaics: Designing Gardens and Habitats.
Eve Pranis, et al. National Gardening Association, Burlington, VT, 2003.

Stalking the Wild Amaranth: Gardening in the Age of Extinction.
Janet Marinelli. Henry Holt and Company Inc., 1998.

Teaching Green Series:
The Elementary Years: Hands-On Learning in Grades K-5.
The High School Years: Hands-On Learning in Grades 9-12.
The Middle Years: Hands-On Learning in Grades 6-8
Tim Grant and Gail Littlejohn. New Society Publishers, Gabriola, BC.

## Books: Reference

100 Easy to Grow Native Plants.
Lorraine Johnson. Firefly Books (1999)

Advanced Birding.
Kenn Kaufman. Houghton Mifflin Company, New York; 1990.

A Guide to Nature in Winter.
Donald Stokes. Little, Brown & Company, New York; 1976.

American Wildlife and Plants: A Guide to Wildlife Food Habits.
Alexander C. Martin, et al. Dover Publications, Inc., Mineola, NY, 1951.

Armitage's Native Plants.
Allan Armitage. Timber Press, 2006.

Attracting Birds, Butterflies and Other Backyard Wildlife.
David Mizejewski. Creative Homeowner, Upper Saddle River, NJ, 2004.

Discovering Moths: Nighttime Jewels in Your Own Backyard.
John Himmelman. Down East Books, Camden, ME, 2002.

Grow Lab: a Complete Guide to Gardening in the Classroom.
National Gardening Association, www.kidsgardeningstore.com

How to Identify Birds.
John Farrand, Jr. McGraw-Hill Book Company, New York, 1988.

How To Spot an Owl.
Patricia and Clay Sutton. Houghton Mifflin Company; New York; 1994.

How to Spot Butterflies.
Patricia Taylor Sutton and Clay Sutton. Houghton Mifflin Company, NY, 1999.

**Worth Repeating** 

*The richness I achieve comes from nature, the source of my inspiration.*

**Claude Monet**

How To Spot Hawks & Eagles.
Clay Sutton and Patricia Taylor Sutton. Houghton Mifflin Company, New York, 1996.

Identifying and Harvesting Edible and Medicinal Plants.
Steve Brill. William Morrow, 1994

Life Cycles of Butterflies, The.
Judy Burris and Wayne Richards. Storey Publishing, 2006.

Native Trees, Shrubs and Vines.
William Cullina. The New England Wildflower Society, 2002.

Noah's Garden.
Sara Stein. Houghton Mifflin, 1993.

North American Birds of Prey.
Clay Sutton,Richard K. Walton. Alfred A. Knopf, Inc., New York, 1994.

Pollinator Conservation Handbook.
Xerces Society, 2003.

Schoolyard Habitats: A How-To Guide.
National Wildlife Federation.

Sibley's Birding Basics.
David Allen Sibley. Alfred A. Knopf, Inc., New York; 2002.

Stokes Guide to Observing Insect Lives. Donald Stokes. Little, Brown & Company; New York, 1983.

Stokes Guide to Observing Insect Lives.
Donald Stokes. Little, Brown and Company, New York, 1983.

Stokes Nature Guides: A Guide to Bird Behavior, Volumes I-III.
Donald and Lillian Stokes. Little, Brown and Company, New York, 1979, 1983, 1989.

The Sibley Guide to Bird Life & Behavior.
Chris Elphick, John B. Dunning, Jr., David Allen Sibley. Alfred A. Knopf, Inc., New York, 2001.

*One of the most tragic things I know about human nature is that 99% of all of us tend to put off living. We are all dreaming of some magical rose garden over the horizon instead of enjoying the roses that are blooming outside our windows today.*

**Dale Carnegie**

# Jane Kirkland's Books, Assembly Programs, and Workshops

By Kae Tienstra

*(Kae Tienstra is the publicist and agent for Jane Kirkland. She books public speaking engagement and school assembly programs. As the media contact for Take A Walk® books, Kae also manages media projects and all TV and radio bookings.)*

Jane Kirkland speaks at schools, conducts professional workshops, and is a featured keynote speaker at conferences throughout the United States. She has been featured on Animal Planet TV, PBS, and NPR, and she is a regular guest on Philadelphia's WXPN radio program, *Kids Corner.* Her programs for schools, her workshops for teachers, and her award winning books can help you and your school to generate excitement, gain experience, and learn about the nature in your neighborhood.

## About Take A Walk® Books

*No Student Left Indoors: Creating a Field Guide to Your Schoolyard* is the educator's guidebook to discovering nature in the schoolyard and *Take A Walk®* books are the companion student guidebooks to discovering nature. This series of award-winning, standards- and inquiry-based, hands-on books help kids (ages 8 to 13) find and identify plants and animals. Designed to take along on explorations, the books include step-by-step instructions (when to go, where to look), instructions and space for taking field notes and creating journals (with examples by other kids), beautiful photographs to help readers identify what they see, and author stories from the field. Written with a very personal voice, readers feel as if the author is walking right alongside them as they explore and discover nature.

Among the many awards bestowed upon the Take A Walk® series are the National Arbor Day Foundation's Education Award, Learning Magazine's Teachers Choice Award for Excellence in Classroom Products, and a ForeWord Magazine Book of the Year Finalist award. Take A Walk® books are recommended by the National Science Teachers Association (NSTA Recommends).

## Who's Using Take A Walk® Books?

*Take A Walk®* books are used in many ways by teachers, environmental educators, reading specialists and homeschoolers all over North America in both science and reading programs. Documentation aligning them to State and Federal Academic Standards is available at **www.takeawalk.com**. *Take A Walk®* books have been adopted by Renaissance Learning's *Accelerated*

**Worth Repeating**

*Sunshine is delicious, rain is refreshing, wind braces us up, snow is exhilarating; there is really no such thing as bad weather, only different kinds of good weather.*

**John Ruskin**

*Reader*® program. You can purchase reading comprehension tests for all of the titles at **www.renlearn.com.**

At Delsea Regional Middle School in Franklinville, New Jersey, teacher Lauren A. Boerlin describes how she plans to use the books in her summer program:

> *Delsea Regional Middle School is excited to be using* Take A Backyard Bird Walk *this summer during our five week summer S.H.A.P.E. Program. The principles of School and Home Achievement with a Partnership for Education are to enrich the Language Arts and mathematics skills of our middle level students in a creative and supportive program that links school, home, and community. This year's theme of instruction will center on our feathered friends that can be found in Southern New Jersey. Our children will be building a backyard bird habitat. We will be building various bird houses, visiting some excellent bird watching sites like Cape May Point State Park, reading and writing about observing birds, solving math problems and calculating percentages of birds we see on daily nature walks, and sharing the learning with others in our community.*
>
> *Our learners will refine their informational reading skills by using* Take A Backyard Bird Walk. *I love the way the book is organized. We will be able to have our students look at charts like the "What's in a Bill?" chart to visualize the bills of different birds. Our math teachers will be able to then have our students use this information to make bar or circle graphs of the different kinds of birds we see on our nature walks. Our technical learners will love the space the book provides for field notes and a backyard school map. After using the book, it is hoped that some of our learners will be able to say, "I saw four birds on my walk today; three out of four were morning doves-that's 75%." I truly believe that this text will greatly benefit our students.*
>
> *What is most import in this kind of multi-disciplinary learning is that the students validate their learning with real concepts that they will be exposed to over and over in the future. Their learning will be a living documentation of math and reading skills needed for life-long success.*
>
> *We anticipate learning alongside our students, and our backyard school bird sanctuary will be available for all of our school community to visit and observe nature in its finest.*

The Commonwealth of Pennsylvania, Department of Education, Bureau of Teaching and Learning Support uses Take A Walk® books at the Governor's Institute for Environment and Ecology. Dr Patti L. Vathis, Curriculum Advisor for the Department of Education, writes this about Take A Walk® Books:

> *Each of these books allows students to explore the world through inquiry, investigative and hands-on applications. The content is rich and extremely appropriate for elementary and middle school students. As the students use the books to study the butterfly and dragonfly or the birds in their backyard or taking a city nature walk, they learn to appreciate each level of these very complex ecosystems.*

**Worth Repeating**

*Come forth into the light of things, let nature be your teacher.*

**William Wordsworth**

*From a curriculum perspective, the books are very standards-based and align well to the science and the environment and ecology content. Using these materials as supplemental books for students will help with the teaching of the nature of science.*

Take A Walk® books are also used in workshops conducted by Dr Lynne Dorfman, Co-Director of The Pennsylvania Writing and Literature Project. Dr. Dorfman calls our books *stellar examples of juvenile multi-genre nonfiction.*

## Take A Walk® Books at a Glance

We hope you'll consider these books for your students—whether or not you undertake a *Field Guide Project.* Stillwater Publishing offers a generous school discount and accepts purchase orders. You can look through the pages of our books online at **www.takeawalk.com**, **www.amazon.com**, and **www.books.google.com**. Take A Walk® books can be purchased from your favorite bookseller or at Acorn Naturalists, **www.acornnaturalists.com**, Amazon, **www.amazon.com**, Follett Library Services, **www.flr.follett.com**, IPG Books (educator discounts available), **www.ipgbooks.com**, Zephyr Catalog, **www.zephyrpress.com**, and, of course, from Stillwater Publishing. You can fax purchase orders to Stillwater at 610-458-4001 or mail them to Stillwater Publishing, PO Box 500, Lionville, PA 19353. For pricing information or other questions, please call us at 610-458-4000 or email *sales@takeawalk.com*. Currently the *Take A Walk®* book series includes five titles. Please check **www.takeawalk.com** often for new titles. Turn the page for descriptions of current titles.

## Take A Backyard Bird Walk

**10 Digit ISBN 0970975406**
**13 Digit ISBN 978097097540**
**Flesch-Kincaid reading level 5.2**
**8.5. x 11**
**Paperback**
**Perfect Binding**
**Full Color in and out**
**32 pages**
**Retail $9.95**

Uncover the exciting world of backyard birds and develop skills for finding and identifying various species. Learn the unique characteristics of birds; where they nest; what they eat; how and why they migrate; how they adapt to survive; their habitat requirements; and more!

### Major Sections or Topics

Aren't All Cardinals Red?
Bird Identification Pages
Birds nest in Trees Boxes and Even Wreaths!
Do Birds Affect Your Life?
Do Not Disturb
Go!
How Will you Find Birds?
Identifying Birds
Identifying Feeder Birds
If you Find an Injured Bird
Interesting Things to Do
Leave Only Footprints
Ready?
Recording Observations
Sample Bird Notes
Set?
What are Birds, Anyway?
What are Field Marks?
What are Field Notes?
What do they Eat?
What's in a Bill?
Which Birds Will You See?

### Vocabulary, Terms, Phrases, Organizations, and Historical Figures

Anting
Backyard Bird
Bird of Prey
Feeder Bird
Habitat
Incubate
John James Audubon
Juvenile
Migrate
Mottled
Nocturnal
On the wing
Ornithologist
Passerine
Predator
Preen
Scientist
Songbirds
Species
Suet
Territorial
Twitching

### Worksheets

List the Birds You Know
My Bird Notes
My Bird Walk
My Field Notes
My Ideas and Questions
My Map

## Take A Tree Walk

**10 Digit ISBN 0970975414**
**13 Digit ISBN 978097097516**
**Flesch-Kincaid reading level 5.4**
**8.5. x 11**
**Paperback**
**Perfect Binding**
**Full Color in and out**
**32 pages**
**Retail $9.95**

Explore the remarkable world of trees and develop skills for identifying various species. Learn why leaves turn color in autumn; how to estimate the height and age of a tree; the various parts of a tree; the shapes of leaves; what trees need to survive; the important roles trees play in our lives; and more!

**Major Sections or Topics**

Celebrating Trees
Flowers, Fruits and Cones
Go!
How Old Is That Tree?
How Tall Is That Tree?
Interesting Things to Do
Interesting Things to Do
Leaf Colors
Leaf Factoids and Oddities
Leaf Shapes of Conifers, Palms, and Broadleaf Trees
Leave Only Footprints
Putting it (a tree) All Together
Ready?
Recording Observations
Recording Your Observations
Seeds and Nuts
Set?
Tree Bark
Tree Identification
Tree Shapes
What Are Field Notes?
What Are Trees, Anyway?
What's a Field Guide?
Which Trees Do You Know?
Who Lives In and On Trees?
Why Are Trees Important?
Why Do Leaves Fall in the Autumn?

**Vocabulary, Terms, Phrases, Organizations, and Historical Figures**

Angiosperm
Anthocyanins
Arboretum
Arborist
Broadleaf
Cambium
Carotene
Cavity
Chlorophyll
Circumference
Compound Leaf
Conifer
Cord of wood
Crown
Deciduous
Dendrologist
Diameter at Breast Height
Forester
Fungi
Gymnosperm
Habitat
Heartwood
Hug a Tree Program
Julia Butterfly Hill
Landscaper
Lobed
Logger
National Arbor Day Foundation
Nutrients
Palmate
Perennial
Phloem
Pigment
Pinnate
Silviculturist
Species
Xylem

**Worksheets**

My Field Notes
My Ideas and Questions
My Map
My Tree Walk
State Tree List
Tree Notes
Which Trees Do You Know?

## Take A Walk With Butterflies And Dragonflies

**10 Digit ISBN 0970975422**
**13 Digit ISBN 978097097523**
**Flesch-Kincaid reading level 6.6**
**8.5. x 11**
**Paperback**
**Perfect Binding**
**Full Color in and out**
**32 pages**
**Retail $9.95**

Discover the worlds of butterflies and dragonflies as you develop skills for finding and identifying eggs, larvae, and adults. Learn unique characteristics of these insects, their fascinating lifecycles, and how they adapt and survive in a changing world. Learn the differences between butterflies and moths, dragonflies and damselflies, and more!

### Major Sections or Topics

Butterfly ID Pages
Butterfly Observation Notes
Butterfly or Moth?
Caterpillar Observation
Caterpillars and Their Host Plants
Dragonfly ID Pages
Dragonfly Observation Notes
Dragonfly or Damselfly?
Get Ready for Butterflies and Dragonflies
Identifying Butterflies
Identifying Dragonflies
Life Cycle of a Butterfly
Life Cycle of a Dragonfly
Migrating Dragonflies
Poisonous Butterflies
What are Field Notes
What is a Butterfly?
What is a Dragonfly?
Where Can You Find Butterflies and Dragonflies?

### Vocabulary, Terms, Phrases, Organizations, and Historical Figures

Adaptations
Aquatic
Arthropods
Camouflage
Chordates
Chrysalis
Cocoon
Cryptic Coloration
Diurnal
Dorsal
Genus
Habitat
Instar
Kingdom
Larva
Lepidoptera
Metamorphosis
Mimicry
Molt
National Audubon Society
Nymphs
Odonata
Perchers
Phylum
Posture
Predator
Proboscis
Pupa
Species
Ventral
Vertebrates

### Worksheets

Caterpillar Observation Notes
Dragonfly Observation Notes
My Field Notes

## Take A City Nature Walk

**10 Digit ISBN 0970975420**
**13 Digit ISBN 978097097530**
**Flesch-Kincaid reading level 6.2**
**8.5. x 11**
**Paperback**
**Perfect Binding**
**Full Color in and out**
**32 pages**
**Retail $9.95**

Examine the incredible world of urban ecology and develop skills for finding and identifying nature in the city. Learn about the amazing variety of plants and animals found in cities; how plants and animals adapt to and survive in cities; which plant improves the quality of life for humans in our cities; and more!

### Major Sections or Topics

Balance in the Ecosystem
Big City or Little Town
Discover Nature In and Around the Water
Don't Forget Your Field Notes
Explore Nature in the City
Explore The Treasures of City Gardens
Find Nature In a City Park
Go! Make a Difference
Let it Be
Look For Nature on Man-made Structures
Look Up for Peregrine Falcons
Meet a City's Most Important Plant (Trees)
Urban Bird Identification Page
Urban Flower Identification Page
Urban Insect and Spider Identification Page
Urban Mammal Identification Page
Urban Reptile and Amphibian Identification Page
Urban Tree Identification Page
What Goes In Must Come Out
What More Can You Do?
What Will you See Today
Why Do We Band Peregrines
Will You See Pigeons Everywhere?

### Vocabulary, Terms, Phrases, Organizations, and Historical Figures

Community and Regional Planning Professional
Ecologist
Ecosystem
Endangered
EPA
Extinct
Homing Pigeons
Iridescent
Lady Bird Beetle
Landscape Architects
Marsh Birds
Morph
National Arbor Day Foundation
National Wildlife Federation
Native species
Naturescaping
Pesticide
Pigeon Milk
Seer
Species
Sustainable
Urban
Urban Ecology Center
Urban Forest Landscapers
Wading Birds
Waterfowl
Watershed
Wildlife Ecology and Conservation Professional
Wright, Frank Lloyd

### Worksheets

Field Notes Page
Nature ID Page

## Take A Beach Walk

Discover the beach in a whole new light! Learn about the littoral zone of the beach, how plants and animals adapt to living on seaside beaches, and the surprising treasures of nature you can find on the beach. Uncover new facts about adaptations and endangered plants and animals, and get a true understanding of why all those signs say "Stay off the dunes!:

**13 Digit ISBN 9780970975447**
**Flesch-Kincaid reading level 5.5**
**8.5. x 11**
**Paperback**
**Perfect Binding**
**Full Color in and out**
**32 pages**
**Retail $9.95**

**Major Sections or Topics**

Are You Ready to Explore?
Which Beach Zones Do You Want to Explore?
It's Your Tern to Tell These Birds Apart
Meet the Mollusks
Crusty, Crabby, Crustaceans
Meet a Beach's Most Prehistoric Character
Don't Forget to Read the Signs
Look for Nature in the Lively Littoral Zone
Discover Nature in the Dynamic Dunes
Experience Nature in the Exciting Estuary Ecosystems
Remember Your Walk with a Nature ID Page
Identify Herons and Egrets
Check Out These Weird Beaks
Build Your Own Best-of List
Focus on Fruits and Flowers
Seek Spiral Shaped Shells
Claim Clam Shaped Shells
Search for Sea Stars
Cash in with Sand Dollars
Make a Difference, Volunteer
Become a Citizen Scientist
Congratulations-You're a Sea Star!
Animal Kingdoms

**Vocabulary, terms, phrases, organizations, and historical figures, writers, poets**

Adaptations
American Littoral Society
Brackish
Camouflage
Cornell Laboratory of Ornithology
Crustaceans
Dunes
Estuaryr
Exoskeleton
Habitatl
Intertidal
Littoral
Maritime
Marine Biologist
Mollusks
National Audubon Society
Naturalist
Oceanographer
Plumage
Project Seahorse
Sea star
Strandline
Sea Jellies
Seagulls
Spawning
Species
Thaxter, Cecelia
Tides
Translucent
Transparent

**Worksheets**

Field Notes Page
Nature ID Page

## Workshops

Jane offers a companion workshop for *No Student Left Indoors: Creating a Field Guide to Your Schoolyard.* The workshop is available in three formats: a one-hour seminar (suitable for conference presentations), a six-hour workshop (with hands-on field work at your location), or a three-day comprehensive workshop.

The workshop helps teachers get up and running quickly on a Field Guide Project™ (FGP) with guided lessons and hands on experiences. They work in independent and collaborative mode as they prepare to lead their students in the study of nature. They'll explore the outdoors with Jane, learn how to use binoculars, see how to find and observe nature, and even learn how to design and assemble their own field guide. This is the fast-track to a *Field Guide Project.* For information on booking a Field Guide Project at your school, organization, or district, please contact me, Kae Tienstra, KT Public Relations, Fogelsville, PA, 610-395-6298, email Kae@KTPublicRelations.com,

## Seminars and Speaking Engagements

Jane has keynoted at many types of professional conferences and dinners, including librarian and media specialist conferences, science and environmental educator conferences, parent-teacher associations, birdwatching clubs, wildlife festivals, and gardening clubs. At the Philadelphia Flower Show, Disney's Epcot Center, The Pennsylvania Governor's Institute for Environment and Ecology, Ding Darling National Wildlife Refuge—wherever she speaks, to groups as small as 30 and as large as 800, Jane's enthusiasm about our natural world and the role we play in it is both infectious and captivating. In 2007 she was one of 1,000 people selected worldwide to receive training by Former Vice President Al Gore in the presentation of his slideshow from the Academy Award-winning movie, *An Inconvenient Truth.*

When you want to treat your group to Jane's self-effacing, wacky stories of nature discovery you'll want her program, ***I Saw a Bald Eagle Soaring Over My Grocery Store***. The underlying message is that most of us are oblivious to the nature surrounding us. When you want to show your teachers a new approach to environmental education in the schoolyard, you'll want Jane's workshop ***No Student Left Indoors.***

## School Assembly Programs

I'm sure you know the excitement that builds when an author visits your school. But imagine that the visit includes an interactive, nature-based, multi-media show by an award-winning author who just happens to be a mesmerizing story teller and who has been on Animal Planet TV (making her a veritable "rock star" among your students). Imagine your students—even the kindergarten—involved in a an hour-long assembly program without wanting it to end! Imagine that your students will learn a very important, simple message about the environment that they'll likely never forget. Imagine that when the author leaves your school at the end of the day, she leaves your students feeling excited about turning off the TV and computer

*Three or four times an hour, eighty or more times a day, a unique species of plant or animal vanishes forever.*

**Scott Weidensaul**
**The Ghost with Trembling Wings**
**North Point Press, Publisher**

the audience, whenever the time of day, Jane's entertaining, educational, and inspiring programs will leave your audience wanting more.

## School Assembly Programs

I'm sure you know the excitement that builds when an author visits your school. But imagine that the visit includes an interactive, nature-based, multi-media show by an award-winning author who just happens to be a mesmerizing story teller and who has been on Animal Planet TV (making her a veritable "rock star" among your students). Imagine your students—even the kindergarten—involved in a an hour-long assembly program without wanting it to end! Imagine that your students will learn a very important, simple message about the environment that they'll likely never forget. Imagine that when the author leaves your school at the end of the day, she leaves your students feeling excited about turning off the TV and computer and heading outdoors to find nature. Imagine a "kid-magnet," someone who looks into the eye of every student, who makes everyone she meets feel significant, who shakes the hands of even your youngest students and who makes your students feel as if their question or comment is the most brilliant thing she has heard that day! Imagine all of this, and you're about half way to the reality of a day with Jane Kirkland.

When you book Jane at your school, she is yours for the day. She can do two assembly programs (K-8) during the day and smaller group visits for question and answer sessions. If you have a student special interest group (such as an environmental club or writers club), Jane would be happy to join them for lunch or a mini workshop. As part of her program, your school will receive a set of Take A Walk® books for your library, posters for your teachers, and nature bookmarks for every student.

On a personal note, I'd like to add that I've been a book publicist for over twenty years. I began working with Jane after Jane published her first book in the series, *Take A Backyard Bird Walk*. Her enthusiasm for the *Take A Walk*® endeavor along with her experience as a bestselling computer book author convinced me that this was a great project. But I did not realize at that time that my collaboration with Jane would prove to be one of the most successful and certainly most exciting of my career. I quickly learned that Jane is as good as her word—her hard work, dedication, passion, and uncanny sense of timing have made her Take A Walk® books a stunning success. Jane is the real thing and it shows in everything she does. I can't wait to see what the next few years will bring! I look forward to helping you to book Jane at your school, event, or conference.

Kae Tienstra
KT Public Relations
Fogelsville, PA
610-395-6298
Kae@ktpublicrelations.com.

**Worth Repeating**

*To me a lush carpet of pine needles or spongy grass is more welcome than the most luxurious Persian rug.*

**Helen Keller**

# Hands-on Science, New Friends Are Magnet School's Draw

Wading into ponds, netting frogs and plant life, might sound like fun for a lazy summer day, but it's serious work at Two Rivers Magnet Middle School in East Hartford, Connecticut. The school, which has a hands-on science curriculum, brings together students from five communities to learn about research and one another. Included: Descriptions of a science-technology magnet school curriculum.

Field research and scientific analysis, complete with computer-generated charts and graphs, is every day work for scientists and soon-to-be scientists, but those activities are rare among schoolchildren. In Connecticut, however, some middle-schoolers already are getting their feet wet—literally—when it comes to scientific inquiry.

Teaching students from different backgrounds to conduct research using the latest technology is the central mission of the Two Rivers Magnet Middle School in East Hartford, Connecticut. Nearly 600 students in grades 6 to 8 are enrolled at the school, which opened in the fall of 2002. The youngsters, who are selected by lottery, come from five area school districts; three of them urban and two suburban.

"We have wide achievement goals; our student achievement [benchmarks] are based on the goals in five communities," said Principal David Pearson. "We want to close the achievement gap and build a diverse school environment. This is a unique opportunity; we're using technology in creative and unique ways."

## A RESEARCHER'S DREAM

Geographically, Two Rivers is ideally situated for its scientific mission; the school was built between the Hockanum and Connecticut Rivers, near flood plains. "It's just an amazing location for field work," said Anne Bartoszuk, the school's community outreach coordinator. The curriculum stresses the environmental sciences, including the rivers' history, geology, and affect on the local quality of life.

"[At Two Rivers], every teacher's biggest goal is to teach to the range of abilities, and to show how science can be challenging at any level," continued Bartoszuk. "Science is approached differently here."

Once every four weeks, for example, students take part in a Bio Blitz, a field-work day. Students might don waders and life vests, grab nets and buckets, and work outside for an extended class period—gathering water, plant, and

**Worth Repeating**

*There is nothing in a caterpillar that tells you it's going to be a butterfly.*

**R. Buckminster Fuller**

---

animal specimens to test the vitality of a pond, for example. Students then compose reports on the laptops assigned to each student and faculty member. "They are using technology to communicate information," Bartoszuk said of the students, who hope to test a pond in each of their five home communities before the year is done.

In some cases, the students' study results are sent to local and state agencies. "We are trying to make connections with outside organizations; we want to interact more with the outside," according to Bartoszuk. The school's motto, in fact, is "changing the world for good."

To facilitate the fieldwork, technology is integrated across the school's curriculum. Students use their laptops in conjunction with the electronic whiteboards teachers employ in the classrooms. Each room has a Tower of Technology, which includes a computer, printer, Web cam, video cassette recorder, and television.

The technical equipment, however, while at first an attraction—and distraction—for some students, now is viewed as just the contemporary cousin of three-ring binders. "Initially, the laptops were seen as a novelty, and there was some inappropriate behavior," Bartoszuk told Education World. "Now the students see them as just another tool, like notebook and paper." Some students even put stickers on their laptops, just as they might decorate traditional notebooks.

"Kids don't come here for laptops," Bartoszuk added. "That's just one small part of a bigger picture."

## TRAINING INQUIRING MINDS

Two Rivers' teachers stress hands-on learning, inquiry, and analysis, an approach tailored to meet the learning styles of young adolescents. Besides their in-depth science work, students take all the core courses as well as some electives. Flexible block scheduling allows for 80-minute class periods; the schedule changes weekly, based on teachers' and students' needs. Members of the school's six teams meet every day. "You cannot be a hide-a-way teacher here," Bartoszuk said. "You cannot shut your door and do your own thing."

"We truly embrace the longer periods," mathematics teacher Robert Storozuk told Education World. "You get more out of students that way; the quality is better if you spend more time with them." During one 80-minute math period, for example, Storozuk's seventh graders used their laptops to create a Jeopardy-style game involving math questions.

Other subjects are approached differently as well. The school does not have athletic fields or after school sports, so the physical education program, called Project Adventure, stresses exploration, fitness, and self-improvement.

**Worth Repeating**

*Like music and art, love of nature is a common language that can transcend all political or social boundaries.*

**Jimmy Carter**

Fieldwork also goes beyond the school year. In the summer of 2003, 80 Two Rivers' students spent two weeks working with professors from Wesleyan University and Trinity College on a Connecticut River monitoring program. The group included some Hartford high school students who had worked with the professors before; they interacted with the younger children as well.

## FROM COPAPODS TO AMPHIBIANS

At Two Rivers, getting hands and feet wet is a mandatory part of studying pond life. In a sixth grade science class one afternoon, students were busy eyeing plants and critters large and small—including frogs and a snake—through glass aquariums and under microscopes. The class collected the samples from vernal pools—temporary containments of water—on the school grounds.

"We're comparing these [samples] with specimens collected from another pool," Joe, 12 of South Windsor explained. "We're trying to identify the specimens based on what they look like."

Another student, Emma, 12, from Glastonbury, was tracking a copapod under a microscope—something she described as "a tiny organism that can go really fast."

"I want to be a marine biologist, and this will help me with math and science," Emma said, explaining why she chose Two Rivers. "I like the school. I'm really into science and I'm fascinated by computers. Every day I find out more about computers."

Students participate in some type of science work every day, and they are curious, engaged learners, teacher Jane Callery told Education World. "It's different and exciting," she said of the school's approach. "It's invigorating to come to work every day, see what's discussed, and share with the children."

The students' technology comfort level also has grown. "Now technology is second nature to them," she said. "Some decide if they want to use their laptops or write or draw in their journals."

## STRIVING FOR QUALITY AND DIVERSITY

Two Rivers' students also are learning to interact with people from different backgrounds and cultures.

A court decision prompted Connecticut to develop magnet schools. In the case of Sheff v. O'Neill, the parent of a student in Hartford's urban school district sued the state, claiming that her child's education was inferior to that of students in non-urban areas. As a result, the state now is under court order to voluntarily reduce racial, ethnic, and economic isolation among all students. The court was not specific, however, about how the state should reduce isolation; magnet schools have been the approach of choice so far. Two

**Worth Repeating**

*I prefer winter and fall, when you feel the bone structure of the landscape—the loneliness of it, the dead feeling of winter. Something waits beneath it, the whole story doesn't show.*

**Andrew Wyeth**

---

Rivers is one of three magnet middle schools in the state. Magnet schools are overseen by the Capitol Region Education Council, a regional educational service that facilitates programs among districts.

"My goal is to close the achievement gap [between ethnic groups]," said Pearson. "We have small classes and unique opportunities, such as a four-week summer program focusing on basic skills. We have a school-wide goal to improve reading. We have no control over what we get [in terms of ability]. It is up to me and my staff to be creative to meet student needs."

Each town is allowed to send 44 children per grade; in the first year, the school had 1,300 applications for 440 openings. In the fall of 2003, 600 students applied for the 220 slots. At the time Two Rivers was proposed, several of the sending districts were running out of space in their middle schools, so they were eager to participate. Two of the towns, South Windsor and Glastonbury, solved their space problems while planning for Two Rivers was underway, but remained involved in the project. "The five superintendents see it as working toward the future," Pearson noted."

According to Bartoszuk, however, Two Rivers is not the place for everyone. In addition to the absence of an athletic program, the school has a strict dress code, which bans jeans, t-shirts, and sweatshirts. Boys must wear slacks and collared shirts; the same rule applies to girls, although they have the option of wearing skirts no shorter than 4 inches above the knee.

## ATTRACTIVE TO STUDENTS, TEACHERS

Several Two Rivers students who spoke with Education World, however, said the school definitely was the place for them. Frankie, 13, a seventh grader from Manchester, said his mother picked the school, but he is happy with her choice. "You get more opportunities and learn more about other people," he told Education World. "I like to draw and I get to do a lot with art. I also like the longer classes."

"I always wanted to go to a magnet school," added Catia, 13, a seventh grader from East Hartford. "I want to be a pediatrician; this school involves science and I love science. And teachers explain things better here."

She also is enjoying meeting new people. "I made a lot of friends," Catia told Education World. "The teams are small, so I'm getting to know kids I didn't know, from East Hartford and from other towns."

Ben, 11, a sixth grader from Glastonbury, said the only downside to attending Two Rivers is a long bus ride—but it is worth it. "The school days go by so fast, sometimes I don't want to take a vacation," he said. "I really like science and I really like technology. I wanted to come. The laptop is a bonus. Plus, I made a lot more friends than I would have at home."

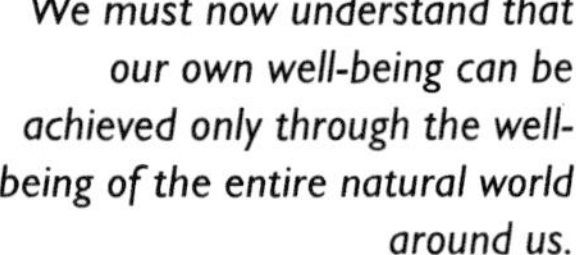

**Worth Repeating**

*We must now understand that our own well-being can be achieved only through the well-being of the entire natural world around us.*

**Thomas Berry**
***The Dream of the Earth***

Even the dress code has fans. "I think it's better than other schools where kids run around in ratty t-shirts," said Joe, 12, a sixth grader.

The chance to teach students from different backgrounds also enticed experienced teachers to Two Rivers. "I loved the chance to work with a diverse population," said Storozuk, who taught in a middle school in South Windsor for ten years. "The classroom discussions are so rich; you get a range of views. This is getting back to teaching where I can make a difference."

"They work side-by-side with people they never met before," added Callery. "They are not afraid to ask questions."

Still, teaching to a diverse population requires some adjustments. "There are more sad stories here, which sometimes makes teaching a challenge," said Storozuk.

The state-of-the-art facilities and equipment also were an incentive for teachers to join the Two Rivers' team. "It was very exciting to hear the job description, involving hands-on science. And it's an opportunity to work with other creative, innovative people," Callery said. Storozuk agreed. "I was dying to get my hands on the technology; it's a chance to do things in a less traditional way," he said. "The technology affords greater opportunities—it's a tool that will be here forever. We are using it here in good ways. It puts all kids on an equal basis."

## A FAMILY AFFAIR

Keeping families involved in the school also is important to the Two Rivers' faculty, though working with parents in five communities can require some creativity.

"We pay for cabs to get parents to PTO meetings [conferences and activities]," Bartoszuk said. "We want parents to get to know the teachers as well as the kids do." Siblings of current students are automatically admitted.

The school also plans to add a health center. "We are here for the entire family," Pearson said.

## LONG-TERM INVESTMENTS

The experience at Two Rivers will help students as they plan for their high school careers and beyond, added Pearson. "They will have more choices in high school -- they will be able to gravitate to courses that meet their needs. They will know what works for them.

"We're not trying to present ourselves as a better option, just a unique option," he added.

Red Clover

Two Rivers is an option whose appeal is growing. "In the first year, we had difficulty attracting students from (suburban) South Windsor and Glastonbury," Bartoszuk said. "Now it is easier. The word is out."

Sixth grader Ben said some of his hometown friends are showing interest in the school as well. "Now other kids want to come here—now they see what I do, and not what I get."

---

# If You Find an Injured Animal

It's a good idea to keep a list of local wildlife rehabilitators in your school office. If you find wildlife that needs immediate attention, you'll be glad you had the list at your fingertips. I keep my list in my glove box of my car, too. Check under look under "wildlife" in the phone book or check on the Internet at the Wildlife Rehabilitation Information Directory **www.tc.umn.edu/~devo0028**. The following charts will help you assess wildlife injuries and actions you can take.

## I Found a Baby Bird ... *Now What?*

***Is bird hurt or sick?***
(Unable to flutter wings, bleeding, wings droop unevenly, weak or shivering, attacked by cat or dog)

Yes → **Call a wildlife rehabilitator.**
→ ***Unable to reach a rehabilitator?*** Call state wildlife agency or a wildlife vet.
→ If unable to reach any of above, **rescue bird** (see instructions on next page).

No → ***Is bird feathered?***

No → **It's a nestling.** (Needs help) ***Can you find the nest? Is it intact?***

- No → **Make a substitute nest.** Poke holes in bottom of a berry basket or margarine tub; line with dry grass, the old nest, or pine needles; hang from nearby tree.
  → **Put baby in nest.** *Observe from a distance.* ***Are parents visiting nest?***
  - Yes → **Leave the area.** Baby is okay.
  - No → **Call a wildlife rehabilitator.**
- Yes → **Put baby back in nest.** *Observe from a distance.* ***Are parents visiting nest?***
  - Yes → **Leave the area.** Baby is okay.
  - No → **Call a wildlife rehabilitator.**

Yes → **It's a fledgling.** (Normal behavior to be hopping on ground; parents will feed it.) ***Is bird safe from cats, dogs, and people?***

- Yes → **Leave the area.** Baby is okay.
- No → **Put bird in bushes or on tree limb nearby.** Watch from a distance. ***Are parents nearby?***
  - Yes → **Leave the area.** Baby is okay.
  - No → **Call a wildlife rehabilitator.**

**If you find a baby duck, goose, quail, or killdeer:**

- If you know the mother is dead, or if the baby is injured, call a wildlife rehabilitator right away.
- If the baby is separated from the mother and you know where she is, place the baby close by so she can hear it. Watch from a distance.
- If mother is not found or does not claim baby within an hour, call a wildlife rehabilitator. If you cannot reach one, rescue the baby (instructions on next page).

# How to Rescue Baby Birds

*(Only adults should rescue baby birds. Before rescuing adult birds, seek guidance from a wildlife rehabilitator.)*

1. **Prepare a container.** Place a clean, soft cloth with no strings or loops on the bottom of a cardboard box or cat/dog carrier with a lid. If it doesn't have air holes, make some. For smaller birds, you can use a paper sack with air holes.
2. **Protect yourself.** Wear gloves, if possible. Some birds may stab with their beaks, slice with their *talons* (claws) and slap with their wings, to protect themselves, even if sick; birds commonly have parasites (fleas, lice, ticks) and carry diseases.
3. **Cover the bird with a light sheet or towel.**
4. **Gently pick up the bird and put it in the prepared container.**
5. **Warm the animal if it's cold out or if the animal is chilled.** Put one end of the animal's container on a heating pad set on low. Or fill a zip-top plastic bag, plastic soft drink container with a screw lid, or a rubber glove with hot water; wrap the warm container with cloth, and put next to the animal. Make sure the container doesn't leak, or the animal will get wet and chilled.
6. **Tape the box shut or roll the top of the paper bag closed.**
7. **Note exactly where you found the bird.** This will be very important for release.
8. **Keep the bird in a warm, dark, quiet place.**
   Don't give the bird food or water.
   Leave the bird alone; don't handle or bother it.
   Keep children and pets away.
9. **Contact a wildlife rehabilitator, state wildlife agency, or wildlife veterinarian as soon as possible.**
   Don't keep the bird at your home longer than necessary.
   Keep the bird in a container; don't let it loose in your house or car.
10. **Wash your hands after contact with the bird.**
    Wash anything the bird was in contact with — towel, jacket, blanket, pet carrier — to prevent the spread of diseases and/or parasites to you or your pets.
11. **Get the bird to a wildlife rehabilitator as soon as possible.**

# I Found a Baby Mammal ... *Now What?*

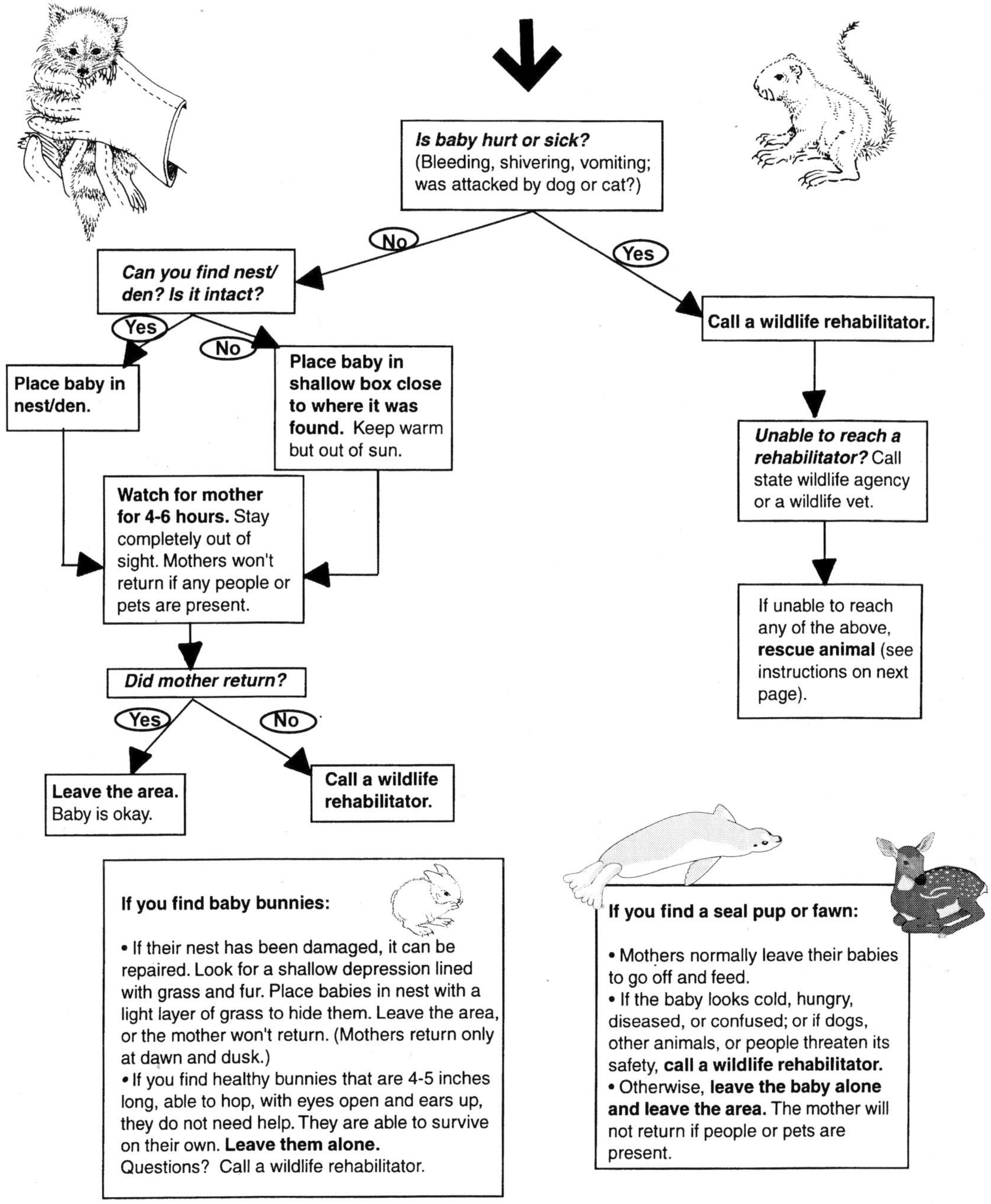

# How to Rescue Baby Mammals

*(Only adults should rescue baby mammals. Before rescuing adult mammals, seek guidance from a wildlife rehabilitator.)*

1. **Prepare a container.** Place a soft cloth on the bottom of a cardboard box or cat/dog carrier with a lid. If it doesn't have air holes, make some. For smaller animals, you can use a paper sack with air holes punched in.
2. **Protect yourself.** Wear gloves, if possible. Some animals may bite or scratch to protect themselves, even if sick; wild animals commonly have parasites (fleas, lice, ticks) and carry diseases.
3. **Cover the animal with a light sheet or towel.**
4. **Gently pick up the animal and put it in the prepared container.**
5. **Warm the animal if it's cold out or if the animal is chilled.** Put one end of the container on a heating pad set on low. Or fill a zip-top plastic bag, plastic soft drink container with a screw lid, or a rubber glove with hot water; wrap warm container with cloth, and put it next to the animal. Make sure the container doesn't leak, or the animal will get wet and chilled.
6. **Tape the box shut or roll the top of the paper bag closed.**
7. **Note exactly where you found the animal.** This will be very important for release.
8. **Keep the animal in a warm, dark, quiet place.**
   Don't give it food or water.
   Leave it alone; don't handle or bother it.
   Keep children and pets away.
9. **Contact a wildlife rehabilitator, state wildlife agency, or wildlife veterinarian as soon as possible.**
   Don't keep the animal at your home longer than necessary.
   Keep the animal in a container; don't let it loose in your house or car.
10. **Wash your hands after contact with the animal.**
    Wash anything the animal was in contact with — towel, jacket, blanket, pet carrier — to prevent the spread of diseases and/or parasites to you or your pets.
11. **Get the animal to a wildlife rehabilitator as soon as possible.**

APPENDIX D:

# Gardening to Attract Birds and Butterflies

By Jane Kirkland

Before there were bird and butterfly feeders, nest boxes, and bird baths, birds and butterflies depended upon their habitats to provide their resources—and they still do. Providing supplemental food in feeders does not guarantee that you'll attract the kinds of birds and butterflies you want to see. If you want a variety of species of birds and butterflies, you have to provide the species of native plants that they need. Of course, you can only attract birds and butterflies found in your region. There's no guarantee that you'll get all the species you want, but you will certainly increase your odds with native plants.

## Attracting Birds

A bird feeder is a great way to attract birds but bird feeders provide supplemental food for birds. Some species of birds never eat the kinds of food you can provide in feeders (seed, nectar, fruit, and so forth). Some are meat eaters. Even with well stocked feeders, most songbirds prefer insects over seed in the summer. If you want to attract more species of birds to your yard, you need to go beyond bird feeders. You need to understand the habitat needs of birds. Once you know what birds need, you can plant bushes, trees, flowers, and other plants that meet those needs. So, what do birds need?

- **Food**. Songbirds eat nuts, fruits, seeds, and nectar. But their number one food source is insects. In addition to providing food, it's important to provide food at the place where individual species eat. For example, some species of birds are ground-dwellers and they eat on the ground. Others stay high in the highest trees. The rest are found somewhere in between. Food sources are needed at all heights.

- **Shelter**. Dense foliage and plants provide safety from predators, cover for nesting, and protection from weather. Shelter is needed at all heights—from low-growing perennials to shrubs and woody plants and trees. Evergreen trees and bushes provide winter protection.

- **Nesting sites and materials**. Some birds nest high in trees, others in shrubs or even on the ground. Songbird nests can be the cup-shaped nests we've all seen in trees, shrubs, or even man-made items such as wreaths on your front door, beams on your deck, and your mailbox. Some species of songbirds build cavity nests—nests in holes in trees or in nest boxes. Different species use different materials for their nests; and materials range from leaves, grasses, twigs, sticks, mud and feathers to man-made materials such as string, laundry lint, even cellophane wrap.

- **Space**. Most songbirds require exclusive territories for nesting. In the fall and winter many songbirds will form flocks, but, come spring, you can be

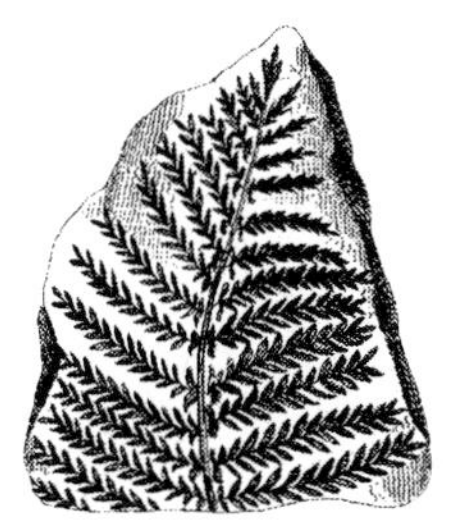

Fossil

sure that most of them will once again separate into pairs and claim nesting territories.

- **Water**. Water attracts birds in a big way. Birds need water for drinking and bathing. If you don't have a stream or a lake in your yard (and how many of us do, after all?), you could construct a small pond or set up a bird bath. If you can run electricity to your water source, consider setting up a heater in winter to keep the water from freezing. Also, birds are attracted by the sounds of water, so fountains, drippers and misters are great additions to your pond or bird bath.

Plants, insects and birds have symbiotic relationship among each other. Plants provide shelter, food, nesting sites, and nesting materials for birds. Plants are also hosts for the insects that are the favorite food of songbirds. Birds and insects pollinate plants. Birds help to propagate plants by dropping their seeds in their feces.

Each species of bird is found in the region or habitat that contains its preferred food sources, shelter and nesting places. You can bring birds closer to your home and in for a better view by planning and planting for the birds and by understanding that birds have plant preferences.

The first requirement for your plants should be that they are native to your region. There is no better resource for birds than native plants; they provide the proper nutrients for the plant-eating birds. They attract the native insects that the local birds prefer to eat. There is no easier garden to keep than that comprised of native plants; they are well adapted to the soil and climate, are low maintenance, require no fertilizer, and should not need pesticides; in addition, they shouldn't need much watering, and they are disease resistant when planted in the right location meeting each plant's light, moisture, and pH requirements. Native plants are particularly good for school properties where gardens are often unattended in the summer and where any time during the year that can be set aside for gardening is at a premium.

Native plants can help meet the needs of birds throughout the year—spring, summer, fall, and winter:

- In the **spring**, birds need food, nesting sites and nesting materials. Insects are a critical food source for migrating birds and the right plants attract the right insects. Plants also provide nesting sites and materials (sticks, grasses, mosses, etc.).

- In the **summer**, birds need food, nesting sites and materials. Depending on the species, nectar, fruit, seed, and insects are important in the summer. Insects are critical to birds at this time of year because hatchling songbirds typically are not fed seed—they are fed regurgitated liquid or insects. Insects provide the growing chicks with not only the protein they need for growth but also the water they need.

- In the **fall**, birds need food—many are loading up for their trip south. In fact, migration actually begins in August for some songbirds. Plants that

**Worth Repeating**

*I once had a sparrow alight upon my shoulder for a moment, while I was hoeing in a village garden, and I felt that I was more distinguished by that circumstance that I should have been by any epaulet I could have worn.*

**Henry David Thoreau**

produce red berries often also have red leaves in the fall to help attract the birds to the berries.

- In **winter** birds need food and shelter. Evergreens are important to birds that this time of year, some providing both food and shelter.

You might want to add plants to your yard gradually over time—a few plants each year—to make your yard and garden more bird-friendly. But don't wait to add a water source. If you don't have one already, add one now. The birds will appreciate taking a nice bath at any time of the year.

## Attracting Butterflies

Depending on where you live in North America, butterflies can be seen year round, or only between the spring and summer. Each species of butterfly has flight seasons and reproduction seasons. Even with a long summer break, you can still see butterflies in your schoolyard in the spring and fall.

Like birds, butterflies depend on plants for their existence. They also need sunny spots to bask, places to seek shelter, and some adult butterflies sip mud for the nutrients. Native plants are recommended to attract butterflies and they need two kinds of plants:

- **Host plants** on which to lay eggs and to feed the caterpillars. Butterflies lay their eggs on their preferred host plant—the one that the caterpillar will feed upon when the eggs hatch. Each species of butterfly has a preferred "list" of host plants. Some butterflies use only one species of host plant. Caterpillars are eating machines and they'll chomp away day and night on the foliage of the host plants. Most leave the host plant when ready for the next step in their life cycle—the chrysalis. Typically a caterpillar will leave the host plant and find a sturdy place nearby (a stick, strong stem, branch, piece of furniture, fencing, and so forth) for this next step.

- **Nectar plants** for adult food. When the adult emerges from the chrysalis, it feeds on flower nectar. In their adult stage, butterflies will pretty much take any flower nectar as well as nectar from a nectar feeder which you can purchase from a local nursery or nature store.

Some native plants do double duty for butterflies; serving as both host plant for caterpillars and as nectar plant for adults, such as milkweed which is the host and food plant for Monarchs.

Adult butterflies also use the leafy foliage of trees and bushes for shelter at night. If your garden contains both host plants and nectar plants, and if you plant a variety of flowers that provide bloom throughout the butterfly season (spring to fall), you'll be rewarded with beautiful butterflies.

Potted plants are good for attracting butterflies. If you pot your plants you can contain any potential invasives. A potted patio or deck garden containing

**Worth Repeating**

*What is a weed? A plant whose virtues have not yet been discovered.*

**Ralph Waldo Emerson**

both food and nectar plants gives you the opportunity to observe caterpillars and adult butterflies closely. If you do nothing else, pot some parsley and some asters and you'll likely get swallowtail caterpillars and adults this summer.

When you visit your local nursery or gardening center to buy plants and seeds to attract birds and butterflies, ask three questions:

1. Is this a native plant?

2. Is this an invasive plant?

3. Which birds and butterflies will this plant attract"

Realize that "wildflower" does not translate to "native" and "native" doesn't necessarily mean "non-invasive". Here's wishing you a rainbow of birds and butterflies in your yard.

APPENDIX F:

# Native Plants in Elementary School Learning

**By Catherine Renzi**
**Yellow Springs Farm**

*Note: Yellow Springs Farm in Chester County, Pennsylvania, specializes in growing native plants and promotes the use of organic fertilizers and sustainable, biodynamic farm practices. This is a great place to purchase and learn about native plants. Visit their Website at:* ***www.yellowspringsfarm.com*** *or call them at 610-827-2014.*

## What are Native Plants?

Each geographical area has a group of native plants that are specifically well-suited to the local temperatures, humidity, rainfall, soil, and air. The native plants provide food or shelter for native insects, birds, and other creatures that live nearby; and, in turn, the plants depend on the birds and insects for pollination. Some native plants might be native to an entire region such as the Middle Atlantic, while others exist only in a small microclimate within a few square miles or less. Native plants might be present throughout a state, or limited to certain areas, such as coastal areas, wetlands, or mountains, for example.

As explorers and settlers visited what we now know as the United States over past centuries, they met native Americans. Together with native people this land also had distinct native plants and animals not known in Europe, Asia, Africa, or other parts of the world.

It is practical to define the native plants are those that were in the United States before the Europeans began bringing plants here. It was very common for settlers and colonists to import plants from other countries that they wished to continue to enjoy in the new land.

**Worth Repeating**

*Man has been endowed with reason, with the power to create, so that he can add to what he's been given. But up to now he hasn't been a creator, only a destroyer. Forests keep disappearing, rivers dry up, wild life's become extinct, the climate's ruined and the land grows poorer and uglier every day.*

**Anton Chekhov**
**[Uncle Vanya, 1897]**

Defining which plants are native to your area requires reaching a consensus regarding the baseline date or date range suitable for the context of your local history. You might use the date when your state entered the Union, or a decade when European settlers colonized an important area. Some will use the 1492 landing of Christopher Columbus as a reference, and other might refer to settlements at Jamestown and Plymouth. For each region's history you will need to pre-determine relevant wars, exploratory journeys or other events that would mark the beginning of plant introductions to America. When a very early date is used, your native plant list will often suffer from a dearth of written documents or other means to catalog and record plants. If you use a date which is in the nineteenth or twentieth century, many plants from Europe, Africa or Asia were already naturalized in the US, and might be mistakenly represented as natives, or the reverse. In either case, the grey areas of confusion in the primary and secondary sources leave you with a difficult task to classify some plants. For most geographical areas, using a baseline date between 1670 and 1770 works well for accurately defining which plants are natives.

When you start to identify native plants, you might be surprised or even daunted at the large number and variety of species. There are about 13,000 native plant species in North America, and 4000 non-native, naturalized species. Of the non-natives about 400 species pose serious threats as invasive plants in the Continental United States today.

## Why are native plants important?

Native plants provide food and shelter to native insects, birds and other animals living in the environment. Together this diverse mix of plants and animals, together with air, water, soil and microorganisms compose a healthy and viable local ecosystem. If diversity decreases significantly, or if a few species become overly dominate, the ecosystem falls out of balance. This stress invites disease, pests and other unhealthy conditions. All living creatures suffer and become more vulnerable in an unhealthy environment.

The native creatures we know in our local regions are here because they find food and shelter to support them, and the reproduction of future generations. This need for basic comforts and security to raise a family is not unlike the reason that most people choose to live in specific area. Native plants provide both food and shelter for butterflies, birds, amphibians, and mammals. Non –native plants can sometimes provide a reasonable shelter for wildlife, but rarely are non-native plants ideal food sources. The berry or fruit a tree produces must fit the size and shape of a bird's mouth. If not, the bird cannot consume it. Among a group of fruiting trees or shrubs, it is often easy to recognize the natives, as these are the ones where the fruit disappears almost as fast as it ripens. Some gardeners mistakenly think their Holly, Elderberry, or Viburnum shrub did not produce fruit in a given year, but instead the truth is the local wildlife consumed the ripe fruit before the humans noticed it was ready.

Another example of native plants' importance as food source for wildlife comes in the Dogwood tree. The native tree (Cornus florida) produces a red, elliptical berry. Many Americans today favor the Asian Kousa Dogwood (Cornus kousa) because its flowers are larger, and it is less prone to mildew. The Kousa Dogwood is a pleasing shape, but its larger fruit is useless to our native birds because they cannot swallow it. In contrast, the native flowering Dogwood produces the right size fruit, and the fruit arrives at just the right time of year when many native songbirds are seeking large amounts of food in preparation for migration. In addition, the native Dogwood foliage turns brilliant red early in fall to help attract the birds to the berries.

**Worth Repeating**

*There is nothing pleasanter than spading when the ground is soft and damp.*

**John Steinbeck**

Native plants are very important food sources for butterfly caterpillars. In the butterfly's larval phase, the caterpillar eats plant leaves. The caterpillar of a specific butterfly typically will eat only about three species of plant foliage. If that food source is not present, then that butterfly species will be absent in the area. Caterpillars choose to eat leaves that provide nutrition they need, but they also need to eat leaves that will give the butterfly that emerges later from the cocoon a distinctive scent and/or taste in its body and wings. The butterflies rely on this scent or taste acquired from the caterpillar's food to repel insects and other predators that would otherwise eat the butterflies.

Many teachers are familiar with the important work plants do in cleaning our air. Photosynthesis takes carbon dioxide from the air, and returns fresh oxygen for the benefit of people and many animal species. Work done by plants' root systems is less obvious, but equally important. As rainwater and stormwater runoff return to the earth by percolating through the soil, native plants' deep root systems woven amidst the soil particles slow the water and minimize waste. The roots are a physical means to slow down water flow, so that less soil erosion occurs. In addition these roots and soil particles fix small waste particles, including pollutants such as heavy metals, excess fertilizers, and others so that water exits the soil cleaner than when it entered. The soil and plants are a large, efficient filter system that is constantly cleaning surface waste water before we re-use it the next time as ground water. Native plants often have deeper, larger root systems than non-native plants and thereby excel at erosion and pollution control.

The native species are well-suited to the soil and climate to their home regions. This is important to the environment, but these same characteristics make native plants easy to care for, saving you time and money in maintaining gardens at school or at home. Native plants are drought tolerant once established, and will require less water to maintain them. This conserves a natural resource. The natives are also able to use nutrition naturally present in healthy soil, so chemical fertilizers are unnecessary. Fertilizers are often a source of pollution because water runoff carries these nutrient-rich chemicals to places they were not intended to feed such as ponds, streams, or even to stands of invasive plants. Diseases and pests rarely plague native plants given they are adapted to the conditions in which they grow naturally. Without disease or pest management, again you can reduce or eliminate the time, expense, and health risks associated with applying chemicals in your schoolyard habitat. Sometimes native plants are plagued by invasive pests such as gypsy moths or opportunistic disease that came to your area with a foreign plant host, such as the early twentieth-century Chestnut blight. In these cases, natives might need interventional support to survive invasive threats.

## National Wildlife Federation's Schoolyard Habitat program

The National Wildlife Federation created a seven-step program especially for schools to support educators who wish to create habitat gardens where they teach. The NWF offers books, brochures, and other resources to help educators learn about Schoolyard Habitats. The Schoolyard Habitat program is similar to the Backyard Habitat program NWF offers for families to create habitat gardens at home. In both cases, the habitat garden can be certified

*The least movement is of importance to all nature. The entire ocean is affected by a pebble.*

**Blaise Pascal**

by NWF if it meets the requirements outlined, such as providing food and shelter for wildlife using native plants. Once the online or paper application is accepted by NWF, you may order a permanent, color sign to post at your garden to let visitors know what your students have accomplished. This certification process is useful in helping students set and meet a goal. Posting the official NWF sign is a reward for a job well done, and the good news is visible to all school visitors. NWF certification also promotes continuity from one school year to the next so that new teachers and students have written guidelines and benchmarks to refer to in maintaining or even expanding the garden area. In addition, building, maintaining or enlarging a NWF Schoolyard habitat garden is a wonderful opportunity for local news coverage to highlight students' positive actions for the environment that might even inspire other nearby schools to start habitat gardens, too.

## Creating your own Schoolyard Habitat Garden

Moving outside the school, the outdoors becomes a boundless classroom for teaching children about nature. The sky, air, soil are easy to find; they are omnipresent and seemingly infinite. If you decide to also teach about native plants, children can learn the plants' names and revisit the plants each time they are outdoors. Plants are child-friendly learning tools because they are found in the same spot as they were left at the prior visit. Birds, insects, and other wildlife species are important in many ways, but because they don't stay put like plants, they are less approachable and predictable aids in the outdoor classroom.

When children start to look for plants, they are likely to first be attracted to trees. Perhaps this is because trees are so large, but it might also be because the bark and trunk don't change considerably during the four seasons. Most trees are easy to find and recognize in any month or season. In contrast, a wildflower or deciduous shrub changes from season to season, as it goes dormant or loses its leaves.

Once you define the outdoors as a learning space beyond the classroom, you will find a pre-existing habitat waiting for observers. No work or intervention is required to start teaching in a schoolyard habitat. Any outdoor area is already a mini ecosystem (a system of all living plants, creatures, and micro-organisms.) It is useful to mark and measure the area you will use as your schoolyard habitat garden. You might also make a simple line drawing of this space on graph paper to note its size and scale. On this same reference site plan mark which direction is North to track sunlight, and include a road, a nearby building, or other landmarks to help with orientation.

**Worth Repeating**

*To forget how to dig the earth and to tend the soil is to forget ourselves.*

**Mohandas K. Gandhi:**

With help from books, field guides and local experts, you can identify the native plants in the schoolyard habitat area each month, and note seasonal changes in appearance and numbers of plants. Finding a new plant species feels like making a new friend, or finding a surprise gift. Take an inventory of the plant and animal species you find in the area you will use for outdoor learning. You might also send a soil sample to your local state university Extension office to learn about microorganisms and nutrients in the soil. Ask experts from local arboretums, nature centers, public gardens, and conservation organizations for assistance in getting a comprehensive and accurate list of the species in your habitat area.

With this baseline plant inventory information, you are likely to find the habitat you are about to work with has both invasive plants and native plants. Most natural areas in urban or suburban settings will be short on biodiversity because building, heavy foot traffic, lawn mowing, and other stress factors have eliminated some native plants. Invasive plants present multiply are aggressive and multiple more quickly than most native plants. If left unmanaged, the invasive plants will crowd out native plants and thereby also effectively lower the diversity of birds and insects in the vicinity. The diversity of the plants species found is usually directly correlated to the number and diversity of insects, birds, and animals found. For example, an area with a large number of plants species will also have large number of insect and bird species compared to an area with a smaller number of plant species.

Some educators will define native plants by showing students examples of specific native species, and others might show what native plants are, by defining what they are not. In other words, native plants are not invasive or naturalized plants. Either method of defining native plants works well when looking at the weeds in your schoolyard habitat. Weeds are usually a combination of invasive plants, native plants, and naturalized non-native plants that are not invasive. In short, weeds are plants you did not put where they are. They are a combination of welcome volunteers, lingering loiterers, benevolent visitors, and pests that refuse to leave. Use a good field guide together with help from local experts to identify the weeds. If a digital camera is available, you might also use photos to help create journals or scrapbooks to document and identify weeds for future reference. With this visual reinforcement, almost everyone will start to call more and more plants by name, just as they readily as they know the names of their classmates.

Like weeds, cultivated ornamental garden plants come in many shapes and sizes. Some are natives, some non-native naturalized plants, and some are invasive plants that threaten biodiversity. Beware that some local nurseries and garden centers sell plants known to be invasive in your region. There are differences in aesthetic preferences, lack of information, and sometimes disagreement among scientific sources that continue to make the quarantine of invasive plants a difficult process. You and your class can make a positive contribution to the control of invasive plants by only adding native plants to your schoolyard habitat.

With thousands of plants to choose from in garden catalogs and retail stores, plus the plants already growing in your schoolyard habitat area, why should you add native plants? Each native plant is not just valued for its aesthetic qualities, but for the food and shelter it provides in the garden for native insects, birds and butterflies. Each native plant has unique qualities such as the time of year it blooms, the quality, shape and amount of the fruit, pollen, or nectar it produces, or perhaps the foliage characteristics. These individual traits each provide one or more particular species of insect, bird or butterfly with food and or shelter that it cannot get from non-native plants.

**Worth Repeating**

*The sun, with all those plants revolving around it and dependent upon it, can still ripen a bunch of grapes as if it had nothing else in the universe to do.*

**Galileo**

## Why Create a "Schoolyard Habitat" Garden?

You might simply use the habitat and plant community you come upon outside the school as your outdoor learning center. But, if you choose to enhance this area by adding native plants, managing invasive plants, the immediate benefactor is local wildlife. When you add some benches, bird feeders,, and other features to encourage people to share in and spend time outside, your schoolyard habitat will be a popular destination for wildlife, students, and adults. If you build it, they will come.

The process of planning, decision making and implantation of garden design will turn students into stakeholders, owners, and creators of the garden. A similar but perhaps lesser reaction might come from parents, local business owners, and local experts who are solicited for help. They might provide advice, materials, or just volunteer labor to help make the schoolyard habitat better. Any project like this that fosters teamwork without competitive goals and isolating winners and losers will build community and encourage sharing and understanding among kids and community members who might not have otherwise been acquainted.

Children can participate and excel in the schoolyard habitat with any or all of their senses. Those who are sometimes shy or marginalized by classmates might find a new leadership role in the class if they have a great ear for birds, or a keen sense of smell for spring blossoms. The ability to touch the things they are learning about will be a new experience for students who customarily learn from books, photos, and video/audio presentations. For urban and suburban children, outdoor time is sparse. Sometimes this is due to lack of safe, attractive places to play and gather with other children, or sometimes the busy schedules families keep make unstructured outdoor time a rarity. The schoolyard habitat garden can serve as a great opportunity for all kids regardless of age, size, ability, or family background to equally share nature collectively and individually.

Native plants offer a chance to define a local aesthetic that differentiates one state or region from the other. For young children forming their own identities and asking "who am I?" the idea that plants growing at their school are unique and different from those in another school is compelling. This is a nice connection to teaching the unique social and political history for your locality, and native plants reinforce the interdisciplinary relationship among the natural and applied sciences.

**Worth Repeating** 

*On every stem, on every leaf —and at the root of everything that grew, was a professional specialist in the shape of grub, caterpillar, aphis, or other expert, whose business it was to devour that particular part.*

**Oliver Wendell Holmes**

Each state has an official state tree and a state flower. These two species might be a good place to start in high-lighting the aesthetic aspects of what defines and differentiates your local area from others, and nice way to introduce native species in the classroom before you move the classroom outdoors.

When considering the specific curriculum requirements you cover, the schoolyard habitat will offer endless opportunities for Interdisciplinary Learning. Your creativity will lead the way, but here are some examples to get you started:

- Math. How many seeds, petals, leaves? What portion of plants, flowers or leaves, etc., are tall vs. short, green vs. red? Create word problems using garden vocabulary. Graph changes over time such as number and size of plants.

- History. What was here before this school?

- Language arts—Journaling; how do plants' Latin names relate to English word roots?

- Creative Arts. Draw or paint inspired by flowers or seasonal color changes. Make collages using plant material and found objects. Write, produce and perform original skits set in the schoolyard garden.

- Social Science. Concepts of biodiversity—how do varied species support and aid one another in plant communities? This is relevant to current events in towns where students live.

- Life Sciences. Nutrition—what do plants eat? What is pollination? What do plants need to live and grow?

## Learning more about Schoolyard Habitat Gardens

If you would like to learn more about creating a Schoolyard Habitat, check your state Department of Environmental Resources/ Conservation (or similar name) and your local chapter of the Audubon Society. Also see Chapter Six, *Resources and Recommendations.*

**Recommended: Stalking the Wild Maranth**

In *Stalking the Wild Amaranth: Gardening in the Age of Extinction* (Henry Holt & Company, Publisher) author Janet Marinelli presents a compelling history of the American landscape, examining how and why as much as one third of native North American plants are considered endangered. For more information on this book, see Chapter Six, *Resources and Recommendations.*

Chicory

APPENDIX F

# Park Forest Inquiry

## "Has the Park Forest Elementary Schoolyard Project affected students' observations of their natural surroundings?"

**Donnan M. Stoicovy**

**Principal**
**Park Forest Elementary**
**April 29, 2006**

**PSU/SCASD Spring Inquiry Conference Presentation**

**Introduction**
**Summer 2005**

Five Park Forest Elementary (PFE) teachers and I participated in the PDS Science Course, Science Ed. 455 Natural History. Dr. Carla Zembal-Saul and the PDS Science Team worked with Shaver's Creek's Mark McLaughlin to design a week-long course exploring the natural history of our area.

During our course, we visited various school sites, looked at school gardens, learned about some of the resources available in Pennsylvania and had guest speakers from PA Department of Conservation of Natural Resources, PA Game Commission, PA Fish and Boat Commission, Millbrook Marsh and Shaver's Creek Environmental Center. As a culminating experience of the course, our PFE team designed the first steps of the PFE Schoolyard Project.

| PSU/ SCASD ANNUAL INQUIRY CONFERENCE<br>Park Forest Elementary School, April 29, 2006 | "If a child is to keep his (her) inborn sense of wonder ... he (she) needs the companionship of at least one adult who can share it, rediscovering with him (her) the joy, excitement and mystery of the world we live in." - Rachel Carson, **The Sense of Wonder**, 1956. |
|---|---|

PSU 455 Field Natural History Course - Taught by Mark McLaughlin. PFE Teachers participating included Michele Daughenbaugh, Amy Gilmore, M.J. Kitt, Ron Meyers, Kim Wilson and Donnan Stoicovy

## Park Forest's Environmental Education History

When I moved to Park Forest Elementary (PFE) School in July 1989, I knew that I was moving to a special area that would allow my interest in the environment to flourish. With its 22 acres of mostly wooded schoolyard, PFE would provide a wonderful location to begin place based education using our school site for learning.

In 1990, one of my first projects was to work on a special Earth Day program. Each classroom designed a quilt patch that was stitched together by a sixth grade student in Mrs. Diane Oyler's class. We sang songs, read poetry, shared the quilt patches and talked about the environment. This became the first of many Earth Day celebrations that we would celebrate. Other celebrations would include raising funds to adopt birds at Shaver's Creek, singing "This Pretty Planet," planting trees, and other earth oriented activities.

Also in 1990, Mrs. Kathy Kerrick and I began the K.I.D.S. (Kids Involved in Doing Service) group. We worked –with a representative group of students who decided that we would do service projects for the local nursing homes and do some environmental projects on our PFE schoolyard. The students selected the name for our group.

In 1991, I met with High School teacher, Dave Kleindinst, who had a group of students interested in helping us develop a nature trail on our school grounds. I met with high school students Jen, Matt and Matt. They worked

### Park Forest Elementary Schoolyard Project's Logistics

1. **Goal**
   To record a field natural history of four sites located on the PFE grounds during the 2005 - 06 school year.
2. **Data Review**
   This data/evidence will be reviewed by the Schoolyard Committee and used to make decisions about how to use each of the sites for the future.
3. **Skills**
   - Journaling
   - Observing, identifying and classifying
   - Recognizing occurring and reoccurring patterns in nature
   - Exploring ecosystems and their interactions
4. **Pennsylvania Academic Standards—Science**
   3.1.4 Illustrate patterns that regularly occur and reoccur in nature.
   3.3.4 Know the similarities and differences of living things.
   3.5.4 Know basic weather elements
5. **Pennsylvania Academic Standards—Environment and Ecology**
   4.3.4C Understand that the elements of natural systems are interdependent.
   4.6.4A Understand that living things are dependent on nonliving things in the environment for survival.
   4.6.4C Identify how ecosystems change over time.
   4.7.4A Identify differences in living things.
   4.7.4B Know that adaptations are important for survival.

**Phenology**

Phenology is the study of regular recurring biological phenomena such as animal migration or plant budding, especially as influenced by climatic or environmental factors that may influence the conditions.

on the trail, labeled and identified trees, and cleaned up the woods. After they completed the trail, our students voted on a name for the trail. "Trail of Life" became the name and two trailhead markers were placed at both ends of the trail.

As we continued to work on the District's Strategic Plan, our PFE staff decided that we wanted to create outdoor learning areas. So in 1992, the first outdoor pavilion was installed on the schoolyard. Teachers began taking their children out to the area for learning activities. It was our goal to develop and build three more sites.

After we began the our outdoor areas, the 1993 K.I.D.S. group began to work on the landscaping around PFE as part of their after school meetings. They worked with a local architect to do some initial planning and to learn what types of native plants would thrive on our schoolyard. They worked on the garden in the front of the school and installed two raised plant beds to plant some daffodils and tulips around some of the clusters.

In 1994, PFE was the host to the Pennsylvania Alliance for Environmental Education's (PAEE) Annual Conference. Over 275 environmental educators and teachers from all over the state attended the conference. Our students benefited by having some of the guest speakers (Helen Ross Russell, author of *Ten Minute Field Trips*, Steve Schuch, musician, etc.) and by being able to go on some field trip with conference attendees to Shaver's Creek, Penn State University, Fisherman's Paradise and Keystone Central's Environmental Center.

To celebrate Earth Day in 1994, Mr. Roy Schaeffer, Mrs. Kerrick and I worked with students to create a raised bed for a tree nursery. Mr. Schaeffer received a donation of trees from the PA Game Commission. After planting the trees, we potted them to take them to the Centre Community Hospital to give to parents of newborns. We called our project "From Our Nursery to Yours." Over several years, we placed over 500 trees in the hands of parents of newborns.

In 1995, a group of fourth, fifth and sixth grade students worked on a WILD Action Grant. The goal of the grant was for Habitat Restoration and/or Inviting Wildlife to A Schoolyard. My role as a facilitator for Project WILD made us eligible for the grant. The students wanted to get funds to buy a Grow Lab so that they could grow native species of plants that they would plant outdoors to attract wildlife to our PFE schoolyard. Students worked diligently to collect data, take pictures, and write supporting information to receive the grant. Theresa Alberici, Education Specialist for the PA Game Commission was impressed with the application and awarded our school the grant in 1996 to purchase the Grow Lab and supplemental materials to do our first plantings. Students were excited about their success and fulfilled the requirements of the grant. It resulted in several school gardens and composting projects being implemented at PFE.

Our first attempt at the Garbageless Lunch Project was an overwhelming success. I worked with a group of students to determine ways that we could reduce the amount of waste that we were producing at PFE. We decided that we would work with students, teachers, food service and physical plants to reduce waste. We would gather data about the amount of waste that we produce on any given day. They audited several lunch times to see how many pounds of waste that we were generating and what types of waste we were producing (compost, recyclable, and non-recyclable). They began to teach students about the different types of waste. They worked with the SCASD Food Service Department to look carefully at unnecessary waste that our everyday practices supported (e.g., paper napkins, straws, etc.) and talked about other ways to replace those that would be less wasteful. Students worked with Mrs. Melanie Fink to help students design earth-themed napkins that could be used for lunch. These would be made from handkerchiefs where students would make designs using fabric crayons that would be ironed onto the handkerchiefs. Students would use these rather than paper napkins. They would also begin sorting trash so they requested from our PFE Physical Plant Department that there be several bins used at lunchtime. The various bins would have compost materials, recyclables, and non-recyclables. They also wanted students to not use straws so students that had difficulty drinking out of the carton were provided with cups that could be washed. They also sent a letter home to parents describing the types of products that could be used for those students packing lunches so that less waste was produced. Students recommended using containers that could be washed rather than plastic that would be thrown away. They placed posters around the building reminding students about waste. They had a graph on the wall near the kitchen where they tracked the data regarding trash. Our most successful day occurred when we reduced our trash from the daily average of 121 pounds to 8 pounds. Students cheered when you heard the waste reduction amount announced over the PA system. Students saved milk cartons to plant trees that students were able to obtain from the Game Commission. A local nursery donated the potting soil that was used for the trees. We continued to monitor lunchtime waste throughout the year and to collect data to show children that we could make a difference by a concerted effort by everyone to change some behaviors.

In 1998, the KIDS group used the Grow Lab to produce plants that they sold to raise funds to buy bird feeders and a bird bath to enhance the PFE schoolyard and to attract other wildlife. We sold about $100 worth of plants for our first fundraiser!

Dr. Gerald Lieberman, from State Environmental Education Roundtable (SEER), came to PFE to interview students about their grant writing, garbageless lunch and the other environmental education projects that we were doing. Students spoke candidly and proudly to Gerry. Information from their interviews became part of the report, *Closing the Achievement Gap: Using the Environment as an Integrating Context for Learning*, funded by the Pew Charitable Trust.

Mrs. Kerrick and I worked with a group of students to write a grant to the National Gardening Association (NGA) in the hopes of receiving a Youth Garden Grant. We were successful with that application and received that grant in 1999. That garden area is now part of Schoolyard Site #3 in our current Schoolyard Project. Each year after the grant, PFE KIDS group students and a local Girl Scout troop maintained the garden and added new planting and bulbs to the area.

Composting had its introduction to PFE in fall of 1999. Ms. Jennifer Ankney had a red worm bin in her classroom. She wrote a $3000 grant to PDE/DEP called "Garbage to Gardens" and eventually had outside compost bins built by our State College Area School District (SCASD) Physical Plant carpenters.

During the spring of 2000, PFE received the Pennsylvania Waste Watcher Award from Lieutenant Governor Mark Schweiker. We were nominated by Joanne Shafer from Centre County Recycling Center. Ms. Ankney and I went to Harrisburg to accept the award on behalf of the students and staff at PFE.

Between 1999 and 2001, a committee of parents, teachers and I raised over $100,000 to establish environmental learning areas and playground areas. The Youth Activities and Recreation Development (Y.A.R.D.) Centre committee held many fund-raising activities to buy playground equipment build two pavilions and establish garden areas. Mr. John Zimmerman's father donated a number of bird houses and bird feeders to the school for use in our newly developed garden areas.

Ms. Ankney wrote another grant to PDE to produce a recycling movie about recycling garbage, "iMovin' Garbage". The school received $3000 in 2000- 01 school year to purchase a Digital Video (DV) camera and some other video equipment.

Summer 2000, students from PFE presented at the Governor's Institute for Environment and Ecology. 5th and 6th graders involved in composting, garbageless lunch and KIDS group spoke to 50 adults about their various projects. I was so proud of them!

In the fall of 2000, Aaron Sheckler, a former PFE student, developed a butterfly garden as his Eagle Scout project. It included a birdbath and other bird houses and bird feeders. The area became a favorite spot for a red tail hawk that frequented the birdbath.

During the spring of 2000, we established new nursery areas with trees donated by the PA Department of Corrections. PFE students and Park Forest Middle School (PFMS) students worked together to plant over 250 trees. It was our hope that many of those trees would be transplanted around PFE. In spring 2004, many of those trees were transplanted to a safe area when it was determined that PFE would be demolished and a new building would replace it.

Summer 2002, PFE received special recognition from PA Department of Education (PDE) for our commitment to environmental education. During the Governor's Institute for Environment and Ecology, Dr. Patti Vathis, PDE Advisor for Environment and Ecology, presented me with a plaque recognizing all of our school's hard work advocating environmental education.

I wrote a grant to Greenworks, an organization that supports Project Learning Tree (PLT) facilitators (I am a PLT facilitator), and received $3000 to support Garbageless Lunch activities and composting. We purchased napkins for everyone in the school, fabric crayons and irons. We started two more worm bins and purchased red worm for in the bins.
State College Master Gardeners and PFE staff members dug up plants and trees to remove from the construction site. They were relocated to a safe zone on the school property. Future garden sites will be started with some of these plants.

PFE receives a Festival of Youth Milken Family Foundation (MFF) Grant to support KIDS group projects. KIDS continued to visit local nursing

Reprinted with permission from Donnan Stoicovy, Principal, Park Forest Elementary

homes and to do landscaping in areas of PFE not affected by construction. KIDS, also, helped to remove trees from the nursery to a new site.

Matt Lanagan, a former PFE student, worked with me to refurbish our PFE "Trail of Life" nature trail. Matt and I identified over 30 trees on the trail. Matt and scout troop members fixed the trail and added markers to help identify the trees. A donation of wood chips and lumber helped to make the trail safer. Matt's work was completed during the summer of 2005 and earned him his designation as an Eagle Scout..

PFE Teachers and I attended PDS course on Field Natural History. Mark McLaughlin, from Shaver's Creek, worked together with Dr. Carla Zembal-Saul to design a course to address PA standards and to support inquiry. Teachers visited various SCASD school sites to see existing gardens and to envision future ideas that could be done. Various resource people from Department of Conservation of Natural Resources (DCNR), PA Game Commission (PGC), PA Fish and Boat Commission (PFBC), Shaver's Creek and Millbrook Marsh shared materials and knowledge about place-based education, biodiversity, songbirds, etc. The PFE Schoolyard Project began to take shape.

When our plan was in its early stages, I contacted Teresa Alberici, from the PA Game Commission, Terri Krommel, from PA Department of Conservation of Natural Resources, and Dr. Patti Vathis, from the PA Department of Education, about a possible funding source. Dr. Vathis contacted me and indicated that if I wrote a proposal, I could possibly have up to $10,000 to purchase the items that we would need to support our program. She, also, encouraged me to contact Jane Kirkland about her assembly program, which she felt would be a great match for what we were trying to do and that her funds could help support her coming.

September 2005, teachers introduced the Schoolyard Project to the staff. I introduced the project to students using a PowerPoint presentation, showing my journal and sharing the story, *Windows,* by Jeanne Baker, which shows change over time to a piece of property outside of a window.

In early October, author Jane Kirkland came to PFE to do her program, "I Saw A Bald Eagle Over My Grocery Store." As stated in her brochure, "during this program, students learn what can happen when people interact with nature in unexpected places and at unexpected times." Jane led discussions about the implications of close encounters with nature, ways that we can help wildlife, and ways we can help the environment. She shared her "20 Second Nature Break" and showed our PFE students how it can benefit our minds as well as the nature around us."

Students began their schoolyard studies, gathering data, which led to this inquiry.

As teachers and students began to embark on this yearlong journey to record phenology, observations and data about our PFE schoolyard, I began to wonder just what the impact of this project would be. I wondered how student observational skills would improve. I wondered if there were areas other than science and environmental education skills that would be addressed from the Pennsylvania Academic Standards. I wondered how the project might impact us as a school community since there were common activities going on from Kindergarten through fifth grade.

I wondered how student journal skills would be improved. I also wondered whether students might be able to draw conclusions about the sites based on the data that was collected and organized. Those various wonderings encouraged me to take the Inquiry course and formally present my wondering, my claims and my findings. Thus began my first formal inquiry into a community activity at Park Forest Elementary School. My goal would be to present at the April 28th PDS Inquiry Conference.

As I began to think about the methods that I would utilize to pursue information about my inquiry, I met with Dr. Bernard Badiali to determine the process I would use to best reach my goals. We reviewed my inquiry brief which was much too ambitious for the time available to me. We narrowed down the different data sources that I would collect and the type of information that would help my inquiry. I selected five classes to focus on by reading a selection of student journals; reviewing the class sheets for each site for all visitations and developing a student survey that everyone in those classes would complete. I would look at observational skills, connections

## Inquiry Classrooms

Mrs. Florence Milutinovic

1st Grade Room 172

Miss Amy Gilmore

2nd Grade Room 173

Mr. Ron Meyers

3rd Grade Room 118

Miss Michele Daughenbaugh

4th Grade Room 225

Mrs.Brenda Khayat

5th Grade Room 210

## PFE Schoolyard Project Resources

| | | |
|---|---|---|
| Barebooks - 1 per student for use as a journal | Fun With Nature Take Along Guide | Field Guides - Wildflowers, Birds, Insects, Butterflies, Animal Tracks, Etc. |
| 4 Binders for each of the Schoolyard Site Class Daily Journal Sheets | Keeping A Nature Journal by Leslie and Roth | GPS units and compasses □Identiflyers & Cards |
| Thermometers and Rain Gauges for 4 Sites | 2 Wagons for Outside Materials | Rulers - Metric and English, Tape Measures |
| One Small Square by Silver | Digital Camera, Binoculars, Magnifying Lenses | Flashlights, Bug Boxes, Lap Boards, Bags, etc. |

to other standards besides environment and ecology and science, impact on our school community and journaling skills through the students and their journals, class journal sheets and the survey.

As I examined my various sources of data, I began to focus in on my actual inquiry

question. At this point I determined that my question to be: *"Has our PFE Schoolyard Project affected students' observations of their natural surroundings?"*

Simultaneously, I was looking at research sources. I located several articles while our class met at Pattee and had then emailed to me. I read David Sobel's *Place Based Education*, Richard Louv's *The Last Child in the Woods; Saving Our Children from Nature-Deficit Disorder, Zenobia Barlow's Ecoliteracy: Mapping the Terrain, and Zenobia Barlow and David Stone's Ecological Literacy.* The last two books I came across when I was at AERA in San Francisco, where I attended sessions with the Environmental Strand.

One set of sessions included a field trip to the Center for Ecoliteracy so I was able to listen to presentations by Zenobia Barlow, Michael Stone, Carina Wong (formerly PDE's Assessment Chief), and Fratjof Capra and to tour the Edible Garden at the Martin Luther King Middle School in Berkeley. Some of the session was spent talking about Rethinking School Lunch, which is the project that the Center is currently expending a lot of its energies. One of the goals in California spearheaded by the Center for Ecoliteracy is to have every school develop a garden. They provided every school with a book called *Getting Started: A Guide to Creating School Gardens as Outdoor Classrooms.* It was their belief that building a school community around the concept of ecological systems made a lot of sense.

**"Before their minds have become marinated in the culture of television, consumerism, shopping malls, computers and freeways, children can find magic in trees, water, animals, landscapes and their own places." - David W. Orr, "A Sense of Place" from Ecoliteracy: Mapping the Terrain, 2000**

Charged with all of this new material to think about while putting together my inquiry, I began to think about my sources of data and how to put that together to support my claims:

- Consistent observations increase student learnings.
- Journaling - both individual and groups journals help keep records of natural events
- Nature is highly motivational for students.
- The PFE Schoolyard Project has given us a schoolwide research project.

At the risk of having too much data, I decided to only use data from five classrooms, which would encompass first through fifth grade. Of those five classrooms, three teachers were involved as part of the Schoolyard Project Team and two were not.

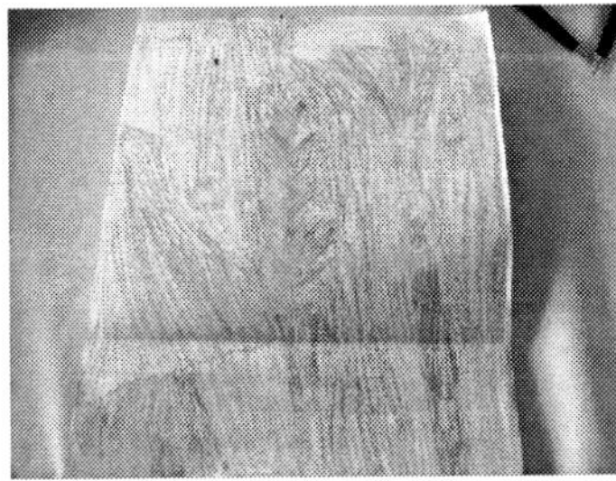

I would look at journals of teacher-selected student journals from those five selected classrooms. I wanted to further explore what students were observing over time and if their journaling was becoming more detailed as their experiences increased.
I would look at journal pages

Field Journal Observations Site # 1
Class: Meyers Grade: 3 Date: 10/5/05
Weather: Haze/W/Sun Temperature:
Sights and Sounds: What do you see? What do you hear?

from the five classrooms of all of the four sites that they visited. I wanted to see what students wrote synthesizing all that their group members had observed into one journal entry for each site during each visit.

I developed a student survey for the five classrooms asking the following questions/statements:

1. What two or more things have you learned while doing our PFE Schoolyard Project?
2. What have you liked about the PFE Schoolyard Project?
3. What would you change if you could about the PFE Schoolyard Project?
4. Please share any other ideas to improve the PFE Schoolyard Project.

My hope was that these data points would substantiate my claims.
As I looked at the various student journals, I found the following to be true:

- Students chose a variety of ways to use journals:
  - some recorded observations, including sights and sounds
  - some drew pictures
  - some wrote poetry
  - many combined all of the above

- Students used journals to record reflections

- Students were thoughtful about information that they recorded. Many would try to carry on thoughts from previous journal entries.

- Students used colors in their journals in interesting ways. In the fall, colors reflected the fall season - many browns, reds, oranges, etc. In the winter, their colors were black, white, brown and occasionally a green. In the spring, they began to use a vast array of colors to reflect everything that they were seeing - greens, reds, blues, yellows, etc.

These finding supported my claims about consistent observations increase student learning and journaling helps keep records of natural events. So my research turned to the classroom pages that students worked in groups to produce from their individual journal entries. Students took turns being the recorder for their group so the quality of these observational sheets varied accordingly.

My general conclusions from those observations sheets of the four schoolyard sites included the following:

- Most data sheets had several observations on them

- Drawing, observational notes and information were dependent upon the child/adult who was the recorder

- As the year progressed, more formal names of plants and animals were used on the sheets.

- All sheets had common information that everyone recorded including temperature data.

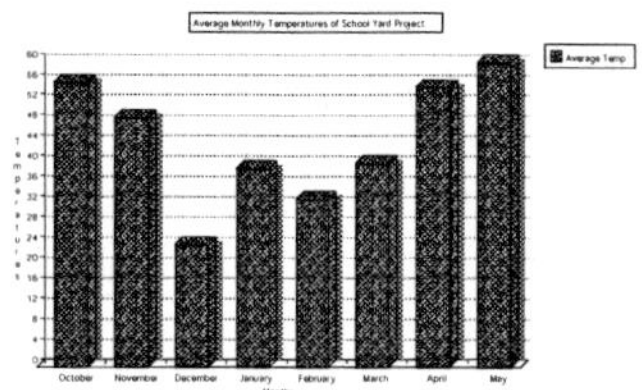


These supported the same claims as the individual journals and also added the idea of school-wide research by keeping track of the temperature data. Next, I wanted to review the data from the student surveys to support those two claims and to support the other two claims about nature motivation and the school-wide research.

When asking the students to identify two or more things that they learned during the schoolyard project, 91.7 % of the students identified two or more things that they learned during the PFE Schoolyard Project. The following pie graph represents the information from the students. Only 9.3 % of the students had only one thing that they had learned.

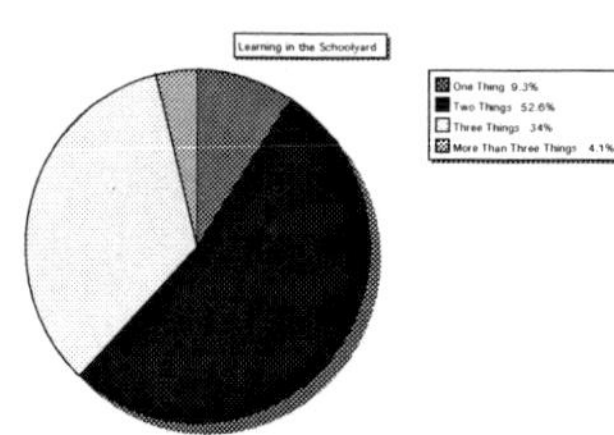


My next data point from the survey involved them specifically identifying what they liked about the Schoolyard Project. I broke the categories down into four main ones based on clustered information review in the surveys. One was "procedural", which included such things as going outside, observing nature, monitoring weather, observing change over time, finding things and journaling. Another was "observations" which included such things as birds, flowers, bugs, animals tracks and the idea of a 20 second nature break introduced to students by Jane Kirkland. Another category was "tools used" which included binoculars, magnifying lenses, the wagons and all the tools that they had available to them. The final category in this area was "everything" where students stated that they liked all parts of the project.

Using their data, 64.3% of the students identified procedural things that they liked, 16.3% identified observations that they had made, 12.2% identified tools that they liked using and 7.1% said that they liked all aspects of the project. Here are graphs representing their information:

Examples of Student Learnings

1st Graders
- I learned that nature is all around me.
- I learned what robins sound like.
- I learned how seasons affect living things.
- I learned how to identify things in nature.

2nd Graders
- If you are quiet, you'll see lots of stuff.
- I learned what bugs do.
- I learned different bird cries.
- There are lots of cool things that we are observing.

3rd Graders
- Nature can change a lot in a month.
- If you look up for 20 seconds, you could see things that you have never seen before.
- Nature is more fun than you think.
- Nature is wonderful and there are many wonderful things to see if you just stop and look.

4th Graders
- Different animals do different things in different seasons.
- Some animals live in the same place their whole life and others go from place to place. (3)
- You hear more birds when it is warm. (2)

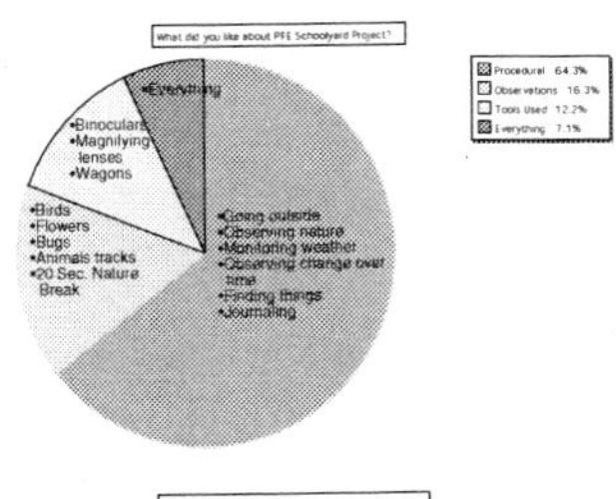


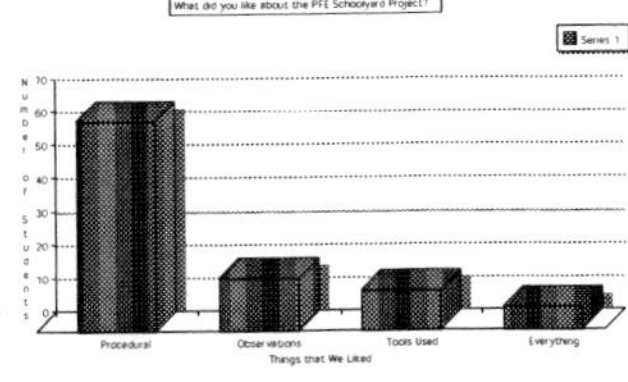

The third questions asked them to identify something that they would like to change about the project. Six areas emerged from their surveys. They included going to more sites (26%), nothing (23%), weather (22%), having more tools (6%), do more projects outside (5%) and go outside more often (3%). One teacher clarified that she has limited the tools that students use each time by introducing a new tools each time so some tools were available but she did not share them with her students until a later time. Another class had two of their observation dates cancelled due to snow days. Their expressed their disappointment in the survey responses and by indicating that they wanted to change the weather. The desire to do more projects outside reflected one class' interest in raking leaves, putting food out for animals, planting flowers and plants, picking up litter at sites, building birdhouses and planting a garden. One important finding from this data is that students would like to go to more sites. The arrangement of site visits was left in the hands of each teacher. Some had students visit only one site while others had students visit two sites. It was clear that students had an interest in seeing all four sites. Although that may be their request, it would be difficult to do in the amount of time a class is outside for the monthly visit. Teachers began to share ideas of how they could share the sites with students in other ways when that data was shared with them during a spring faculty meeting.

Here is a graph of that data:

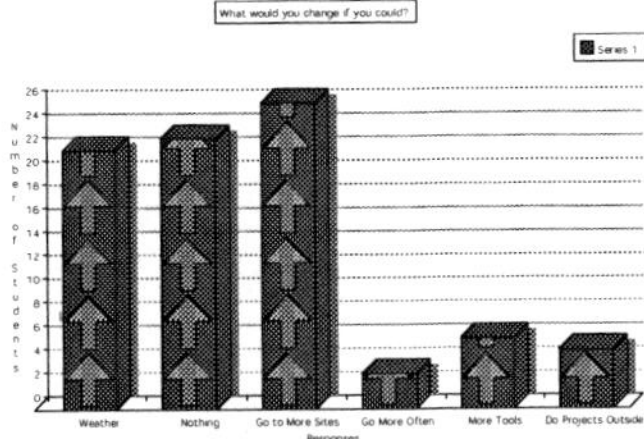

The final part of the survey invited students to provide ideas to improve the project. Six main ideas emerged from their information. The categories included no changes (29%(, attracting wildlife to our schoolyard (21%), providing more tools for their scientific exploration (16%), more sites per visit (11%), weather (8%) and more time outside during observational visits (8%). Here is a graph representing that data:

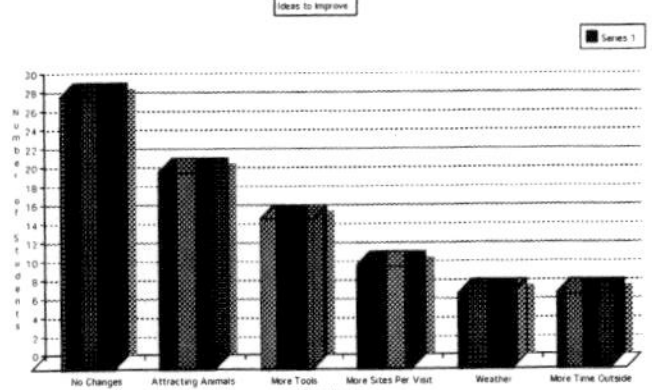

These four survey questions embodied all the claims that I had initially made and results supported my claims. My evidence clearly demonstrated that:

1. Students became better observers as the year progressed.
2. Students typically repeated familiar observations either in individual journals or on classroom observation sheets.
3. Student journals were personal things - students wrote and drew pictures as much or as little as their interest allowed them.
4. Our PFE community has an area of study that everyone K-5 shares with common data.

> **"Our relation to the natural world takes place in a place and must be grounded in information and experience."**
> **Gary Snyder**

After my inquiry presentation, one of our interns, Mavis Yap, shared her journal that she kept during the year. Her use of the journal modeled for the children in her classroom.

On June 6th Jane Kirkland returned to PFE to present a program especially developed to accompany our Schoolyard Project. Her program, *The Most Extreme Nature in Your Schoolyard* highlights information that I shared with her from student journals identifying ten different plants, animals and insects that were commonly found at PFE. Jane's presentation had her playing against the students to use the clues to identify the things. Jane scored points if the children did not get the answer in the allotted time. In both presentation (K, 3 & 5 and 1, 2 & 4) students were able to identify most of the objects and "win" the quiz.

Students in the first grade class that was part of my study also participated in Journey North, where they gathered data about the robin migration and shared that information with other participating classes via the internet. Students in the fourth grade class that was part of my study also participated in Project Feeder Watch through the support of Dr. Carla Zembal-Saul. They also shared their observations and data with other participating classes via the internet. I am sure that aspects of the Schoolyard Project were enhanced by their teacher's interest and participation in these programs.

## Conclusions and Next Steps

Based on the inquiry information and data that was shared with the staff, our Schoolyard Committee determined that we will continue our PFE Schoolyard Project next year and for years to come. Here were some recommendations made:

- Our newly purchased materials will continue to be shared resources for everyone through the use of the wagons.

- Some materials will be stored in a box so that teachers may select items that will best suit their goals for the observational day.

- Our students voted to give names to the schoolyard

sites rather than call then Sites #1, #2, #3 and #4 they would be called Chipmunk Getaway (#1), Tree Towers (#2), Bet Landing (#3) and Lost Land of Leaves (#4). We will create a map to use with those names on it.

• Information from the Schoolyard Observation Sheets will be shared weekly at our PFE Community Gathering.

• A bulletin board will be created to share Bird, Tree, Plant, Insect and Animal of the Month.

• Monthly information will be shared to help teachers with ideas about what types of things to direct student attention to during the visitations.

• Teacher resources will be explored during an Open Space Session during our monthly Open Space Faculty Meetings.

The Schoolyard Committee met to bring closure to their work by discussing their summary sheets from the State College Area Teacher Alternate Evaluation Program. Their narratives reflected the significance of the project to them and their vision of it for the future. They also send an email to staff giving them some closing thoughts:

• Thanking everyone for cooperating with the project.

• Asking teachers to have students keep their journals in their portfolios for use in next year's project.

• Announcing the Open Space Session for the fall using some of the new teacher resource, particularly the *Keeping a Nature Journal* book.

**The objective (of education) is to teach the student to see the land, to understand what he (she) sees, and enjoy what he (she) understands.**
**- Aldo Leopold**

We surveyed the teachers with the following:

1. Please share some strategies that your students used during their site visits that you found to be successful.

2. Which tools have you found to be most useful?

3. What have you liked about our PFE Schoolyard Project?

4. What would you change, if you could, about our PFE Schoolyard Project?

5. Please share any other ideas to improve our PFE Schoolyard Project.

6. Have your initial thoughts about our PFE Schoolyard Project changed? If so, how?

Our results will be shared during our first Open Space Session in the fall from the 15 out of 22 surveys returned (note: 4 of the 5 members of the Schoolyard Committee did not return their surveys). Information from these will also help shape next year's project.

Finally, we began some projects that would develop a butterfly garden and restore and establish natural habitat areas. With the support of our PTO and Fox Hill Gardens Nursery, we were able to start a butterfly garden. Fox Hill Gardens donated the services of their Landscape Architect, Lynn Torretti to design the garden. Our fifth graders in Brenda Khayat's mathematics class tackled the project to take her drawings and to make them real on the plot of land identified for the garden. Students mapped out the garden using grid sheets. They placed stakes to identify places where plants would be planted as they were provided. They mulched the walkway for the garden. Next our PTO encouraged parents to purchase plants for the garden by donating them in the name of their child's teacher/intern/paraprofessional. To date, a large number of the plants were donated and planted. Students from various classrooms took time over the last few days of school to completely cover the plant area with mulch. Over the summer, the garden will be maintained and the PTO will work to complete the project next year. They allocated funds to add such things as a bench, watering stones, a bird bath and other plants. Our school will be providing mulch, bird feeders and butterfly boxes.

As for habitat restoration and establishment, numerous bird feeders were added to six sites surrounding the school. Two bluebird boxes became homes to two bluebird families. Our bat box was reinstalled after being removed during construction, in the area now named Bat Landing.

We see our PFE Schoolyard as an ever-evolving project. Information from this inquiry has provided support for continuing to involve students as active participants in activities involving the natural world.

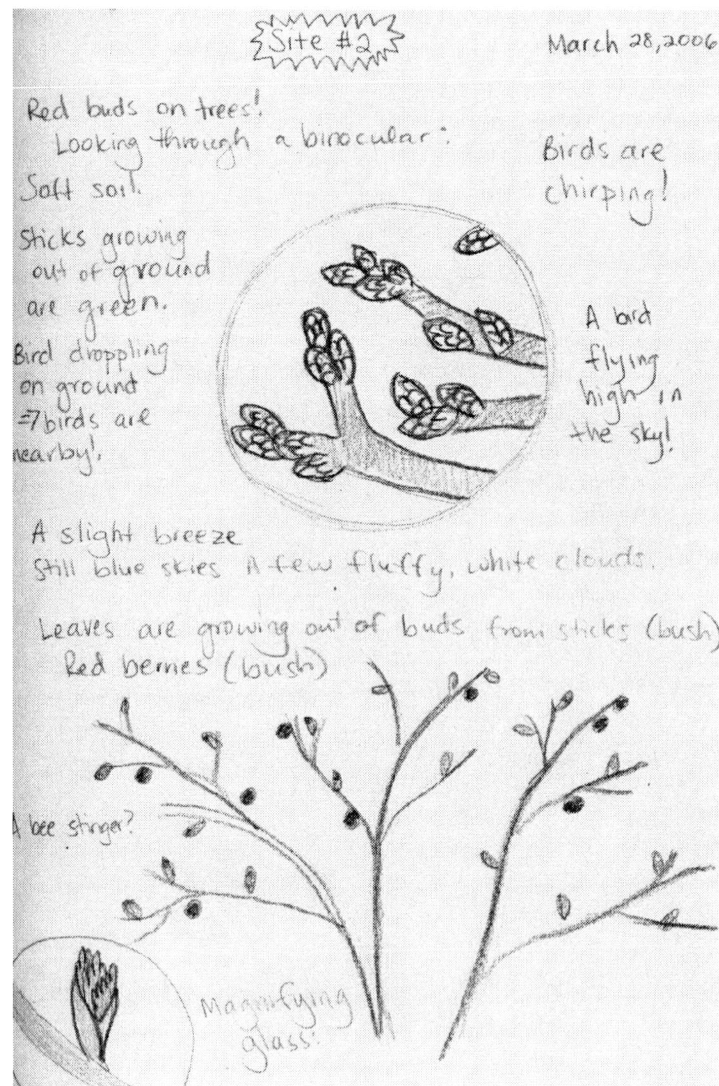


**"Education in our time should aim at nothing less than the renewal of wisdom, the rebirth of gratitude, and the sense of beauty large enough to embrace esthetics and justice."**

Reprinted with permission from Donnan Stoicovy, Principal, Park Forest Elementary

# Index

100 Birds and How They Got Their Names, 121
100 Easy to Grow Native Plants, 124
101 Ways to Help Birds, 121
20-Second Nature Break™
 Teaching, 37
Acorn Naturalists, 29, 34
Adobe PDF, 59, 65, 68
Advanced Birding, 124
Advice from a Tree, 121
A Guide to Nature in Winter, 124
American Wildlife and Plants: A Guide to
 Wildlife Food Habits, 124
Ants, 21
Aristotle, 68
Armitage's Native Plants, 124
Attracting Birds, Butterflies and Other Backyard Wildlife, 124
Audubon. *See also* National Audubon Society
 Local chapter, 2
Avian flu, 18
Ayres, Colin, 57
Berry, Thomas, 142
Bethlehem Area Vocational Technical School, 2
Binoculars, 4, 29, 32
 Acorn Naturalists Field Binoculars, 40
 Eye cups, 40
 Harnesses, 40
 Interpupillarly distance (IP), 39
 Lens diameter, 39
 Magnification, 39
 Minimum focus length, 39
 Prices, 39
Bird feeders, 17, 18
 Mobi Mesh feeder, 19
Birds
 Avian flu, 18
 Books about
  How to Draw Birds, 18
  That Quail Robert, 18
 CDs about
  Birding by Ear, 18
 Documentaries about
  Life of Birds, 18
 Migration, 20
 Number of species in N.A., 16
 Observing, 45
 Urban Birds, 48
 Websites about
  PigeonWatch, 22
Birdwatching, 16, 17
Bodily-kinesthetic Intelligence, 8
Boerlin, Lauren, xv, 130
Bridges to the Natural World, 13
Burpee Seed, 22
Burroughs, John, 115
Butterflies, 21. *See also* North American Butterfly Association
 Observing, 46
Byer, Dana, xv
Caldicott, Helen, 55
Caminite, Dario, 39
Camus, Albert, 70
Carnegie, Dale, 27, 125
Carter, Jimmy, 140
Carver, George Washington, 109
Character building, 5
Chekhov, Anton, 153
Chicago Manual of Style, 26
Citizen scientists, 22. *See also* Cornell Lab of Ornithology
Civics, 5
Clean Water Act, 49
Clipart.com, 67
Community and place-based learning, 7
Constructivism, 7
Contests, 110
Copyright, 67
Cornell Lab of Ornithology, xv, 18, 48
 Citizen Scientist Programs
  PigeonWatch, 22
  Bird Sleuth, 89
Creative arts, 5
Curie, Marie, 65
Curious Naturalist: Guide to Understanding
 and Exploring Nature, The, 121
Curriculum integration, 7
 Curriculum Web, 6
Damage Control, 48
Da Vinci, Leonardo, 121
Delisio, Helen, 139, 140, 141, 142, 143, 144
Delsea Regional Middle School, 130
Dichotomous keys, 43
Direct instructions, 7
Disabilities, 17
Discovering Moths: Nighttime Jewels in Your Own Backyard, 124
Discovering the Naturalist Intelligence:
 Science in the Schoolyard, 9
Distribution, 10
Dover Publications, 18, 67
Downingtown Area School District, 12
DPI, 66
Duiker, Lina Ruth, 64
Earth Day, 34
Education World, xv, 139
Endangered Species Act, 49
Equipment
 Comparison shopping for
  Bizrate.com, 34
  Pricegrabber.com, 34
ESL, 3
Everybody Needs a Rock, 122
Excel. *See* Microsoft Excel
Exercises
 Bird Sleuth, 89
 Creating a Dichotomous Key, 95
 Explore your Public Lands, 108
 Glorious Weeds, 85
 Habitat House Hunt, 82
 Making Maps, 98

Quick Quadrat, 102
Experiential learning, 7
Famiglietti, Daniel, 116
Field Etiquette, 51
Field Guide Book (FGP Book)
Binding, 68
Content, 23, 24, 26
About Our Schoolyard, 25
About Our Students, 25
Foreword, 25
Map to Schoolyard, 26
Our school page, 25
Project History, 25
Copies and Distribution, 67
Design
Index page, 23
Templates, 56
Title Page, 23
Files for the Web, 69
Layout, 60
Using PowerPoint, 58
Field Guide Project
By Task, 5
Choosing Subjects, 18
Database, 54
Defined, 1
Disciplines, 2, 4
Funding, 34
Images, 67
Clipart.com, 67
Dover Publications, 67
Istock.com, 67
Launching, 34
Participants, 3
Steps to creating, 2
Worksheet. *See* Planning Worksheet
Field Guides, 1, 4, 29
Choosing, 43
Recommendations, 44
Fly Away Home, 110
Forms
Bird Observation, 76
Butterfly Observation, 78
Caterpillar Observation, 77
Field Notes, 80
Nature Observation, 79
Planning Workbook, 72
Tree Observation, 81
Frank, Anne, 36
Frogs
Learning calls, 32
Fuller, R. Buckminster, 139
Galileo, 157
Gandhi, 156
Gardens, 21
Creating a Schoolyard Garden, 156
Gardner, Howard, 7
Intelligence Reframed, 7
Geist, Kathleen, xv, 13
Ghost with Trembling Wings: Science, Wishful Thinking, and the Search for Lost Species, The, 121
GIF, 69
Gingerich, Kathy, xv
GISS, 45
Golden Guides, 44
Grants, 111
Green Teacher Magazine, xv, 128
Green Woods Charter School, 13
Grey Nun Academy, 35
Growing Flowers Series: Flowers, Leaves, Seeds, and Stems, 122
GrowLab: A Complete Guide to Gardening in the Classroom, 123
Grow Lab: a Complete Guide to Gardening in the Classroom, 124
Hansen, Denise, xv
Happy Feet, 110
Harris, Cait, xv
Hartford University School for Urban Exploration, 48
Healers of the Wild, 145
Hearing Impaired. *See* Disabilities
Heintzelman, Gail, xv
Holmes, Oliver Wendell, 158
Howard Gardner, 9
How to Identify Birds, 124
How To Spot an Owl, 124
How to Spot Butterflies, 124
How To Spot Hawks & Eagles, 125
Huey, Michelle, xv
Identiflyer, 32
Identifying and Harvesting Edible and Medicinal Plants, 125
Illustrations
American Toad, 28
Black Oak, 20
Box Turtle, 43
Bull Thistle, 17
Canada Goldenrod, 123
Canada Goose, 110
Chickadee, 7
Chicory, 159
Common Green Darner, 113
Dandelion, 38
Eastern Cottontail, 16
Hemlock, 49
House Finch, 54
House Sparrow, 29
House Wren, 9
Hummingbird Moth, 114
Luna Moth, 26
Mallard, 4
Milkweed, 47
Monarch, 18
Orb Spider, 117
Poison Ivy, 51
Praying Mantis, 118
Queen Anne's Lace, 11
Raccoon, 8
Red Clover, 143
Rock Pigeon, 22
Snail, 3
Stellar's Jay, 23
White Pine, 33
Images. *See also* Field Guide Project
Scanning, 64
Sourcing, 67
Independent study, 7
Indirect instructions, 7

Injured Animals, 49
Birds, 145
Mammals, 147
Insects
Number of species in North America, 21
Insects and Spiders, 21
Intelligences. *See* Multiple Intelligences
Interactive Instruction, 7
Interpersonal Intelligence, 8
Intrapersonal Intelligence, 8
Jenny, Don, 2
Johnson Books, xv, 145
Journaling, 53
JPEG, 69
Judge. Mary, xv
Kaufman Focus Guides, 44
Keeping a Nature Journal, 6, 28, 53
Keller, Helen, 138
Kirkland, Guy, xix
Language arts, 4
Last Child in the Woods: Saving Our Children from Nature-Deficit Disorder, 10, 123
Launch party, 34
Laws and Acts
Clean Water Act, 49
Copyright, 67
Endangered Species Act, 49
The Migratory Bird Treaty Act of 1918, 49
Learning about Spring with Children's Literature, 123
Learning from the Land: Teaching Ecology through Stories and Activities, 123
Legacy of Luna: The Story of a Tree, a Woman, and the Struggle to Save the Redwoods, The, 121
Leggett, Lois, xv
Life Cycles of Butterflies, The, 125
Life in the Undergrowth, 110
Life List, 46
Life of Birds, The, 110
Life of Mammals, The, 110
Lindbergh, Charles, 56
Linguistic Intelligence, 7
Logical-mathematical Intelligence, 7
Longfellow, Henry Wadsworth, 63
Look What I Did with a Leaf, 122
Look What I Did with a Shell, 122
Lorax, The, 122
Louv, Richard, 10
Lower Merion Conservancy, 34
Lubbock, Sir John, 37, 120
Mammals, 22
Man Who Planted Trees, The, 122
March of the Penguins, 110
Math, 5
Math in the Garden: Hands-On Activities That Bring Math to Life, 123
Meyer, Maggie, 8
Migratory Bird Treaty Act of 1918, 49
Mind of the Raven, 121
Mitchell, Joni, 1
Mitchell, Joyce, 19
Monet, Claude, 124
Muir, John, 62, 71
Mullins, William, 69
Multiple Intelligences, 7
Musical Intelligence, 8
National Audubon Society
Field Guides, 44
Field Guides to Your Region, 16
National Gardening Association, 21
National Science Teacher Association, 34
National Wildlife Federation
Schoolyard Habitat Program, 155
Native Plants, 153
Native Trees, Shrubs and Vines, 125
Naturalist Intelligence, 8
Nature
Defined for the FGP, 9
Finding, 10
Nature at Your Doorstep: Real World Investigations for Primary Students, 123
Nature deficit disorder, 10
New Horizons for Learning, 8
New Jersey Audubon Society, xv
Nikon U.S.A, xv
Noah's Garden, 125
Nonfiction Signposts, 24
Norris, Barbara, 12
North American Birds of Prey, 125
North American Butterfly Association, 21
Observation
Frequency, 26
Skills, 12
One for Sorrow, Two for Joy, 123
On the Wing: To the Edge of the Earth with the Peregrine Falcon, 121
Pale Male, 123
Documentary, 110
Park Forest Elementary, 33, 54
Equipment Purchases, 33
Meet Park Forest, 14
Observation schedule, 28
Pascal, Blaise, 155
Peanut Allergies, 19, 41, 47
Permit, Wildlife Salvage, 49
Peterson Field Guides, 44
PFE. *See* Park Forest Elementary
Photosynthesis, 155
Physically Impaired. *See* Disabilities
Picasa, 69
Pigeons, 10, 47
PigeonWatch, 22
Planet Earth, 111
Planning Workbook, 16, 23, 24, 28, 34, 40, 54
Downloading and using, 16
Planning Worksheets, 72
Plants. *See* Native Plants
Plants and Animals of Mid-Atlantic Suburban Schoolyards, 11
Pollinator Conservation Handbook, 125
Problem-based learning and critical thinking., 7
Raabe, Christine, 3
Reading, 4
Red-Tails in Love: A Wildlife Drama in Central Park, 123
Renzi, Catherine, 153
Richard Louv, 10

Rocks, 22
Rosillo, Cary, xv
Rowan, Linda, xv, 35
Royalty-free. *See* Field Guide Project
Ruskin, John, 129
Salvage Permit, 49
Scanner
    Resolution, 65
    Scanning, 64
School nurse, 3
Schoolyard
    About Our Schoolyard page, 25
    Habitats, 155
    Map, 25
    Urban, 10, 22
Schoolyard Habitats: A How-To Guide, 125
Schoolyard Mosaics: Designing Gardens and Habitats, 124
Science, 4, 92
Seasonal Guideposts, 30
Seasonal Guide to the Natural Year, 50
Selective reading, 24
Sense of Wonder, The, 122
Shakespeare, William, 119
Sibley, David, 44
    Birding Basics, 125
    The Sibley Guide to Bird Life & Behavior, 125
Silent Spring, 121
Slotterback, Sue, x, xv
Social studies, 5, 7
Spatial Intelligence, 8
Squier, Robin Dennison, 48
Squirrels, 18
Stalking the Wild Amaranth: Gardening in the
        Age of Extinction, 124. 159
Steinbeck, John, 154
Stoicovy, Donnan, 14, 33
Stokes
    Field Guide to Birds, 44
Stokes Guide to Observing Insect Lives, 125
Stokes Nature Guides: A Guide to Bird Behavior, 125
Stone, Megan, 66
Storey Publishing, xv
Stranger in the Woods, 123
Stress management, 12
Suet, 19
Take A Walk Books, 34
    Take A Backyard Bird Walk, 17, 19, 23, 26,
        37, 44, 45, 51, 52, 76, 130, 132
    Take A Beach Walk, 136
    Take A City Nature Walk, 22, 23, 37, 44, 47,
        48, 49, 51, 52, 53, 79, 80, 135
    Take A Tree Walk, 20, 21, 23, 26, 37, 44, 46, 51, 52, 133
    Take A Walk With Butterflies And Dragonflies,
        18, 23, 37, 44, 46, 51, 52, 78, 134
    Using, 129
Tankus, Adam, 61
Taxonomic order, 43
Teaching Green Series, 124
Technology, 5
That Quail, Robert, 123
Thermal Warriors: Strategies of Insect Survival, The, 122
Thoreau, Henry David, 111, 150
Trees, 20
    Number of species in North America, 20
    Observing, 46
Trees in My Forest, The, 122
U.S. Department of the Interior.
    Bureau of Land Management, 108
Urban Birds. *See* Birds
Urban Naturalist, The, 122
Urban Schoolyards. *See* Schoolyard
Vargo, Tim, 11
Vathis, Patti, iii, 130
Visually Impaired. *See* Disabilities
Watershed, 25
Websites referenced in this book
    www.acornnaturalists.com, 29, 34
    www.amazon.com, 44
    www.bhwp.org, 113
    www.birds.cornell.edu, 18, 22, 92
    www.bizrate.com, 34
    www.blm.gov/education/LearningLandscapes, 108
    www.books.google.com, 131
    www.copyright.gov, 67
    www.copyrightkids.org, 67
    www.cornell.edu/birds, 18
    www.cyberbee/com/cb_copyright, 67
    www.dover.com, 67
    www.enature.com, 46
    www.epa.gov/surf, 25
    www.flr.follett.com, 131
    www.Google.com, 69
    www.greenteacher.com, 82, 83, 84, 85, 86, 87, 88
    www.ipgbooks.com, 131
    www.kidsgardening.com, 111
    www.lmconservancy.org, 34
    www.naba.org, 21
    www.NGA.org, 21
    www.nikonusa.com, 41, 42
    www.nps.gov/plants, 113
    www.nwf.org, 111, 113
    www.plants.usda.gov, 113
    www.pricegrabber.com, 34
    www.wildflower.org, 113
    www.WildsideToursInc.com, 42
    www.zephyrpress.com, 131
Weidensaul, Scott, 137
Wells, H.G., 112
Wild Bird Center of America, 19
Wildflowers, 21
Wildlife rehabilitators, 50
Wildlife Salvage Permit, 49
Wildside Tours, 126
Winged Migration, 111
Winter World: The Ingenuity of Animal Survival, 122
Wordsworth, William, 130
Wright, Frank Lloyd, 122
Writing, 4
Wyeth, Andrew, 141
Yellow Springs Farm, 127, 153